STOP WHINING;
START **WINNING**

STOP WHINING; START **WINNING**

FOR TEACHERS AND COACHES

BY

TOM ANSTETT

STOP WHINING, START **WINNING**

Please contact publisher for permission to make copies of any part of this work.

Windy City Publishers
2118 Plum Grove Road, #349
Rolling Meadows, IL 60008
www.windycitypublishers.com

Published in the United States of America

ISBN:
978-1-941478-36-3

Library of Congress Control Number:
2017936741

WINDY CITY PUBLISHERS
CHICAGO

To Carl, Christine, Bill, Susan, John, and T.J.,
Six of my best teachers.

Contents

This is some fellow,
Who having been prais'd for bluntness, doth affect
A saucy roughness and constrains the garb
Quite from his nature: he can't flatter, he!
An honest mind and plain,—he must speak truth!
And they will take it so; if not he's plain.
These kind of knaves I know, which in this plainness
Harbor more craft, and far corrupter ends,
Than twenty silly, ducking observants,
That stretch their duty nicely.

~Wm. Shakespeare
(*King Lear*, II. 2)

Wisdom is one treasure no thief can touch.

Japanese Proverb

FOREWORD

TOM ANSTETT HAS BEEN A successful English teacher for over 40 years, including holding the chairman position for 14 of those years. He has presented at the Illinois Association of Teachers of English's annual conference six times and has been published four times in both poetry and prose for the *Athletic Journal*, the *Illinois Association of Teachers of English*, and the *Poetry World National Gallery of Writing*. He also has had seven mentions for *Who's Who of American Teachers* and was nominated for a Golden Apple award.

I watched Tom play during his Illinois Basketball Coaches Association's Hall of Fame high school career at Chicago's Quigley Seminary North. I then had the opportunity to work with him in basketball camps and watch his teams play in his Illinois Basketball Coaches Association's Hall of Fame career as a coach. Very few people are in this Hall of Fame both as a player and as a coach.

I have spoken often with Tom about his teaching career because we both were college English majors. Tom was a totally dedicated teacher and department chair. Unfortunately, many coaches do not give the same commitment to their classroom teaching as they do to their coaching. Tom would have none of that nor would he allow teachers in his charge give anything but their best effort every day.

There is a maxim in the coaching world that states, "Coaching is teaching." That was exactly how Tom felt about his teaching. Whether he was at a teacher's institute or a basketball clinic, he was constantly looking for concepts that he could integrate into his teaching and coaching.

A superintendent of schools once told me, "With all the technology we have today, we can teach teachers how to teach; but we still don't know how to teach them to like kids." Tom was a great teacher because he genuinely cared about the students in his classes. He taught more than the curriculum; he taught young people.

Stop Whining; Start Winning is a book every teacher and every coach should read. We often get educational books written by college professors who have never taught in a high school. They teach students who are the best of the best because they are pursuing their college degrees. However, high school teachers must work with every type of student, from the highly motivated to students who have no motivation for learning whatsoever.

Stop Whining; Start Winning is a pragmatic book, not a theoretical book. It is replete with practical examples of things that really happen in schools throughout our country. Tom is in a unique position to write this book as he has taught in five high schools, each with a different educational culture.

For teachers, Tom gives insights into how you might deal with the unmotivated student and how your influence may change his entire outlook on life. You will meet a Marine who came back to visit Tom's class because of the "tough love" Tom used to change his life.

How does a teacher deal with a difficult class? It seems like every year teachers have that one class that they feel they are not reaching. Tom gives insights into how teachers might change that class into their most rewarding class.

You will read a different perspective on the "Three R's" (Relationships, Rapport, Rigor) that will give you a number of excellent teaching insights and recommendations.

For coaches, Tom answers questions such as:

- What kind of dedication must an athlete have to be an outstanding player in his or her sport? You will read memoir chapters on Tom's personal journey through his high school and college basketball years and see the commitment it takes to excel in a sport.

- Some other questions he ponders are:

- What three things should high school coaching be about?

- What is the significance of seventeen inches?

- Why is "impatient patience" such an important part of coaching?

- Why is it critical for coaches to answer the question, "Why do I coach?"

- Finally, he explains, "What is the end game?" When your teaching and coaching careers are over, what would you like to have accomplished? You will read a quote from Cardinal Francis George that may give you an answer.

The above represent a very short synopsis of the wisdom found in this book.

Tom Anstett has been a winner all his life as an athlete, as a coach, as a father, and as a teacher. In *Stop Whining; Start Winning*, he has written a book that is just like he–an absolute winner!

~Pat Sullivan
Author of *Attitude*
Head Basketball Coach, Retired
University of St. Francis
Joliet, Illinois

PREFACE

TEACHING AND COACHING COMPLEMENT EACH OTHER.

IN THE SPRING OF 1976, I applied for head coach of the basketball program at Immaculate Conception (I.C.) in Elmhurst, a Catholic parish high school of about 750 students. I did so feeling too much the novice, having been coaching and teaching for just three years, and never as the head coach of a basketball program. The late Bill Schaefer, my high school basketball coach and mentor during my post-college/Quigley years, pushed me to apply. I did so as cautiously as a non-swimmer approaching the deep end of a pool as his only option. When I heard I was the chosen one, I did not know whether to cheer or fear. So I did both. Before I left Quigley for my new position, Bill gave me a piece of wisdom I cherish to this day, "Tom, never let the administration be able to fire you because you are a lousy classroom teacher. If they disagree with your coaching style or you don't win enough games for whatever reasons, that's one thing, but be the best teacher in your school. Then they can never use that against you. You are paid for your English teaching, not the basketball coaching. The better teacher you become, the better coach you will be."

I began to realize this truth through various trials and triumphs. Eight years later, after a very successful run in Elmhurst, I accepted the head basketball position at Glenbrook North High School, my first public school venture. My initial interviews consisted of the principal, the assistant principal, the athletic director, and the English department chairman. When I spoke with the chairman, one of his first remarks was, "I suppose I will have to have you, being the head basketball coach. Can you actually teach English?"

Question understood. I was insulted and peeved, but that remark ignited my competitiveness. "I will be one of your best teachers," I responded. So it began. I enrolled at Northeastern Illinois University to start a Masters in

Literature program. That journey took five years of taking courses in the spring, fall, and summer. Winters were out because of the time and commitment of basketball. Those five years were some of the roughest I experienced. Even though the players were very enthusiastic and willing to learn, the coaching was tough since I had taken over a program with players with little varsity experience. Winning became a special dessert, instead of the main course. The majority of the parents were supportive, as are the majority of parents in every school district. There were three sets of parents, however, who made my coaching very trying and frustrating. On the other hand, the classroom teaching was terrific. My colleagues in the English department were outstanding: always curious and optimistic and supportive. With the resources available in that district, possibilities were endless. The students, for the most part, were highly driven and energetic. Through both arenas, I was beginning to see Bill Schaefer's words as my personal bible. Moreover, to my everlasting ignorance, I was starting to employ methods from one arena to the other. I was also beginning to understand the importance of clear communication among student-players, parents, and myself.

In my second year there, the chairman asked me to explain to my colleagues at a future date some of the coaching methods I used in my English classroom. When he first approached me with this request, I blanched. I found that question curious. My team finished 5-19 in my first year; why would anyone be interested in my methods when I had such a poor season? In the weeks ahead, I pondered this task. I reflected after a day's work what coaching techniques I used within the day's lessons. Nothing was coming to me. Then a few weeks later during my fifth period English 3 Basic class consisting of fourteen boys and two girls, three of the boys barged in fifteen minutes tardy. Two of them, quite inebriated, stumbled into desks. Their stench of alcohol permeated the room. I ushered them down to the dean's office.

After their two-week suspension, I sat down with each boy to discuss his status in class. Little did I realize it then, but my coaching techniques were in full display. I spoke to these boys like a coach to his player who might be struggling in his confidence. That is all these boys needed: someone who takes some time to listen to them and hear their stories. One of the boys, Andrew, remarked to me, "My dad is never home and when he is, I never talk to him or really see him. He never asks me about school, so I don't care much. At least you want to know me a little." Within our discussion, I countered with the three questions I ask of athletes:

1. "Are you a hard worker?"

2. "Are you a team player?" (and/or) "Are you a good example in class?"

3. "Do you give up too easily? What is your degree of mental toughness?"

These prompts engender relevant feedback from students, players, or parents. In Andrew's case, he changed his entire attitude: his effort, production, and skill accelerated. Passing the course became a reality. Those three questions became ones I fell back on repeatedly throughout my career, no matter whom I was addressing. Parents, colleagues, students, and children all heard the same prompts. Those questions became the backbone for my becoming a quality teacher. Sure, I knew my curriculum. Selling that curriculum became authentic when my audience knew me as more than a teacher.

From the other side of education, I've watched many coaches over the years, worked closely with many more. If I had one wish, I would want *all* coaches to hear those questions before they start their careers and consider their repercussions. I realize that most new coaches have heard those questions from a player's perspective, but asking those same questions as a coach offers a new prospect for learning. In truth, I never used classroom time to prepare basketball practice, write down plays, or do anything else basketball-related. It was all English, all the time. I quickly discovered that there was no time to waste as an English teacher; there was far too much to prepare, to grade, and to learn. As I gained experience, Schaefer's parting words gained more and more relevance and meaning. Teaching and coaching had a strange, yet wondrous partnership, a connection that assisted my public school experiences.

Unfortunately, I have witnessed the Darth Vader side of coaches who concentrate on their sport all the time. Teachers who slight their classroom obligations are discouraging for the kids and for the school. I recall one particular moment when I, as the department chairman, was having a conference with one of my English teachers who was also an assistant football coach. I had paid a visit in an informal observation to his class and discovered his lesson very haphazard and unprepared. I called him into my office to discuss the reasons for this lack of preparation. During our conversation he mentioned that his focus on football had diminished his luster for his English teaching. Not the words I wanted to hear. I proceeded to inform that teacher that if he could not keep up with his first priority, his classroom instruction, that he should not coach. I even told him that I would consider his status as a non-tenured teacher on very shaky ground if I did not see immediate improvement. Happy to report that this teacher responded well and his methods and brilliance began to skyrocket. As a department chairperson, I expected all my teachers to improve. That improvement began with my own effort and modeling for superior teaching. How could I blame any of my teachers for a lack of production if I was a poor model? I had to be the best teacher in the department, just like I had to be the best coach in my program.

Furthermore, if more attention from administrations was given to the teaching end, i.e., just how good a *teacher* is each coach, coaches would understand what the priorities are in their schools. Some of the priorities are school-driven with pressure from the administration to win games. I offer these concepts not as a blanket criticism, but as a source for evaluation. Leadership with integrity always is the bottom line for any healthy balance between academics and sports.

Some might argue that coaching is harder than it's ever been. I will not argue with that because it begs the question; coaching has always been, and will always be, difficult and challenging. The pressures of time, family, outside influences, parents, and administrators have always presented challenges to a career as a coach. In contemporary society, the overuse of social media must take some accountability for raising every educator's blood pressure. This book wants to help teachers and coaches do their jobs better. If coaches can discover methods to improve their teaching ability, their relationships with their athletes, their ability to communicate with parents, there will be less room for whining and blaming. Clarity will emerge. Coaches who find and sustain real priorities and develop the inner toughness to secure and to teach a valid belief system for their sport become the true winners. That winning attitude transfers to both students and athletes. Healthy relationships with school colleagues also assist a coaching career.

Teaching and coaching share similar traits (See Appendix D for a warmup), and can thrive as one persona despite being in contrasting physical environments and using different terminology. Moreover, one of my trusted colleagues with whom I had the pleasure of being both a teaching colleague and a member of his basketball staff for eleven years at Lincoln-Way East believes one *should teach more on the court and coach more in the classroom.*

I never had the opportunity to explain my coaching techniques applied to the classroom to my Glenbrook North Spartan English teammates. Since that time, however, I have had plenty of moments to apply the aforementioned tenet as it increased in value to me throughout my career. That tip serves as one antidote to the entitlement venom. This book contains similar serum.

SECTION 1-A

TEACHERS, EXPECT NOTHING HANDED TO YOU.

CONTEXT

THROUGHOUT THE EDUCATION SYSTEM—AND I might surmise in the culture in a majority of families—a discomfort exists about being a first-hand witness or a supporter of struggling students or children. We dislike this feeling. Whether we are parents, teachers, or coaches, we become uncomfortable watching kids battle through dilemmas or difficulties. In effect, we love them too much. We sometimes separate good discipline from love when those two components are actually authentic partners in the rearing of children. Consequently, we tend to enable, to alibi, or to excuse the students from their initiative and subsequent ability to find solutions and follow through on those solutions. Within those foibles lies the welcome mat to entitlement: we expect everything from everyone else; we tend to blame instead of empower; we can lack the relentlessness to help the strugglers grow up and face their problems with some level of maturity and grit. I do not write this book out of meanness, just honesty; not out of criticism, just support. I faced what you are facing, educators. I did smile before Christmas once in a while, but balanced my enthusiasm with my very high expectations. So as their teacher, you supply a unique form of love, a distinct caring they might never witness again after high school.

On Facebook in June of 2016, I saw a post containing a picture of a yellow legal pad. The sheet was blank; the title of the post was, *Here is a comprehensive list of everything you're entitled to and what the world owes you.* Thus the fools' gold of entitlement provides the motivation for my writing. The world of teaching and coaching throughout my forty-two year career provides the context. The disease of entitlement is nothing new. However, combining that machine with the materialism present in this country makes for a rough combination that entices society to use it for an ever-present and convenient alibi for its lack of discipline. Throughout my teaching/coaching career, I witnessed an increasing swell of entitlement: parents who will make any and all excuse(s) for their kids' lack of commitment, children who follow their lead and avoid personal responsibility, teachers who crave the paycheck but not the work, coaches who assume too much and do too little. Each section and chapters describe an issue of this problem with some suggestions for eliminating or lessening those issues. I also include personal stories to embellish and support the particular section's focus and other tales of significance from the many people who contributed to this effort.

Why does entitlement require such a study and response? Why is whining so debilitating to a productive career in education? In one of my earlier years as a teacher, I returned graded essays to the students. One young lady took a look at the grade, crumbled the paper, threw it on the floor, pronounced her eternal hatred for her teacher, and began weeping. For an example as a basketball coach, I once told a player who had a proclivity for unnecessary dribbling, *Every time you dribble, you weaken the nation.* He responded with arms outstretched, palms upward, wondering why he was being criticized. In both examples the recipients believed they were deserving of something better, and perhaps they were. However, both reactions professed something altogether dismaying, disheartening. I saw similar reactions twenty and thirty years later, only with many of the more recent ones, parents and sometimes administrators became involved to an unnecessary degree. I have concluded that every time a player raises his arms, palms outstretched to God; every time a parent pleads with an administrator about his child's personality conflict with a teacher; every time a coach shields a player from that player's ownership of responsibility, America takes one giant step backward. Thus, I feel entitlement with its inherent whines needs to be discussed, addressed, and *rejected*. Entitlement poisons the flavors within that delicious recipe called the education process.

Researchers maintain that a human being's primary emotional need is to feel appreciated, but in this current era, appreciation and support are as frequent as a NASA moon shot; thus, the discomfort level rises. So too does the world of entitlement, a rising development in the twenty-first century, a major illness fostered by delusional parents, nurtured by careless and spineless adults, sometimes emboldened by educators, and delivered in daily doses across the United States. This book's list contains just a few examples of ways entitlement fractures the quality of education. The list also includes ways to combat it. The great Hubie Brown, ex-NBA coach and current ESPN pro basketball analyst, once stated, "Give a loser an excuse and he'll use it every time." I have found that statement accurate. *Expect nothing handed to you; blame no one; (and) do something* represent cures for entitlement and begin the path to less whining and more winning.

When my older son John entered high school, he had an Individual Education Plan (I.E.P.) for additional time for big tests. Large tests with a mass of content strangled his inner calm. These tests typically diminished his final grades. My first and only reaction to this plan was, "I want him removed from this accommodation as soon as possible." I never wanted him to use anything for a crutch; adult life does not allow for that convenience. We discussed ways to solve this issue, but knew that that process would be gradual. As he gained confidence, he was the first to ask to be treated like everyone else by the end of sophomore year. When he came home from his first ACT test as a junior with a score of 21, he was devastated, a word I have come to dislike. Earthquakes are devastating, so are floods, so are cancer-victims. Devastated has become the everyday descriptor for hassles we all experience. He went to work and with the help of some extra tutoring, earned a 28 on his next ACT. Allowing children to struggle, then helping them plan to alleviate that struggle, then stepping aside to allow them that struggle are the best gifts parents can supply.

Unfortunately, instead of allowing the struggle and acting as a facilitator or an advisor, many parents will alibi, believing that this course of action provides a necessary buffer, believing they have to step in and speak up for their student or athlete. Their student's C in math devastates those parents; others feel traumatized when their star athlete sits on the bench or does not receive the playing time they feel he or she should. Such situations surface every day throughout homes in America. As a teacher, as a coach, and as a department chairman, I was privy to many conversations about such circumstances. One commonplace episode would be the phone call to my chair phone from a venting, disgruntled parent whose student felt slighted with a grade or a remark from the classroom teacher. On one hand, I always wanted to hear the parent out; on the other, I always volunteered the question of whether that parent had spoken yet to the classroom teacher. Usually, the answer was no. So there I was, the man-in-the-middle, with little direct knowledge from the teacher's point of view. I took my teacher's side until proven otherwise.

From there, I directed the parent to call the teacher. After that conversation, I sprinted to find the teacher involved to set up a powwow or at the very least to find out the teacher's side and tell him or her that a call was forthcoming. In 98% of the cases, one direct phone discussion between the two parties cleared any misunderstandings. Appropriate communication from the start will diminish hurt feelings and promote a positive direction for the student with that teacher. In any event, when conflicts develop, as they certainly will, honest and timely talk between the parties involved tend to soften hard feelings and provide good models for student or athlete maturity.

In another case, I discovered that one of my AP students plagiarized his research paper. I sat him down and provided the proof. He could do nothing other than admit the sordid deed, a concession I appreciated. As he sat in my office, I made him listen to my phone conversation with his mother. I wanted complete transparency. Instead of just giving him a zero without any learning, I decided to have the student complete a new paper, a paper he had to complete or fail the entire course. I provided the topic and we discussed a timeline when he had to submit the appropriate steps all the students had to complete in this process. If he missed one step or one deadline, the deal was off. The mother was supportive and appreciated the fact that I was giving her son another chance, instead of just dropping him off the academic cliff without any experience in fixing the problem himself. As it turned out, the student completed each step on time and the final project with a fine result. I still see the mom around town today; she sometimes revisits that situation and compliments me for the way I handled it. In short, parents provide a lifeline between student and teacher. Dealing with difficult situations means teachers acting immediately to provide appropriate communication and a solution. Most parents appreciate those steps.

I freely admit I am not an expert on this topic. I have no Ph.D., for whatever that degree is worth. I realize people learn at different paces. I understand that there are thousands of parents out there who raise their kids with responsibility and allow them to struggle and to figure things out. There are thousands of teachers and coaches out there who daily commit their minds, bodies, and souls to their charges with integrity. My objection surfaces when people from any walk of life use the same excuses again and again for circumstances over which they can exhibit ownership and possible solutions.

Finally, I first heard the title of this book in 2000 when I assisted the varsity level for boys' basketball at Lincoln-Way Central High School in New Lenox, Illinois. I thought of the same words again at 2:33 a.m. in January of 2016. That team grew into a powerhouse, reaching the super-sectional in 2001. They possessed a collective determination to win, had good floor leadership, and exhibited a relentless camaraderie that surfaced most in the direst game situations. The head coach repeated the three sentences often, and the players believed in them. That mantra translated into wondrous seasons for that group; they felt entitled to nothing, and played that way, with the proverbial chip on their shoulders. The only whining they did was to each other when one player might have felt another wasn't playing as hard as possible. Thus, I have borrowed those motivators-*expect nothing handed to you; blame no one; (and) do something*-with the hope and the expectation you will discover these concepts as guides leading to roads of personal significance: finding the means and ability within your chosen career of teaching and/or coaching to help others become successful and purposeful.

A CONSTANT CONFRONTATION: WHINING VS. WINNING

WHINING PRONOUNCES,
"YOU ARE MY TEACHER; OF COURSE, YOU WILL WRITE A LETTER
OF RECOMMENDATION FOR COLLEGE FOR ME."

A Winning Frame of Mind

A few years ago, a student marched into my office without a knock at my department chair door. I was in the middle of some trivial matter such as the creation of a master schedule, the budget, or a formal evaluation. "Mr. Anstett, I need a letter of recommendation, preferably by Friday. I can get you the address. I figured that since you already wrote one for me, you can just change it a bit and give it to me." Please notice there were no questions in the student's words, no interrogative sentences, no supplications with a dose of humility, just statements of need and want.

I paused to look at the student and said, "Good morning. Is there a greeting and a question somewhere here?"

After some discussion including a brief lecture about first knocking on a teacher's door and a review of correct conduct we had role played in class, I agreed to write the letter. Nowhere in my job description is a statement about writing letters of recommendation. Teachers do this task because they develop a healthy relationship with those students requesting the letters, and also because teachers are really nice people. These letters take time and effort, the former being a constant pressure in every teacher's psyche and daily operations. Every one of the hundreds of letters I have written for students was original. I owed that effort to each student. However, if you are in the profession long enough, you realize both the joy and the angst of teenage naiveté. The state of naiveté can be very refreshing, exhibiting astounding moments of creativity and innocence. It can also provide provocative lessons in manners, civility, and decorum. We all do *stupid* things when we know better but do an action anyway. Stupidity reinforces entitlement, a disease running loose in schools, in business, and in life.

The above scenario is an example of stupid (not a stupid example) since I had mentioned to his class the point of letters and the correct ways to request them. The student in question neglected to remember the difference between a declarative, an imperative, and an interrogative sentence. He was reminded of those essential differences in our discussion.

After I wrote the letter and gave it to him, I received an inaudible thank you, two words teachers might hear on occasion, but rarely at the end of the school year. We discussed that particular nuance as well. As a matter of fact I received an average of one thank-you note for about every fifteen to twenty letters I completed. I realize I might be whining a bit here, but I did not dwell on the lack of appreciation. I adjusted. I determined to acknowledge every possible way I could appreciate people's actions. When in doubt, model. Doing a job well leaves no regrets and is reward enough; that concept reinforces the urgency to battle entitlement. The greater sense of entitlement, the fewer thank-yous can be expected and/or deserved. Such courtesy, once known as common, should once again become the norm, rather than the exception. People deserve recognition, or at least a thank-you, for a job well done.

WHINING DECLARES,
"I DO DESERVE AN A FOR THE SEMESTER. DO YOU REALIZE I HAVE NEVER
RECEIVED LOWER THAN AN A IN ANY CLASS UNTIL YOURS??"

A Winning Frame of Mind

It seemed like every year this comment would surface at least once around report card time. Many times the comment came from a very capable student, one who had high expectations. High expectations are fine, as long as the work ethic supports those goals. I usually reserved the sandwich method for these students. I began with a positive ("You have been doing a good job in class and I am enjoying teaching you."). Then, I filtered one substantive way the student can improve. ("I have noticed that your booknoting had been incomplete. Are you spending sufficient time on that assignment?). I concluded with another positive. ("I am sure that if the annotations improve, your learning will, and the grades will follow.")

Deserving can become a toxic mental detour. Earning supplies the antidote. Earning anything coincides with more sturdy self-confidence since very few things that are earned do not come without a steely and resilient work ethic. Do a diagnostic on the level of preparation for the task required. Center student conversations around work ethic; many students fall short in this area. See if that level needs an oil change. Supply through the discussion the steps necessary for improvement.

A couple of more salient points about *deserving*:

1. Teachers: Start fair and tough; finish tough and fair. Ever have the urge to be kind and give the student a B– on his essay or project when he really deserves the C+, especially early in the year? I tended to grade lower; in that way, I tested students' resolve for improvement rather than their quest for a high grade point average. I discussed that challenge with them. The only time I wavered from that course of action was at semester grades. *If* the student had exhibited persistence and improvement over the course of the months of study, I would award the higher grade *if* the student was on the fence between grades and the percentages were within a point or two. If I could restart my career, I would guide my students with the mantra of the Rolling Stones: *You can't always get what you want, but if you try sometime, you get what you need.*

2. There is a saying, *Children spell the word love as t-i-m-e.* So, parents, how often do your children *deserve* your time in the area of

study, homework, or preparation for class? Adults can overdo it; they communicate the message to their children that they, the parents, will figure everything out for the kids. From the parents' perspective, the temptations are constant. Children will moan that they lack the understanding for the homework, that the teacher never explained the problem. Parents hear these angsts and decide to help their kids complete the homework, help them to write the paper, help them analyze the concept. What happens in many cases is that the help translates to parents' spending their time wracking their brains while the student watches.

Perhaps these temptations begin in early childhood years when parents decide to overstructure the child's daily schedule. Individual playtime, downtime, whatever one might call that time of decompression for kids, is valuable. There is no need for kids to participate in every camp known to man every day of the summer. Kids need to learn to initiate their own games, organize their own pickup contests or neighborhood frolic, argue about rules with their peers, learn to respect others from their own confrontations, at times get into a fight. Perhaps all parents should watch the movie *Sandlot* a few times so that they begin to understand that the contemporary approach of total time manipulation for their children can be unhealthy. *Mommy will always be there for them* is an utter falsehood and propels children toward the unholy sense of entitlement. Put another way, a healthy balance of *independent-dependence* is in order. In the teenage years, this type of parental leadership will find mutual trust. However, parents must know where their kids are at night and know their friends.

Grades have to be earned through struggle, the struggle from the student. I would rather have my student receive the D or the incomplete within the struggle, find out what went wrong, redo the task, and then earn the higher grade, than just have Mom or Dad do the work for them. Students might learn about photosynthesis in science by completing the assignment, but they will learn more about their character by supplying the elbow grease themselves. The payout will come later in life.

WHINING PROCLAIMS,
"I STARTED ON THE TEAM LAST YEAR AS A JUNIOR.
OF COURSE, I WILL START THIS YEAR AS A SENIOR.
WHY SHOULD IT BE ANY DIFFERENT?"

A Winning Frame of Mind

This attitude is part of the inexperienced thinking of an adolescent, but the source for it has to be shared. I compare that whine to a similar sound when I overheard parents think aloud about the skills of their freshman son, proclaiming his right to the keys of the kingdom as a varsity player who will average twenty points a game, be the M.V.P., win the state title, play Division-I basketball, ad nauseam. The problem with the expecting returner is the potential lack of commitment during the off-season, if his thinking enters the land of entitlement. It is true that there are many good players who continue to improve from one year to the next without that sense of deserving any one position the following year. However, with the increase in player skills, competition, physical growth, and outright talent from year to year, players and parents cannot assume anything. I had one player I brought up to the varsity as a sophomore who started every game. He was 6'4" and strong with good skills. He blended in well with the juniors and seniors. Two years later, he was relatively the same player in his skill level, a bit overweight, and most importantly, did not assume the mantle of leadership required from a two-year starter with the experience level he had acquired. In short, he flailed from the pressure of being a go-to guy when the game was on the line. As my high school coach once proclaimed, "You never know what a player will show, once the Friday nights glow. Practice has its say, but game time will hold its sway."

Just like the great students who start their lessons assuming they know nothing, so too the best players learn to relish each day as an opportunity to improve. Speaking purely from a basketball standpoint, how often do players have the discipline over summers to shoot *alone* with game speed, or find the tough competitor for some hard one-on-one-in addition to their attendance at school camps? Each sport an athlete plays has its own level of excellence and the precise work that is necessary for success at that level. Integrity is doing the right thing without being watched. When that integrity is applied, deserving becomes earning, a reward that comes without a trophy or ribbon, but with plenty of intrinsic rewards.

WHINING ANNOUNCES,
"I HAD "MR. SO-AND-SO" LAST YEAR. HE DIDN'T LIKE ME,
SO WE DID NOT GET ALONG. OMG, MY DAD WENT BALLISTIC
WHEN I CAME HOME WITH A C AND HE CALLED THAT TEACHER
THE NEXT DAY, REALLY GAVE IT TO HIM."

A Winning Frame of Mind

The education translation for that particular whine is personality conflict. Do parents ever contemplate the damage that can be done in conversations like this one? Not getting along has two sides and many times the teacher's side is not heard. As a department chair, I received many calls from parents whose children claimed they had a personality conflict with one of the teachers. I listened, then asked one question: "Has your student completed all of his/her work in that class?" I received one of two answers. "No, not all," or, "I don't really know." Both answers revealed a lack of communication at home. My answer was simple: If students try to complete all their work, personality conflicts often disappear. In many cases, the angry parent had not yet spoken with that particular teacher. One phone conversation, not ten emails, can provide sufficient clarity about the situation and a positive meeting of the minds.

Teachers also create more conflict than is necessary. Not returning phone calls promptly from a parent, treating a student disrespectfully (especially if that student is respectful), talking too much and saying too little, answering emails with too many emails, or being unprepared for class so that students have avenues for creating disturbances are all sure-fire methods for possible, yet unnecessary conflicts that students misinterpret. Remember, what one says is many times not what listeners hear. Then, the mixed message arrives home, and all hell breaks loose.

Being born in 1951, I came from a nuclear family where the teacher was always right. Period. No discussion. As my teaching career progressed, I was privy to more and more complaints similar to the one described in the above scenarios. Whining and blaming have become the familiar drinks of choice, the lack of responsibility fostered in homes where Johnny is never wrong. However, this type of situation is in the minority of teacher-student/parent conflicts. Most parents are willing to make the effort to understand the reason for a personality conflict before waging all-out war on the teacher. I just wish if a conflict occurs, that both parents and teachers be more proactive and show the patience and wisdom to discover the other side of a story.

Consider… *WHICH PARENT ARE YOU?* (Anonymous)

"I got two As," the small boy cried.
His voice was filled with glee.
His father very bluntly asked,
"Why didn't you get three?"

"Mom, I've got the dishes done."
The girl called from the door.
Her mother very calmly said,
"Did you sweep the floor?"

"I've mowed the grass," the tallboy said.
"And put the mower away."
His father asked him, with a shrug,
"Did you clean off the clay?"

The children in the house next door
Seem happy and content
The same things happen over there,
But this is how it went:

"I got two As," the small boy cried.
His voice was filled with glee.
His father very proudly said, "That's great;
I'm glad you belong to me."

"Mom, I've got the dishes done."
The girl called from the door.
Her mother smiled and softly said,
"Each day I love you more."

"I've mowed the grass," the tallboy said.
"And put the mower away."
His father answered with much joy,
"You've made my happy day."

Children deserve a little praise
For tasks they're asked to do.
If they're to lead a happy life,
So much depends on you.

WHINING ARGUES,
"THE RULES ARE FOR EVERYONE ELSE, BUT LITTLE OL' ME!"

A Winning Frame of Mind

Various social media have displayed posts of parents' notes to teachers excusing their child for something everyone in the class is obligated to do. The posts occur in instances of teacher refusal of some request from the student and point the finger at the teacher for making the student's life unbearable. Rules must be fair; moreover, they must be enforced, but there can be some individual application for rules. For example, when I was a dean at Lincoln-Way Central, I conferenced at times with first-time offenders, students who made a mistake but had never even been in the deans' office, much less even know where that office was in the building. Those students did not whine about being there; they knew they were wrong and were willing to accept their punishment. The issue was the repeat offenders. Those hooligans were *never* guilty, whining to the ninth degree and blaming everyone for their problems. They had learned no conscience development. Typical of blamers and whiners, they had become too lazy to confront and then to correct their faults.

Adaptability remains an essential attribute; teachers can help students learn and practice this virtue. This quality is especially essential for the troublemaker or disruptive individual who feels rules are made to be violated whenever possible. Establishing a friendly, yet academic relationship between student and teacher or between player and coach is a two-way responsibility. The depth of any relationship is the extent it survives throughout a crisis. Teachers must promote an open door, encouraging their charges to seek help when necessary. One method I used was a two-minute intervention. I established time within my bi-weekly planning to talk to each student in class for two minutes each. This conversation was informal: "How has your week been?" "Is there anything I can help you with?" "What is going on with your family? "How are all your classes going?" "I was at the concert on Friday; I could hear your oboe in the back row. Nice work!" These short talks communicated that this teacher cared about that student. I was sure to find the students who were failing or having trouble keeping up, etc., as my first priority for these interventions.

Another method to promote relationships I employed each five-day week was *checkins* and *checkouts*. On Mondays, we began class with each student saying something about his/her life; this comment was to be brief and as personal as the student chose. Thus, after five minutes, *each student* had already participated in the class. It was a joy to witness the progression of these comments as the year continued. We discovered the class humorist, the class storyteller, the class complainer, etc. Eventually, the students were disappointed if we had to skip this part of the week. On Fridays we had checkouts the last five to seven minutes. Same idea. I planned these quick bursts every full week of school. Yes, the teacher participated. I cannot underestimate the wholesome and enjoyable effectiveness of this activity. This strategy was another way to build trust; students saw the persona of both the teacher and their peers.

One more: Fridays were for me a *High-Five Friday*. No one, not even an administrator, entered my room without giving me a high-five. Once this ritual became habit, many unknown students would give me one as well. Simple, easy, purposeful fun.

If healthy, proactive relationships exist, rules become second nature and unnoticeable; they become for everyone. Smiles decrease whines. When conflicts invariably rise, the more sound the relationship and class atmosphere, the greater chance that conflicts and class disturbances that interfere with lessons diminish. The winning faculty will go out of their way to say hello to *all* students in hallways or during passing periods, not just their own. We will never know what a simple, friendly greeting can do to the lonesome, despondent student. That greeting and smile might be the only ounce of friendship the troubled students see all week.

Whining pronounces,
"That class is too hard;
my Johnny won't get into X-University."

A Winning Frame of Mind

High school is not supposed to be easy. Furthermore, there is always the question of the quality of junior high schools for preparing their students for the necessary rigor of high school work. I tutor a seventh grade student now and his study habits are inadequate. He takes little pride in his work, yet that work is accepted at his school. His habits will not help him in high school. On the other hand, I realize that there is a great deal of growth from freshman through senior years, so all is not lost. After many years as a teacher, I believe that freshman year is one of the most significant for a secondary student. Many times by the end of freshman year, a student buys what high school is selling or does not. So often I listened to a senior bemoaning the fact of a wasted first two years. His or her G.P.A. floundered due to silliness or laziness, and now it was too late to redeem the grades for college acceptance. Whether a student has floundered throughout four years or has excelled, high school does more for kids in terms of preparation for real life than does college. The constant schedule with its subsequent quest for astute time management is just one area that coerces high school students into forming more self-discipline. Personally, I never found college as demanding in terms of time management as high school. Academics might be more career-specific and challenging in college, but high school forces students to do or to study some things they dislike. Nothing wrong with that demand.

Complaining about anything being too hard dilutes focus. Sure, a certain task just might be difficult, but finding unnecessary fault is useless. Work ethic is the bottom line. Moreover, in a study done by *Forbes* in 2015, work ethic was one of the top five characteristics employers desired in their new hires.

Moreover, life can detour in some marvelous ways: witness a 1973 Boston College graduate who began post-secondary life majoring in education. He did not like that and switched to Arts and Sciences. He disliked that route, so switched to the School of Business, graduating with a B.S. After a year of playing pro ball in Belgium, he went to med school for dermatology, eventually opening a practice in the Washington D.C. area. Today he stands as one of the country's leading MOE's surgeons for treatment of skin cancers.

Sure, attending a good college helps set a path for a career, yet how many students are out there today, saddled with debt, and jobless? A good college helps, but some clarity, risk-taking, patience, and work do much more. Those qualities begin to develop in high school; those qualities students take to college with greater weight than what's in their luggage. Furthermore, one high school class does not determine the outcome of a college decision. A mature balance of academic ability and improvement, community service, intra-school teamwork, and healthy relationships compose the winning ticket for college acceptance. That ticket determines whether the student picks the college or the college picks the student.

Whining states,
Exhibit A: "I just coach; I don't have to teach much."

Exhibit B: "Standards? What standards?
Those are for English and math."

Exhibit C: "Do you think you can pass Joe Athlete?
I need him for Saturday's game."

Exhibit D: (Knock on door while I am teaching)
"Tom, can I take Joe Athlete out of class for
fifteen minutes? Mr. Recruiter is here to talk to him."

A Winning Frame of Mind

Many other examples of debilitating self-talk abound. Talk about expecting nothing. Whining in many cases is embedded in selfishness supported by a lack of work ethic.

Work ethic is the principal component of self-respect. The rest will follow. Work ethic has ties to an oxymoron. Seen in a negative slant, work is a four-letter word, something human nature would love to shun. Ethic seems more positive, a trait most people would admire and hope they would possess in many areas. When this pair is put together, we have a term discussed and applied in a plethora of contexts. Consider the denotation of the word, ethic. Mr. Webster defines it as, "the discipline dealing with what is good and bad" and "the principles of conduct governing an organization or individual." The word discipline underscores the essence of this word.

I heard Coach Hubie Brown, one of the best teachers of basketball in the world, say to a basketball clinic in 1986, "Coaches and teachers need three inherent qualities to be the coach or teacher they want to be: pride, ego, and great work capacity." Those qualities remain prime concepts of any teacher's philosophy. Let's consider each one.

PRIDE

Breaking Bad has been one of my favorite television dramas. In one scene, Jesse, Walter White's meth partner, recalls a moment in high school when he was asked by his shop teacher to make a small cedar box. On the due date, the teacher looked at Jesse's product and remarked, "Jesse, is that the best you can do?" Jesse pondered that question in silence. In the next few weeks he reworked and revised his product until he was finally satisfied, until his internal pride pronounced clarity and finality.

I had the habit of asking students the first thing they wrote on a piece of paper for an assignment.

They typically answered, "My name." Correct. One right answer.

My response was, "How many names do you have?"

"One." Second correct response.

"Then, have the pride to do your best work. If you put your sacred name on anything, you are guaranteeing your best effort. Would you not agree?" We then discussed what pride really meant and the ways it manifested itself in a school or in a person. Consider the following poem:

Your Name
You got it from your father.
Maybe it was all he had to give.
But it's yours to use and cherish
For as long as you may live.
You may lose that which he gave you;
It can always be replaced.
But a black mark on your name, son,
Can never be erased.
So guard it very closely
For when all is said is done,
You'll be glad the name is spotless
When you give it to your son. (Anonymous)

Pride is a learned asset. It develops through good role models, conscious thinking, patience, adversity, and humility. Pride's close cousin is stubbornness. Many times a first attempt falls short; improvement does not just happen. Teachers, students, players, or people in business need the right balance of work, pride, and stubbornness to ensure that a goal might be met. However, we all realize no guarantees exist that any goal will be met. It is in the doing and the striving that growth occurs in a career or a family. Pride is often the difference between success and failure.

There have been countless examples of false pride, as well. The book *Stories for Preaching* describes the Roman Empire, one of the more powerful to rule the world. For hundreds of years the Romans dominated the Mediterranean, building magnificent cities, constructing roads that remain today, and imposing their form of peace upon those they conquered. At the time of Jesus and in the following centuries, the power of Rome seemed unassailable. By the fifth century A.D., the citizens of Rome had enjoyed eight centuries as a superpower. Regaled with tales of victory by their armies in far off places and convinced of their superiority to the barbarian hordes, they were convinced their city would never fall. Then in the first decade of the fifth century, they awoke to find Alaric, king of the Visigoths, standing at their gates with his army.

What a preposterous man to believe Rome would fall to his power! Envoys were sent out to conduct negotiations to have him move away. They began with threats: an attack on Rome would be met by the almighty strength of its innumerable warriors.

Alaric's reply was simple, "The thicker the grass, the more easily scythed."

The envoys realized Alaric could not be fooled by their empty threats. What then would be the price of his departure? Alaric explained that his soldiers would move through the city taking all the gold, silver and anything else of value that could be moved. They would also take with them every barbarian who had been enslaved.

The envoys became hysterical. "But what would that leave us?" they demanded.

"Your lives," Alaric replied. And with that Rome's centuries as an apparently unbeatable superpower came to an end. (end *Stories*)

Rome was missing one vital trait: humility. No doubt the challenge of staying on top of one's game relies on a certain level of pride, and time can diminish that very level. As Olympic decathlon champion Bob Richards says in his book, *The Pride of a Champion*, "Pride is the most important thing in life." Coaches often will talk about this asset with their athletes, classroom teachers not nearly enough. What a relevant topic for a written response from students during the first week of school!

Ego

Doctors find all kinds of information about an individual's health by examining blood. I wish that a finding existed within that red juice to examine the current of energy running through the respective person. To me, that current represents ego, the energy quotient for accomplishment. All people need some level of this trait to strive to be the best in a department, school, business, or organization. Here I retell a brief anecdote from Mark Frost's compelling book, *The Grand Slam: Bobby Jones, America, and the Story of Golf.* Bobby Jones was one of the first true money winners in professional golf. He designed Augusta National, the home course for the annual Masters tournament, arguably the most prestigious competition among the four major golf championships.

'On the second day Jones lapped the field and finished thirteen shots ahead with Smith in distant second place. Bob had stretched his lead to eighteen with only three holes left, when a half-hour delay on the sixteenth tee blunted his concentration. While killing time with Keeler, Granny Rice, and a privileged, interested spectator by the name of Ty Cobb, Bob ignored the fiery Cobb's suggestions that he stay on his feet and swing the club to keep loose. Instead, Bob lay down on the grass and lingered while he chatted with his old friends. When play resumed he hooked two of his final three drives into the weeds and tossed away three strokes on two of the finishing three holes. Later that evening over cocktails at Cobb's house in Augusta, the recently retired baseball immortal took him aside and, as Bob later described, 'I got the dressing-down of my life. It was not Ty's idea just to win, but to win by the most you could. That's what made him such a great player' (Frost).

Ty Cobb had an ego as large as the Grand Canyon and at times was considered rather ruthless in his quest for greatness, but he did not achieve the Hall of Fame by wishing for it. Not everyone can reach a Hall of Fame, but everyone does have a ceiling for greatness. Having an ego with balance-"It's nice to be great, but it's greater to be nice"-can be the buffer for the times when events or situations stand in the way. Ego keeps the engine humming toward set goals. It motivates the achievers to find out everything about what they are doing, so that they stay at or near the top. Ego will contemplate, but not worry about consequences.

I look at some of my coaching heroes (Hubie Brown, the late Rick Majerus, Mike Krzyzewski, the late Bill Schaefer, Pat Sullivan, just to name a few), and my personal heroes (my dad, my mother, Larry Bird), and I find a sufficient amount of ego that energized their daily lives. Those egos were never obnoxious, just balanced; never selfish, just sharing. Teachers need some ego to stifle the bad days and to respond with inner strength to the obstacles so that these problems become advantages and impetus for improvement. As a department chairman, I witnessed many occurrences where ego replaced work ethic. Most of those times it was the veteran teacher whose ego became stagnant. That teacher relied on past experience to recreate stale lessons, did not cooperate in new ventures or ideas, and thought that his/her way was the only way to teach a certain skill or subject. Cynicism results. Would it not be wondrous for all veteran teachers to retain the vigor and eagerness exhibited during their first few years as a teacher? Some do; many do not.

GREAT WORK CAPACITY

"GROWING UP, MY BIGGEST FEAR WAS BEING AVERAGE.
I WANTED TO BE RICH. I WANTED TO BE A MILLIONAIRE.
I GET WHAT I WANT, ONE WAY OR THE OTHER.
SO I BECAME A MILLIONAIRE—MANY TIMES OVER, I MIGHT ADD.
HOW?
HARD F——— WORK!"

~LEN DYKSTRA
HOUSE OF NAILS, A MEMOIR OF LIFE ON THE EDGE

For people to possess G.W.C., a muscle builder for the mental muscle required for a significant career, they have to be just as lucky as they are good at what they do.

Why lucky? We are all born without our consent. Once we realize we are alive, we find ourselves surrounded by this group called a family. We learn all kinds of lessons, beliefs, motivations, and knowledge from that intimate society. My father was a tool and die maker for over forty years. He established his own successful business with his brother in Chicago. Dad left around 5:30 and came home after a twelve or thirteen hour day. I worked for him during the summers throughout high school and college and saw the effort he would put into his career. Sweat and hard labor were an everyday challenge, but he performed what he needed to do without complaint. As soon as he walked into our house in the evening, he dropped being a boss and became my dad, helping with some chores around the house, but always having time to toss the baseball with me in the alley behind our house. He was unafraid of work; he welcomed it. Mark Twain's words are accurate when he said, "When I was a boy of fourteen, my father was so ignorant I could hardly stand to have the old man around. But when I got to be twenty-one, I was astonished at how much he had learned in seven years." Our stay-at-home mother handled the three of us, cooked scrumptious meals, made sure we did our homework and trusted we did it right, had time to volunteer at the local hospital, and kept the house humming and clean. She was the engine in the family. From those two giants I witnessed the value of hard work; they would not accept minimal effort. Children either misunderstand the examples from their parents, or underestimate their steady influence. Many children have not been as fortunate as I was; however, if people with less auspicious backgrounds observe closely, they can find the mentors and models they need. It is one thing to have good models, another thing to take advantage of them.

How might this apply to teachers or coaches? One example is my experience with two student teachers, in effect, "a tale of two cities, the best and the worst of times." First impressions can last. My first protégé, currently an English teacher at Ottawa High School in Illinois, earned his degree at Elmhurst College. As my first student teacher at York High School, he was a shining star from the start. Unafraid of the workload, time pressure, and overwhelming preparation for a student teacher, he entered school every day with a smile and usually left with one, enhancing his rapport with that daily demeanor. He was a sponge, absorbing everything I advised him. Once he advanced to the point of taking over my five classes, he asked the right questions and revealed maturity beyond his years with astute and relevant lesson plans. One particular episode germane to every student teacher's experience captured his potential. He had prepared a lesson to his three English 2-Honors classes. The first two classes unfolded according to the plan; the third one was during fifth period, a very intelligent, eager group. His plan flamed out and crashed after twenty minutes. In his words, "Those kids did everything I had planned; I was at a loss for what to do over the next thirty minutes, and I told them so." I happened to be in the classroom at that time, so I walked up to the front, put my arm around him, and asked the class, "Can you tell why Mr. — is going to be an outstanding teacher?" After a few responses, I answered, "Because he is honest. He leveled with you and you responded well." I gave him an extender for his planned discussion; he took flight once again with that suggestion, and the class enjoyed a profitable discussion for the rest of the period. When all was said and done, I had no doubt he would flourish as an English teacher because he was honest; he was meant for that calling, not just for that career. Today he is one of the most respected teachers at Ottawa High School as a department chairman. I also know his warmth and care as a father of two boys.

Take all the positives from that tale, subtract them from my next student-teacher experience, and you have candidate #2. It is one thing being over-whelmed; it is quite another to let that feeling be the guiding force. My second protégé lasted about a month. There was little work ethic but a laundry list of excuses. In our final discussion where we decided to end the experiment, his parting words were, "I will never underestimate again what teachers have to do." At least he learned something.

I knew one particular teacher who could not wait to leave the building every day. He was out the door by 2:55; the last bell rang at 2:52. One time he was in such a hurry he left his keys in his classroom door. He was a very average classroom teacher. Just mentioning. Contrast that to the majority of staff who sacrifice their free time just to coach or tutor students, to run the after-school clubs that give many a shy student some confidence, to stay for forty minutes after a practice to work with that soccer player for his dribbling improvement, to go home then return to school in the evening for four hours to show a film for a social science class, or to get up thirty minutes earlier than usual in order to arrive at school to meet with a student for some extra writing tutelage. Examples abound revealing what a true G.W.C. looks like.

G.W.C. is not something innate. People learn this from examples, from experience, from their own effort, and from the evaluation of those results. I used to tell my players, "Hustle is a talent. Not everyone can be as strong as the other or as quick, but everyone can hustle. Learn how." I used to tell my English teachers similar points: increase your ability to work, reread the same books again and again, keep your promises, finish what you start, reflect each week, and explore the details of your craft. Try to keep in mind: *If the road is easy, it might be leading in the wrong direction.*

Teachers and coaches, as you approach the door to your job each morning, see it as a door of opportunity for expanding the values which help a teaching and/or a coaching career evolve, sustain, and empower those people under their guidance. This attitude will increase your respect and humility for expecting no handouts and the self-fulfilling power within that maxim.

Whining remarks,
"Listen to your body when training and when it gets
too hard, let up. Your mind doesn't know
what it's talking about."

A Winning Frame of Mind

Ahh, the constant battle between mind and body. I have heard the theory that mental is to physical as four is to one. The mind drives the body, that robot adhering to the many commands the mind feeds it. When I was basketball coach at Immaculate Conception High School, one player disliked distance running during pre-season conditioning. He would complain to me constantly. The more he complained, the greater the need for him to do that type of running. Some coaches might shy away from that type of strategy. Not me. I saw it as an opportunity for this player to develop more mental toughness. So, the young man ran…ran a lot. Doing what he disliked the most hardened his will to compete. He became one of the most reliable players I ever coached and earned a basketball scholarship to Northeastern Illinois University. He became one of the nation's leading foul shooters as a senior in college. He had won the battle against his mind's foibles, and has taken that triumph to new heights as one of the most successful salesmen in his company.

The same was true in my classroom. My students wrote. And wrote. And wrote more. The expectation was firm: they did the work or did not pass. Whether the task was journals, formal papers, response writing, peer revisions, notes, or written essay tests, my students worked the pen. Writing is the truest test of students' ability to think. Writing takes time. Writing takes work. Writing takes re-writing. One of my first points as the English department chairman at Lincoln-Way East was that writing had to be a minimum of 50% of a student's semester assessments for every teacher, no matter the course. Writing blends the abilities to read with comprehension, to develop revision skill, to improve depth of thought, and to incorporate modes of expression. The students who improve as writers-and if the students write about their readings in various ways, they will improve-bring an efficiency and a confidence to college often unmatched by their peers from various parts of the country. We often heard from our graduates at Lincoln-Way that they were asked to help their peers revise papers. The graduates were often asked, "How did you learn to write so well?" That praise was earned through the efforts of the outstanding teachers in the Lincoln-Way English departments.

Why are many faculty reluctant to challenge their students with quality work and written assignments on a consistent basis? If the answers are: "no time for all that grading", "I'm not an English teacher; writing is their job", "I don't know how to grade all that stuff", or "They won't do the work anyway, why should I break my own neck?" perhaps that career is on life support. I write more about the necessity of writing as the baseline for a school's overall curriculum later in the book.

When teachers and coaches get to a point where students complain about the workload or blame the teachers for the students' lack of time for anything else, those educators know they are getting someplace. That pivotal point tests the relentlessness of those teachers and, in an odd way, tests the love teachers have for their pupils. Conscience asks, *Should I ease up, am I giving too much?* Do not listen. Maintain the course. Remember the mantra: Work hard; recovery is quick.

WHINING REMARKS,
"I AM SOOO SATISFIED WITH WHAT I'VE DONE,
EVEN IF I'VE ONLY BEEN AT IT FOR TWO YEARS.
I WANT THE CHANCE TO DO WHATEVER,
SO I AM LEAVING WHATEVER TO BECOME A, LIKE, WHATEVER."

Department chair responds, "Why not give your choice of career, much less your speaking ability, a chance to blossom? You have barely scratched the surface. You are doing a solid job, but you will really understand some of the nuances of this profession if you give it more time. Also, in that way you will have more experience to fall back on if a new venture falls through or if you do apply for the desired position."

WHINING REPLIES,
"No, I CAN MAKE MORE MONEY AND I WOULD NOT HAVE THE HOURS I HAVE
NOW. BESIDES, ALL THOSE PAPERS TO, LIKE, GRADE REALLY INTERFERE WITH
MY, LIKE, SOCIAL LIFE."

A Winning Frame of Mind

At times I dealt with younger, inexperienced staff expressing a desire for greener pastures. Many times it was the siren call for an administrative position. Most of these occurrences occurred with the teacher having just a few years in the classroom. The conversation asked my opinion on which second degree to earn: an English Masters or administrative certification. My answer was always the same.

I asked about goals; most times the people in question could not define any. Good time to ponder such a thought.

I would repeat the tried but true adage, "The grass is always greener on the other side of the fence." Administration looks good from the outside: no grading, no lessons to prepare (Ever see an administrator present something to the entire faculty?), no essays (Ever have to write a grant?), no report cards (ever see the state report cards?), fewer parent calls (really?), no kids (you sure about that?).

Why be a jack-of-all-trades and a master of none? Excellence means learning as much as possible about what you are doing. Having two years of teaching experience qualifies that teacher for nothing other than two years of experience. Learn *the trade*. Develop an accurate and relevant awareness of what classroom teachers endure on a daily basis, year after year. My wish list for making the jump from classroom teacher to front office would contain these guidelines: 1. After a teacher has had a minimum of ten years of classroom experience, then that teacher can think about administration; 2. All administrators have to teach one class every two or three years, so that they can stay attuned to changes in culture, in kids, in standards, in their colleagues, and in themselves. Unfortunately, with the surplus of teacher turnover and the lack of respect teachers receive, administrators become younger and younger. Young teachers sometimes see administration as the only sure way to make money. Is making money the reason you chose teaching?

Don't be a jack-of-all-trades. *Learn the trade.*

THE RECURRENT, REPETITIVE WHINE
HEARD IN THE 80S, 90S, AND 21ST CENTURY:
"THE STANDARDS ARE CHANGING AGAIN!?? %*##!!
WE JUST GOT USED TO THE OTHER ONES!"

A Winning Frame of Mind

I freely admit I did my share of whining as a teacher and a chairman every time the dictum fell on our shoulders about a new set of standards. My whining, complete with some inner cursing, lasted about fifteen minutes, and then I went to work. However, I wondered if we could ever settle on one group of intelligent, accurate, relevant, insightful standards that encapsulate the desired goals for a child's education? Probably not. Standards that education officials create and enforce cannot cover the various demographics and economies of the hundreds of districts in the U.S.A. That being said, I do believe that the current Common Core State Standards (C.C.S.S) are the best group of goals I have studied and applied, but once again, it is up to teachers and communities to supply the support, the energy, and the relentless pursuit of nurturing and expanding their students' work habits.

In short, *somebody* has to supply standards. Standards signal levels of quality, norms, or models for comparative study, but they begin with *why* one teaches. Here is more factual background:

According to Marzano and Kendall (1996), many educators consider the publication of A Nation at Risk (National Commission on Excellence in Education, 1983) as the "initiating event of the modern standards movement." With the passage of the Goals 2000: Educate America Act in 1994, U.S. lawmakers acknowledged the importance of high standards in improving education. Since that time, the call for higher standards has come from all areas: administrators, teachers, teachers unions, state-level and national-level educational organizations, business and community leaders, parents, and students.

The push for standards has guided change efforts at all levels of education and has brought about positive results. "The standards-based movement in America is on solid footing and is slowly but surely changing the way we think of teaching and learning in America's classrooms," notes the American Federation of Teachers (1999). "Nearly three-fourths of the teachers who have worked with standards for at least six years say the standards have had a positive impact on their schools." (p. 12). Ravitch (1995) adds, "Standards can improve achievement by clearly defining what is to be taught and what kind of performance is expected" (p. 25). Many efforts to improve education begin with the process of integrating standards into the curriculum (Berkas & Pattison, Internet).

When curriculum and standards meet, teachers cringe, and anticipate-with good reason. How many times will standards change? On one side, teachers are suspicious of the source of the standards. Politicians and administrators do not have an accurate ear on what is happening in the classrooms since they might have been removed from that arena for a number of years, nor might they solicit sufficient feedback from teachers regarding what skills are more essential. How frustrating for teachers to align a curriculum, only to have the state or federal government dictate a few years later new standards for all to follow, meaning a new realignment. Thus, both teacher effectiveness and their reactions to standards compare to a sudden storm: varied, unpredictable, surprising, and scary.

But no matter the weather, standards are necessary. Do we not follow the Constitution as the law of the land? The founding fathers designed those standards we agree to and live by today. Someone has to be accountable for making standards. If every teacher went his or her own way in the classroom, what kind of system would we have? Chaos. How would be able to give a similar experience to all students who take the same course? If teachers spent the time studying the standards and integrating those standards within their own creativity and lesson designs, instead of complaining about them, perhaps their charges would be better prepared.

Excellence means learning everything one can about what one does. Standards are steps to excellence. Standards state expectations. Without them, how would we realize improvement in our teaching and in our students? Standards are necessary parts of that equation. They are stepping stones toward that Holy Grail: the positive influence teachers possess for every student under their charge, with that influence leading to the large range of improvement students experience over four years of high school or eight years of elementary-intermediate-junior high education. It is unfortunate that the federal government tries to enlist students' motivation through an avalanche of standardized testing, when the motivation for learning should be facilitated by the teachers and their curricula. Assessments should be made and kept by local districts/teachers with the CCSS as the *measures* for successful learning. The teachers are the experts; every district within every state possesses a variety of demographics that create unequal playing fields. The present pressure of comparing one state to another, one school to another is the government playing, "My dad is better than your dad." Any expert knows that the constant comparing between one student to another leads to useless results. Not every student has the same talent for any one part of curriculum, just as some are destined to be mechanics, or stockbrokers, or police officers. The government seems to think that the C.C.S.S. should be the entire outcome; however, the C.C.S.S. are simply *measures*, not outcomes. It should be up to the leadership of each district's administrators to engineer the formulae necessary for the needs of their communities to educate their children with the C.C.S.S. as a guide, as ways to meet students' needs. Isn't helping each student learn what teachers try to do anyway?

There is one step I would have recommended to the experts who designed the C.C.S.S. to have within its standards. It is a value teachers subtly instruct to their students; it is like a silent vapor permeating any quality curriculum. That step is *persistence*. Angela Lee Duckworth (https://youtu.be/H14bBuluwB8) promotes the essential quality of *grit* as an asset for students. Grit is one rock that students should be acquiring through the instructional rigor of their teachers. Students rarely realize that this quality is being fostered as they trudge through high school. There is no mention of grit or persistence in the Common Core. How many teachers will discuss this quality as an *essence* to their classes? That virtue is just as essential as learning any math parabola, English metaphor, or history date. It is so worthy for inquiry, a term and method promoted and desired in today's classroom. The more grit a student has, the higher level of learning is possible. The grittier kids many times have less talent, but a greater willingness to persist despite challenging obstacles.

Pressure makes diamonds. Finding the value in both positives and negatives has its influence. That influence is called enrichment. Enrichment lasts well beyond a final grade, and standards are steps toward that enrichment.

EXPECT DIFFICULTIES

Perhaps we have heard the saying, "Within difficulty lies opportunity"? Many times the opportunity appears with pain and hardship. Many times the lessons within those difficult moments are the latent springs of growth Henry David Thoreau described in the *Conclusion* in his journal *Walden*, the unheard whispers that carry us through mountains of challenge later in life. A particular moment of difficulty appeared one winter morning at St. Ferdinand on Chicago's northwest side. I was a seventh grade altar boy for the parish and during that particular week in January, I was assigned the 6:00 Mass. My bungalow on Roscoe Street was seven blocks from the parish, a walking distance of about fifteen to twenty minutes. Not that morning. Overnight ten inches of snow had fallen, and had not diminished. I could have called in sick, but my parents did not allow that; I never bothered to ask. My dad had already left for work, so there was only one way to go-on foot. I trudged through the snow, through the dead, unplowed walks and streets to serve Mass. It took me over thirty minutes to get to church. I was the only altar boy. The organist, three elderly ladies, and the priest were in attendance. The Mass took fifteen minutes. I felt a sense of pride that I not only overcame the weather, but also felt a sense of obligation. That sense has never relinquished its hold on me and kept me churning through many a difficult class, task, or student.

The difficult —— can be the cause of many sleepless nights, ulcers, and teacher abandonment. Abandonment? Harsh word. Yet, this emotion occurs when reluctant students skip assignments, accumulate dean referrals, and disrespect themselves and others. They do not give that class their total effort; consequently, teachers abandon those students to the failure list or to next year's teacher. If any class or student deserves a total effort on the part of the teacher, it is that one class whose students are crying for discipline, enthusiasm, attention, and love. Want to really learn how to teach? Take on a few collaborative classes, the basics, or the Special Services groups. Want to really learn what it takes to coach? Take on a few bad teams or a program in need of serious resuscitation. Those classes or players will reveal all aspects of both a teacher's strengths and character flaws, and from those experiences, teachers either grow or wither on the vine.

Fourteen boys, two girls, and a mountain of a paper trail constituted one of my first classes at Glenbrook North High School in 1984, my first public school position. I also had two other classes of junior basic students, but that fourth period was grist for the mill. Some of my colleagues warned me to never turn my back and had more pointed advice about certain boys. My department chairman advised me numerous times to divide and conquer. One colleague advised, "Don't tell them anything about you"; another said, "Let it all hang out." I took the middle road and that decision saved me. The students were intensely curious about who I was, whom I loved or idolized, what I did away from school and in summers, why I became a teacher, what girls I dated (I could only provide a very short list!), and on and on. They cared not about grammar, reading, literature, or anything else remotely connected to English. This class occurred in the middle of the day. So my charges came to class hungry, horny, amorous, angry, tired, bored, or desperate. Notice the word *studious* is absent, and would be for the majority of the time. The first week became a war with a relatively inexperienced teacher of eleven private school years and a sneaky band of marauders. They denied the reality of any homework. They interrupted, "Hey, Mr. A-, you ever get a speeding ticket??" in the middle of the definition of a simile. They would tease each other incessantly: "Ha, you trying to be teacher's pet?" when one student had the gall to answer not one, but two questions in class. I left this class every day with the incessant drumbeat of failure. Group work was out of the question; they could not talk about an academic topic in small groups, much less any other subject with any focus, without personal attacks disrupting any harmony in the class. I started to give them class time for homework, which gave me a chance to talk to them individually to build up some rapport. I narrowed an actual lesson of teacher talk to fifteen minutes on a vow that students would cooperate during that time frame. I started reading aloud to them every day and this proved a worthy supplement to most lessons. If a story from my life happened to surface, I went with it. If a student actually asked a relevant question, I answered it with as much embellishment and praise as I could. Those methods created interest for both of us. Why? I was meeting them where their spirits sojourned as I tried to reconnect to English. The two managed to unite more fully as the year progressed. I realized that all students focus and supply a level of cooperation if they have a reason for learning and if they felt the teacher cared about them *and* their learning. I tried to give them both.

Only by Thanksgiving did the class concentrate together for more than twenty minutes, other than on Mondays when they were too exhausted from their weekend shenanigans. Unlike many teachers, I treasured Mondays; I felt that the beginning of the week provided a fresh start. So, I treated Mondays as I would the first five minutes of every class, that time when students know whether that particular class will be one of curiosity or boredom. By December, the students were calmer and beginning to acknowledge each other with some respect. They were working together well; I was down to only two discipline reports a week on average and only two phone calls home to discuss student conduct. Most of the time when I had to phone a home, I could not reach the parent and rarely received a call back. By the end of the year, the class had diminished to eleven students. A couple of students were dropped due to various reasons. That failure drumbeat diminished as my confidence improved.

By the end of the year, I looked forward to this class because my own use of strategies and personal stories had elevated the rapport and the trust. We were able to have some fun together, but achieve some progress in learning at the same time. The outcomes far exceeded the actual journey, but without the journey, the outcomes possess little satisfaction or significance. *Relish* might be too hopeful a descriptor for the difficult class that has a habit of appearing every year in a teacher's schedule. *Love* the difficult class? *Challenge* the difficult class? I let you decide. Whatever the word, the level of toil combined with the integrity of the relationship will influence the level of mutual respect and love. See challenges as opportunities.

On another note, what do teachers do with the very willing, yet unskilled student? Talk about difficult. These challenges will test the patience of instructors and the very reasons why they teach. I maintain that in any lessons with these novices, the material teachers try to communicate with various methods pales in comparison to the lessons of grit and perseverance they are communicating to their willing learners. Those themes stick. I once met weekly with a student who had little confidence in her writing ability, and with good reason. Her writing was lifeless. She had command of sentence structure and spelling, yet her organization and writing said nothing. We spent time writing short poems, focusing on verb choices, turning short sentences into long ones and vice versa, understanding purpose, examining pictures and trying to detail the imagery. She began to enjoy writing, and perhaps that ingredient was what was missing. These lessons were not easy for either of us, but the reward for her was not becoming a better writer; the reward was the necessity of relentless pursuit when one is aspiring to a level of art or ability. For me, the reward was realizing that traditional methods were/are sometimes insufficient. Teacher creativity and bold risk-taking are the lifelines of any good teacher.

For a provocative and humorous book on teaching reluctant or the willing, yet untalented students, read *Teacher Man* by the late Frank McCourt or listen to some of his talks on *YouTube*. McCourt, a Pulitzer Prize winner and entertaining speaker, said one of my favorite maxims about teaching, "If you're teaching and not learning, you're not really teaching." Maybe that reason describes why teachers need to *relish* the difficult class or the challenging students. Teaching, after all, is about teachers finding their professional identities, that part of their souls that elevates the relentless pursuit of the unattainable.

YOUR TURN

Describe ways you can help particular students confront their problems wisely and patiently instead of avoiding them or blaming others for those issues.

FATIGUE

I was fortunate to have met numerous tests of will as a high school athlete. Fortunate, you say? Yes, for unknown to me, these tests built my endurance for teaching and coaching. For starters, my physical education curriculum in high school consisted of this agenda: first quarter nonstop calisthenics for the whole period, five days a week for nine weeks; second quarter gymnastics, complete with mats and parallel bars (we learned it all); third quarter wrestling, all the crippling holds complete with a weight-class tournament at the end of the quarter; fourth quarter track and field and some softball…if we behaved. After four years of that brutality, even the worst of the shapeless were eager tornadoes. Then there was the brilliant idea of Coach Schaefer: next year's team running ten miles with ankle weights on the last day of my junior year (1968). I mention that the temperature was 94. He mentioned to us as he lined us at the starting line, "We could be pretty good next year. Let's start today and get in better shape."

Ten miles? Forty laps? In two hours?? And the Olympics were still a couple of years away! We accomplished the feat, not without some nausea, dizziness, dry heaves, and muttered vulgarities of all sorts. We helped each other through it. We battled fatigue and survived. We conquered our improvised *Unbroken*.

Of course, teachers do not have to run the track to determine their worth, at least not physically. Teachers' tracks take many twists, paths, mountains, and valleys. More like a marathon. From the people who appear at the August institute tanned and fresh, eager and inspired; come October and the subsequent months, those same people appear bedraggled, anxious, more melancholy, and yes, t-i-r-e-d. Raising families, teaching students, grading, meeting demands of supervisors, coaching or facilitating teams and clubs, running special events, and volunteering to help students' activities all pull teachers' gas gauges down to E quickly.

Battling fatigue is never easy, but it is a battle to *win*. No seconds here. One interaction with a struggling student can turn a life around; teachers cannot afford fatigue. Personally, I avoided the actual word and any of its synonyms. I felt those mental blocks lowered my resistance, developed a crack in my mental armor, an armor I was always careful to protect. I had plenty of days where fatigue was a factor, but I refused to let my students or peers detect that. Some of my best teaching days were those that came after the longest nights. I tried to relish fatigue, taking it as a personal challenge. Some of my worst nights came the night before a formal evaluation. Sound familiar? Practicing my lesson as a lullaby never worked. I tossed and turned, awakened hours before the alarm, and gagged my way through a nervous breakfast. Usually, the lesson worked because I worked. As I walked into the door every morning, I told myself, "Get going. People count on you."

What is more important to the kids: grading five more essays past midnight or getting some rest so you are eager for the next day? Over the years I overheard plenty of teachers come into the office saying, "I graded until 3 a.m. last night and did I get a lot done." I worried about that person that day. Would that individual run out of steam by noon? How accurate were the comments and grades on those essays? Was the same energy used for each one?

Speaking of energy, ever wonder why teachers are by nature an optimistic group? Besides being around the innocence of kids, teachers enjoy *summer vacation*, the very thing the majority of the general public dislike and/or criticize about the profession of teaching. In the June 1, 2015 edition of *Time*, Jack Dickey writes about the past and present status of summer vacation in America. Here are some provocative pieces from that essay:

- "Ninety-six percent of American workers recognize the importance of taking a vacation (according to a study by the U.S. Travel Association). Elementary research suggests that it's restorative and good for the heart health. But over the past 30 years, the U.S. has become the no-vacation nation…stressing both employers and employees how endure greater turnover and lower productivity when their workers get little time off" (46).

- "In 2013 the average American worker with access to vacation was sixteen days worth. Compare that to Bureau of Labor statistics from 1976-2000 which show an average of 20.3 days taken over that period" (46).

- "The quality of vacation time has eroded along with the quantity. Technology now perpetually tethers workers to the office; the smartphone never takes time off. 61% of workers, according to a 2013 survey, say they typically keep working, even if they are not at work. Throw in high school sports starting earlier, two working spouses, and a longer average school year, and vacation time becomes a minor miracle" (64).

- "The U.S. is the only advanced economy that does not require employers to offer paid holidays or time off. No paid vacations. Zilch. Not even a single U.S. state has a paid-vacation law on the books. So what, you may say. This is not Europe where Luxembourg guarantees workers 35 paid days off, Norway 29 days, and Switzerland 28, according to the Organisation for Economic Co-operation and Development. Those three nations happen to be the three OECD economies that finished ahead of the U. S. in 2013 in gross domestic product per capita, the favored metric for workforce productivity" (47).

OK, enough of the startling statistics. What they might suggest is that teachers not only thrive with some time off, but also can the same fact be linked to the overall work force. It is one thing to battle fatigue during the actual working hours; it is another to have the actual time off to recharge and battle it that way. In short, just as workers need time away from their jobs to recharge, so too do teachers need summers. If you are still in doubt and not a teacher, go try teaching for reassurance.

Fatigue is a factor in teacher retention and turnover. Examine the following:

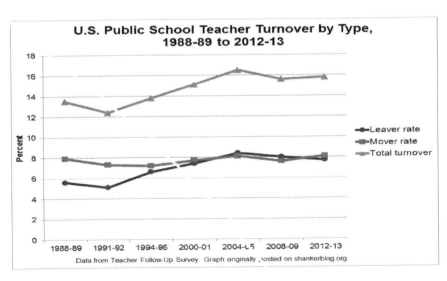

Update On Teacher Turnover In The U.S. by Matthew Di Carlo—January 22, 2010

The chart reveals that teacher turnover has leveled some in recent years. However, that stat does not identify the issue with retaining young/new teachers. Teaching experiences severe turnover, especially during the first five years of a teacher career. In "Building a Better Teacher: Michigan Classrooms Loaded with Rookie Teachers who Soon Wash Out" in *Bridge Magazine*, Ron French notes, "In 1987-88, the most common amount of experience for U.S. teachers was 15 years, according to the U.S Department of Education; twenty years later, it was one year. The state does not track the percent of educators who drop out of public schools. But it does record the longevity and age of teachers, which serve as proxies for the scope of teacher churn." Michigan being just one example, the problem of teachers' leaving the profession can be attributed to some of the following factors: lack of training, lack of mentoring, the recruitment and placement of industrial people into teaching jobs, and lack of respect for the profession. When was the last time we saw education as a top priority in a presidential campaign? All of these factors lead to mental anguish on the part of staff; mental fatigue is to physical as 4 is to 1. Does an astronaut need a spacesuit? Does a car need brakes? Do teachers need recoup time, improved mentoring, respect for the profession, increase of salaries, and administrative support? Each of these improvements will lessen teacher burnout and increase teacher efficiency.

Teachers, since this book expects no handouts, expect none of the aforementioned. You *can* expect to become tired. Welcome that feeling. *Increase* your expectations on those days. Have your best days when you are most fatigued: the baby never slept, the child is ill, you just could not sleep after that great Cubs win, etc. Excuses and whining have the same number of letters. On your hardest days, expect a lot, so that the day becomes a winner. Anticipate greatness, no matter the physical condition.

APPROACH

We become what we think about. At our August Institutes during my years at Lincoln-Way, the previous superintendent said as much with his statement, "I do not go to work; I go to school." Thinking of school as work poisons the brain. What could be work when teachers are with young people for a part of their day? I venture to say that readers/teachers across the country would refute that question with a plethora of evidence, and of course, not every day is nirvana. How many times have we left school in a much darker mood than when we entered that morning? Record keeping, misunderstandings, one student's blatant, thought-less outburst can make a day miserable. At each school I taught, I had some of those anxiety-drenched phone calls with parents caterwauling about how terrible a teacher I was, about how I should pursue another occupation, about how I could not teach, about how unfair and nonhuman I was, ad infinitum. At one school where I was the head basketball coach for five years, I had the privilege of coaching many fine young men with excellent parents; however, just three sets of parents made my coaching life unpleasant. One particular ax-grinder would sit five rows behind me to cheer for the *opponent*. Imagine the confusion and anxiety level of his son, who was one of the better players, but naturally did not get enough shots. It only takes a couple disgruntled people on the outside for any teacher or coach to question why he/she ever chose teaching as a profession, but thoroughbreds carry on, knowing each day carries a new attitude and new possibilities. Through all the rough parts, thoroughbreds keep the faith.

As I approached the doors at my various schools, I had a pit in my stomach. This feeling qualified my determination to succeed that day, to help one student I was not reaching, to say hello and learn one more unknown teacher's name, to be more pleasant to all the unsung heroes in the school: the secretaries, maintenance people, cafeteria ladies, bus drivers, etc. I could not wait to get to school to open new doors to opportunity. I expected nothing from anyone; I expected myself to grow. My growth was realized through the friendship, partnership, and love from the following incomplete sampling of colleagues and mentors through the years. Perhaps you will find a nugget to activate for yourself from these treasures, these exemplary teachers who expect(ed) no handouts. They approached each day, opened new doors with vigor and optimism.

My Mother and Father
(the *classroom-houses* on Keating Ave., Dickens St.,
and Roscoe St. in Chicago and in Des Plaines)
~discipline, love, togetherness~

Mr. Richard Geist
(my cooperating teacher during my student-teaching experience at
Newton South High School in Newton, Massachusetts)
**~my first example of a real teacher in the work force,
ready every day to teach and to inspire~**

Professor Albert Duhamel
(Boston College, Shakespearean scholar)
~*Power corrupts; absolute power corrupts absolutely* (Lord Acton)…
his favorite quotation—he was a master at making Shakespeare
both enjoyable and thoughtful~

(The late) Rev. William Sheridan
(Quigley Seminary North-Latin)
~the ease and humor he transferred to his students while
communicating a difficult subject~

Roger O'Brien
(Quigley Seminary North—English, retired)
~"You can write, Tom"~

Bishop James P. Keleher
(Quigley Seminary North—Social Studies)
~his clarity in teaching cultures worlds apart~

(The late) Bishop Thaddeus Jakubowski
(Quigley Seminary North-Latin)
~the best *Jeckyl and Hyde* persona. His gruff demeanor
as dean of students belied his charm and grace
as a person and his love for students~

Matt Blackall
(Glenbrook North High School—English, retired)
~ready every day, supportive every day,
never sought reward or attention, quietly effective~

Peg Forbes
(Glenbrook North High School—English, retired)
~loved what she did and the students knew that~

Ken Mularski
(Glenbrook North High School—English, retired)
~the simplicity and the effectiveness of differentiated instruction
with the power of knowledge~

(THE LATE) GERRY LOMBARDO
(York High School—English)
~ahead of his time with his incorporation of media,
especially music, into his lessons' goals~

JEFF KELLER
(Lincoln-Way East High School—Math Department Chair)
~giving his whole self to the school through expert instruction, steady
leadership, extra participation outside of class, and smiles~

DOMINIC BELMONTE
(York High School as the English Chairman,
Current CEO at Golden Apple Foundation in Chicago)
~caught a snapshot of every student and presented multiple ways
for each student to show that picture~

CLARK FISCHER
(York High School—Assistant Principal, retired)
~the patience, work ethic, knowledge, and empathy required
for excellence as an administrator~

RICH KOLIMAS
(Lincoln-Way East High School—English)
~the excellence at his daily readiness for the classroom and the court—
one never interfered with the other. Both of my sons took his sophomore
English class and freely admitted to me without any bribery,
"Mr. Kolimas was one of my best teachers!"~

MRS. KAREN MCCONNELL
(Lincoln-Way East High School—English)
~fostering a classroom environment straight from *The Three Bears*—
not too cold, not too hot, just right~

MRS. KATI NAKAMURA AND MRS. NICOLE DANGMAN
(Lincoln-Way East—English)
~the power of teacher-teamwork to revise curriculum and assessments
and create good lessons without complaining. Often these two
cyclones volunteered to experiment and were two of the first in
the department to attempt new, suggested strategies.~

Dr. Susan Anstett
(Lincoln-Way East High School—Chairman of Health, P.E., Drivers Ed.)
~ability to handle crises with foresight, clarity, and poise~

(THE LATE) Mr. William Schaefer
(Quigley Seminary North—Physical Education, Boys' Basketball Coach)
~faith and foresight, incredible humor, relentless work ethic~

(THE LATE) Mrs. Linda Porick
(Lincoln-Way East High School—English)
~a prime example of the statement credited to
President Theodore Roosevelt, *People don't care how much
you know until they know how much you care*~

Don Young
(Lincoln-Way East High School—Math)
~the down-to-earth empathy required to bolster
students' readiness to learn~

Mrs. Laura Slusarski
(Lincoln-Way East High School—Spanish)
~enthusiasm, enthusiasm, and enthusiasm embolden her instruction~

Dr. Jerel Howard
(Northeastern Illinois University, retired)
~the combination of knowledge, communication skills,
enjoyment and encouragement for the instruction of writing.
He was far ahead of his time~

Josh Holder
(Lincoln-Way East High School—Social Studies)
~great example of both popularity and respect~

John Terry
(Lincoln-Way East High School—Math)
~the ability to step out of the formal teacher and reveal
a fun side to students and faculty~

Mrs. Stephanie Natalie
(Lincoln-Way East High School—Physical Education)
**~incredible drive and adaptability to harness special skills for
Special Education adaptive P.E. students~**

Mr. Experience
(the ever-present influence)
~taking what you know and applying that to the newness of each day~

For the following event, I was the one searched out, and to say I expected nothing was a true understatement. First a bit of context: the student/Marine of focus in the article below was in my English 3 class as a junior and failed both semesters. He did not take summer school for make-up. When the following school year began, the opening institute gave staff their rosters for their classes, "a day of infamy," to quote a great President. I saw Brandon's name; I felt that unqualified doom that teachers feel in those spots. Smile evaporated, stomach tightened, blood pressure skyrocketed. As that first class commenced the following day, I greeted Brandon at the door, took him aside, and mentioned that it might be in his best interest to change his class to a different English teacher. No baggage that way, fresh start. I used every convincer I had. Brandon responded, "No, Mr. Anstett, I asked for you. I wanted to prove to you I could pass your class."

I told Brandon that there would be no special treatment; he had to do all his work, read all the novels again, etc. After all, history has a way of repeating itself. In Brandon's case, I believed he would provide more evidence to further substantiate that premise. Talk about expecting nothing!

"OK, Mr. Anstett, I understand." And so we began.

Thus, I am reprinting my *Voice of the People* article titled *A Teaching Reward Beyond Measure*, published in *The Chicago Tribune* on September 27, 2002. It seems relevant here to reemphasize that there is always more than the curriculum. Moreover, expecting no handouts has its own rewards, many surfacing in unexpected, surprising ways.

*Certain moments shine as epiphanies for many of us who serve
in the teaching profession over he course of years. September 11,
2002, was a moment for me.*

One of the many ironies of teaching is the student(s) who never seem to "get it." They struggle and test us; they fail and fight us; they wander and confuse us.

They make us uncertain about our talent and expertise. We figure that it must be something we don't do well as teachers. They sit in our class a second time or even a third, and one day— perhaps only through the grace of God—finally walk across the platform on an evening in June and continue their lives. They disappear into the future as black marks in a grade book or a data system with our scarred psyches in some tatters. We think we have had no impact, and that hurts.

September 11, 2002. American flags, signatures to the people of New York, writing from John McCain, "America the Beautiful" over the intercom, replays of the crumbling World Trade Center and Pentagon, scenes of a remote Pennsylvania field afire. Permanent images of a world in chaos. Then a young Marine knocks on my classroom door during my third period English class.

Mouth agape, I open the door, my students curious. He walks in. I shake his hand. He stands erect, clean-shaven, hair cropped, shoes and uniform crisp as a new bill. He wears a smile of inner peace and satisfaction. The two-time flunkee, the kid who could not get it, has emerged, ready for life, balanced, poised, and pushup-tested.

"I just wanted to make sure you saw me, Mr. Anstett."

Brandon, thanks for making sure I saw you. Take care of yourself. Don't be late for drills. Keep the shoes shined. Protect your buddies. Watch your back. Write to your mother. Come back from wherever our country sends you. Thanks for making September 11 a better day in my life, a day that won't be one of perpetual sadness.

You have all had these students in your classes; they are there. One day, they will knock on your door. In the meantime, keep knocking on theirs.

YOUR TURN

Use this space to write some reflections for this section. What concepts might you apply to your own lessons, pedagogy or self-motivation?

SECTION 1-B

COACHES, EXPECT NOTHING HANDED TO YOU.

CONTEXT

I ADORE MY BELOVED CUBS and have done so since the womb. Until this past season of world championship baseball, that statement was grounds for insanity. During the summers and fall, I check the standings as often as I might eat. As a nine-year old in 1960, I attended a Cubs-Cardinals doubleheader with two older friends, ate my way through all my money, saw the Cubs' Don Cardwell pitch a no-hitter in the nightcap, lost my friends as they ran onto the field in celebration, and ended up walking home the twelve miles straight west on Addison Street. My parents had called the police to report a missing boy. My mother scolded me; my father enjoyed the moment and suggested that I needed to wake up. I watched the Cubs play 27 times at Wrigley Field in the grandstands in the summer of 1969, only to leave for college in the fall and have a miserable first semester in Boston watching my pitiful heroes blow the pennant. Cub failures never diminished my enjoyment of the national pastime, so this past season felt particularly joyous.

My loyalty to baseball probably surfaces from my playing softball almost daily in the alleys and at the parks with buddies in the neighborhood. We had nothing else to do in the summers before my daily working days for my dad, other than to serve Mass occasionally or endure whatever tortuous chores our parents gave us. So we played 16-inch softball or fast-pitch against one of the public school's walls. No one drove us to these events; we walked or biked. If the tennis court was empty at Mozart Park, we played softball on it where a home run was parking the ball over the high fence. That way you jogged around the bases and hurled insults at the opposing pitcher. Sometimes we brought our baseball cards to the park and spent time trading them. "You got an Ernie Banks???!! How about I give you one of my Sandy Koufax and two others for that??" Having doubles of a baseball kingpin engendered respect and power in the trading game. My getting on the hands and knees to beg for a coveted card was always an option I employed with regularity.

Before all the regulars got to the park or the court, or at least enough for a game, we spent the time playing peggy-move up or homerun derby. I was the first one there. I had plenty of stomachaches from gulping down Mom's dinner (four minutes stands as my personal best), dashing on my bike to the park while carrying my ball and bat, and hitting that softball. Being the first one, I would repeatedly toss the ball up and hit as hard as possible. Of course, that action meant chasing the ball down with the bat in hand, so I could reverse my field. Hitting one home run provided the Rolaid. My enjoyment of base-ball has never really diminished. If it was not softball, a couple of close friends and I would always find some time to play fast-pitch against some garage door or public school wall. We needed a rubber ball, a bat, and some imagination for hours of competition and fun. Playing in high school as a pitcher and a first baseman continued to satisfy my baseball fix. I was never inside much after school or in the summers. I learned durability, endurance, and long hours while enjoying myself.

During those formative years, I was innocuously acquiring the habit of arriving first and staying late, just to hit that last ball. When I fell in love with basketball in high school, I would spend three hours a night playing or shooting, either at Cragin Park, at St. Patrick High School's outdoor court, or in the gym at Notre Dame High School for girls near my home. Often my hours at Notre Dame's gym were alone. I left my workouts winning many games in my mind, thus developing my proclivity for wanting the last-second shots for my high school team, for striving for playing time at Boston College, or for helping my amateur team after college, Midwest Bank, become a powerhouse. If I was at the park, I relished the fact that the nearby denizens would threaten to call the police; I was intentionally unaware that the park closed at 11:00.

Little did I know that that habit sustained my competitiveness as a teacher/chairman/coach throughout my professional career. For example, there is always a specific time that a teacher has to be in the building per the contract. Didn't matter to me. I was there early. When I was English chairman at Lincoln-Way East, the administration created a staggered schedule due to the explosion of enrollment. While Lincoln-Way North was being built, Lincoln-Way East had to absorb the extra population for two years. East's enrollment swelled to 4,100.

Senior and juniors began at 7:00 and were dismissed at 1:30. Sophomores and freshmen started at 8:20 and ended at 3:30. What did this change mean for the department chairs? The unwritten rule was that chairs had to be there before school started; that rule meant 6:30. Was I paid more? No. Did I feel the responsibility to be there? Yes. This undesired change was part of the game and the responsibility. I did not question the extra burden, even though we had plenty to complain about. I felt that as a teacher there was always something to do or to prepare, and the last thing I wanted to feel was a lack of preparation. With sound preparation comes more confidence. That thought was not just for me, but a precept I tried to instill within each teacher in my English department and with each coach I worked with. Confidence is a distinct level of being and self-worth that people have to work for; there is no doctor's prescription or secret for attaining it. Expecting no handouts is one main ingredient for attaining any degree of true confidence.

Any teacher, coach, or career person worth his/her salt is unafraid of the long hours. Good people thrive on those tests of stamina. There is always the concern of another stipend for extra work. Yes, that is important. My first year as varsity coach at Immaculate Conception, I kept track of my per hour salary during the basketball season. It amounted to about $0.09/hour. That figure never bothered me, more my wallet. However, if one of my players needed extra work, I was ready. Is that the attitude of teachers today? Is that attitude yours, no matter the career? On the one hand, coaches are always at the low end of salary and respect, commensurate with their responsibility. The same can be said for factory workers, fast-food employees, you name it. Coaches, as well as professionals from all occupations, choose that profession with a love for kids, with a love for nurturing youth, or with a love for their talent. That love overrules the time. Good coaches do what they must, knowing that learning and maturation for each athlete constitute a long journey. Good coaches also understand that they are just players in a long-running drama; some are major characters, most are minor ones, but each plays a distinctive role.

Perspectives…

CIRCUMSTANCES THAT UNDERMINE INTEGRITY IN COACHES
WHO TRY TO DO IT RIGHT

Head coaches in any institution expect cooperation among their coaching colleagues in other sports. After all, they are all in this coaching effort together: helping young people find their way, developing discipline, learning teamwork and unselfishness, etc. In many cases, that aura of cooperation exists. In other cases, it does not. Expecting full cooperation is difficult, if not unrealistic, when the pressure to win or to look good overtakes common sense and the excessive egos of some coaches. The following perspectives display a few areas of concern regarding lack of integrity, in other words, my turn to whine!

Perspective One—Recruiting

In this area, the entitlement factor is alive and well. Take early February each year, the time when high school football players commit to sign to a university. If there is a more revolting demonstration of unwarranted entitlement, I do not know. And I hesitate to place culpability on those eighteen-year olds; the problem, as usual, lies in poor adult models. ESPN, are you listening? Einstein's theory of relativity should go far beyond math and physics. How relative to real life is placing teen football stars on that heavenly pedestal, promoting such entitlement, inflating fragile and immature egos to the expectation of super-stardom before even entering college? The entire show reeks, and that event is just one example. The impetus for such ridiculous vaudeville emanates from coaches and college presidents who ignore academics with the lure of millions of dollars for their school. The entire system is rudderless and these thoughts are coming from a former scholarship basketball player. When I signed at Boston College in 1969, there was no coach sleeping over at my house in order to get the drop on the rivals or any marching band saluting me on that day. My parents were thrilled, but both of them said, "You are going there to study! Make sure you do." Those words ended the celebrating. When college football coaches make more salary than the President of the United States, something is wrong. Sure, these indicators are, in one sense, signs that capitalism works. In our society people have the power to earn as much money as possible. I do not begrudge anyone of that power. Yet, what message do adults communicate to teens about what is truly important in areas of sports and academics when the lure of stardom, millionaire status, and self-promotion are at the forefront of young people?

Perspective Two—Specialization

Club volleyball, a leader in the "let's make kids specialize" department, provides some background about the problem of specialization. Now here is a grand entrance for the devious coaches, those who hoard glory and winning records, thus steering kids away from multiple sports with all kinds of nefarious reasons, college scholarships being the pick of that litter.

Specialization hurts kids in two main areas. Numerous studies exist revealing the high risk of physical liability to the same muscles in athletes who play one sport all year long. Here are a couple of samples:

> Participation numbers are dropping for many traditional youth sports, in part because children are focusing on a single sport at earlier ages.

> Driven by year-round travel clubs and the availability of indoor practice facilities, parents are spending more money and time in the expectation that their children can rise to the highest levels.

> USA Football encourages young athletes to play multiple sports. According to medical experts, taking part in a variety of activities—whether structured or not—leads to greater skill and muscle development.

> The lateral movement that basketball players use to stay in front of defenders is the same skill that shortstops develop to field ground balls and offensive linemen work on to better pass protect.

> Parents who hope their children could one day earn a college scholarship should take heed of a recent study that showed that varsity athletes at UCLA began specializing at a single sport on average at age 15.4 while undergrads who played sports in high school but not at the college level began limiting themselves to one sport on average at 14.2.

Focusing on a single sport hones the skills required for that particular activity but doesn't necessarily develop a better athlete and the fundamental movement skills required in all sports.

Kids who play multiple 'attacking' sports, like basketball or field hockey, transfer learned motor and anticipatory skills- the unconscious ability to read bodies and game situations-to other sports,' David Epstein, author of *The Sports Gene* wrote in a *New York Times* opinion. 'They take less time to master the sport they ultimately choose.

(http://usafootball.com/blogs/joe-frollo/post/8942/playing-multiple-sports-builds-better-athletes)

A second reason for promoting a decrease in specialization lies in the study *Is It Wise to Specialize*. Kirk Anderson, Director of Coaching Education for the U.S. Tennis Association states:

Even if parents and coaches know and understand age-appropriate principles for children, I think they would be reluctant to accept them because they would fear their child would fall behind the kid in a more structured program that focuses on training, competition and deliberate practice.

This fear has forced kids into sports that often are not of their own choosing, and in many cases compels them to remain in activities that are not enjoyable, not intrinsically motivating, nor are congruent with their actual athletic abilities. This path fails to consider many of the physical, emotional and social costs to children who only play a single sport.

There is a different path. It is the one based in science, psychology and best practices of athletic development. It is one that serves the needs of children for a lifetime, reduces injuries and burnout, increases enjoyment and motivation, and produces better athletes. Sound appealing?

It is the path of multiple sport participation and less structured play. But don't take my word for it. Below are some eye popping facts and statistics that should make every parent think twice about early sport specialization in sports like football, soccer, baseball, hockey and basketball, where athletes peak in their 20s.

First, here are five research excerpts that demonstrate how early specialization may negatively affect your child:

1. Children who specialize in a single sport account for 50% of overuse injuries in young athletes according to pediatric orthopedic specialists

2. A study by Ohio State University found that children who specialized early in a single sport led to higher rates of adult physical inactivity. Those who commit to one sport at a young age are often the first to quit, and suffer a lifetime of consequences.

3. In a study of 1200 youth athletes, Dr. Neeru Jayanthi of Loyola University found that early specialization in a single sport is one of the strongest predictors of injury. Athletes in the study who specialized were 70% to 93% more likely to be injured than children who played multiple sports!

4. Children who specialize early are at a far greater risk for burnout due to stress, decreased motivation and lack of enjoyment

5. Early sport specialization in female adolescents is associated with increased risk of anterior knee pain disorders including PFP, Osgood Schlatter, and Sinding Larsen-Johansson compared to multi-sport athletes, and may lead to higher rates of future ACL tears (added May 2014).'

If that is not enough for you, here are six research-based reasons for multi-sport participation:

1. **BETTER OVERALL SKILLS AND ABILITY**: Research shows that early participation in multiple sports leads to better overall motor and athletic development, longer playing careers, increased ability to transfer sports skills to other sports and increased motivation, ownership of the sports experience, and confidence.

2. **SMARTER, MORE CREATIVE PLAYERS**: Multi-sport participation at the youngest ages yields better decision making and pattern recognition, as well as increased creativity. These are all qualities that coaches of high-level teams look for.

3. **MOST COLLEGE ATHLETES COME FROM A MULTI-SPORT BACKGROUND:** A 2013 American Medical Society for Sports Medicine survey found that 88% of college athletes surveyed participated in more than one sport as a child

4. **10,000 HOURS IS NOT A RULE:** In his survey of the scientific literature regarding sport specific practice in *The Sports Gene*, author David Epstein finds that most elite competitors require far less than 10,000 hours of deliberate practice. Specifically, studies have shown that basketball (4000), field hockey (4000) and wrestling (6000) all require far less than 10,000 hours. Even Anders Ericsson, the researcher credited with discovering the 10,000 hour rule, says the misrepresentation of his work, popularized by Malcolm Gladwell in *Outliers*, ignores many of the elements that go into high-performance (genetics, coaching, opportunity, luck) and focuses on only one, deliberate practice. That, he says, is wrong.

5. **FREE PLAY EQUALS MORE PLAY:** Early specialization ignores the importance of deliberate play/free play. Researches found that activities that are intrinsically motivating maximize fun and provide enjoyment. They are incredibly important. These are termed deliberate play (as opposed to deliberate practice, which are activities motivated by the goal of performance enhancement and not enjoyment). Deliberate play increases motor skills, emotional ability, and creativity. Children allowed deliberate play also tend spend more time engaged in a sport than athletes in structured training with a coach.

6. **THERE ARE MANY PATHS TO MASTERY:** A 2003 study on professional ice hockey players found that while most pros had spent 10,000 hours or more involved in sports prior to age 20, only 3000 of those hours were involved in hockey specific deliberate practice (and only 450 of those hours were prior to age 12).

Top youth sports researchers Jean Cote and Jessica Fraser-Thomas provide an additional thought. They suggest that at no time should a young athlete participate year round in a single sport. While they recommend that athletes in sports whose competitors peak after age 20 need to accumulate around 10,000 hours of general sports participation, no more than half of that needs to be deliberate practice of their chosen sport. As a general rule they recommend the following age breakdown for athletes trying to achieve elite status in a specific sport:

- Prior to age 12: 80% of time should be spent in deliberate play and in sports other than the chosen sport!

- Age 13-15: 50/50 split between a chosen sport and other athletic pursuits

- Age 16+: Even when specialization becomes very important, 20% of training time should still be in the non-specialized sport and deliberate play.

http://changingthegameproject.com/is-it-wise-to-specialize/

Thus, athletes should be encouraged by their head coaches to play at least two sports. Players can work for college scholarships, but coaches should never promise anything of the kind to any athlete. Too many things can go wrong, one of those being the hopeful-to-delusional mentality of the parents. I recall that when I went to college, my parents promised me one thing, "We promise to kick your ass if you do not do a great job in the classroom and study hard." I know, I know, different generation...we just cannot tell kids these things today. There are better, more positive ways to communicate. Where's the kindness, coach? The problem with all the kindness is a lack of direct honesty. Without honest communication, whining and blaming are easy, and for the most part, the recourse losers turn to when they are beset with problems. Thus, we help children feel entitled to things they have not earned. Bluntness as a form of honesty and fairness eliminates gray areas; people will know where they stand, and that knowledge pushes progress. That type of child rearing has served me well. For one, I developed a conscience.

Moreover, highlight videos made by parents are relatively useless. These videos do not reveal how players react when things are not going in their favor, a situation college coaches want to see so they can evaluate the entire player. Coaches should be able to watch entire games, so they can evaluate players with balance and fairness.

PERSPECTIVE THREE—ATHLETE SHARING

I worked at some schools where some head coaches coveted their athletes like Scrooge coveted his money in *A Christmas Carol*. They sermonized about their willingness to encourage their stars to play more than one sport–their sport–but when summers came around or when promising sophomores became juniors or very good juniors became seniors, the sermon took a far different tone and message: Specialize now or sit the bench. Far too often, this scenario made me wonder what words were told to their fellow coaches who desired those stars to play multiple sports and what words were told to the actual players. Thus, the unfortunate words from a good player to his/her head coach, "I want to concentrate on _____, so I am quitting your team," have become part of the uneven tenure of any coaching career. These words are especially painful when a particular coach enters a season full of juicy expectations for lots of winning. These words have blindsided and hurt coaches, pushing coaches to explore why they even put such effort into their low paying, underappreciated extra-curricular teams.

Throughout my final stint at my last school, I assisted the boys basketball program. The varsity team regularly consisted of anywhere from 3 to 7 football players. As a general rule, the school's teams shared athletes. Once January came around, and our basketball team had a couple of key football players for next year, especially if we had the quarterback, one or more assistant football coaches would take the liberty to invite said quarterback, many times a starter on the basketball team, to early morning quarterback drills in a one-on-one situation. I guess it wasn't enough that the quarterback had a two or three hour practice waiting him after school after six hours of school. Talk about overemphasis. I guess basketball was not as important as football. I would keep my place and say nothing, but inside I seethed. I did suggest that during the following fall maybe the basketball coach should invite the quarterback to ball-handling and shooting drills at 6:15 a.m. a couple of days a week. This was yet another example of selfish handling of athletes by people who should know better.

Thus, some coaches expect cooperation with their peers involving the sharing of athletes, one-way cooperation. Athlete sharing should be an open dialogue among the appropriate coaches. That dialogue surmounts to almost a treaty. This type of collegiality heightens the spirit and the unity in schools.

PERSPECTIVE FOUR—THE AAU (AMATEUR ATHLETIC UNION)

I found AAU to be stimulating in two aspects: first, players less fortunate than others can find the good competition for determining the level of their skills and second, colleges will scout those tournaments. As a basketball purist, however, those points are where the advantages stop. If I had been involved in AAU as a high school player, I do not believe I would have earned a scholarship for college basketball. I am probably an exception to this, considering I only played three years before my game and motivation blossomed, but I needed a ball in my hands throughout the summer. Because I knew I had to improve my shooting, my physique, and my endurance, I spent the hours working, many times alone, in a gym or at a park, with my imagination and goals as my guiding lights. I improved in every way through self-discipline and hard work, very hard work. Would being on an AAU team where I might take five or six shots a game, played maybe half the game, and practiced twice a week have given me the preparation I needed? AAU takes the ball out of the participant's hands; consistent 5 on 5 basketball in the summer makes players worse. It is fools' gold for the majority of average players.

Players have come to believe that AAU is the only tool they will need to become good players, and many AAU coaches will feed them that nonsense. Players need much more than that. Daily regimens of ball handling, hundreds of *made* shots, weight training, one-on-one or three-on-three against good competition are the keys to the basketball kingdom of excellence. Most AAU practices do not provide those necessary workouts or instruct the precise fundamentals necessary for that skill development.

The lack of skills has trickled down to the college game, then to the high school level. Where is the hard screening and movement? Does anyone know how to fake before dribbling? Where are the pure shooters? Can a player who is a very good rebounder actually bring the ball up the court and make a fundamental, effective move to create a shot? Where has the post play gone? Is there another offense other than ball screening? College basketball has gone the way of the NFL-lots of specialty players who are jacks-of-all-trades, but masters of none. Thank the God of Roundball for model like Stephen Curry of the Golden State Warriors who actually knows the fundamentals, in addition to his shooting ability. Other than the Warriors and a handful of other NBA teams (the Utah Jazz, the Brad Stevens-led Boston Celtics, and the San Antonio Spurs among those teams), the game of basketball has taken a back seat to money and unskilled players. AAU makes its yearly donation to those unworthy causes, blowing hot air to very mediocre players, players who overnight believe they are Division-I talents, then take those inflated egos back to their high schools where they and their parents place undue and misguided pressure on their high school coaches. Basketball has become all about *me* and winning championships and scholarships, and we have AAU to thank for much of that notion.

I had hands-on experience participating in AAU when my younger son was in his early teens. I coached his teams in AAU competition for a few years. I witnessed much of what I have already described. I tried to play each player an even amount. I instilled in my son and my players that AAU games were not nearly enough for his acceptable strides as a player. We lost more than we won, but my entire focus centered on the development of each player on the team.

This is not just one man's rant. In an article on *ESPN.com* (January 2015), Kobe Bryant of the Los Angeles Lakers compares European players to America's, labeling Europe's as "more skillful." He further blames the culprit, "AAU basketball—horrible, terrible AAU basketball. It's stupid. It doesn't teach our kids how to play the game at all so you wind up having players that are big and they bring it up and they do all this fancy crap and they don't know how to post. They don't know the fundamentals of the game. It's stupid."

What's the solution, Kobe?

"Teach players the game at an early age and stop treating them like cash cows for everyone to profit off of," he said. "That's how you do that. You have to teach them the game. Give them instruction." (Web)

On one hand, I realize that AAU can provide kids who might never have a chance to show what skills they might possess an opportunity to do so, but on the other, AAU is worshipped as the means to the end. Many players of AAU sterilization come to expect to be stars or to gain interest from college scouts just because they play AAU. The focus of improvement in skills is lost. Thus, we have replaced the process with the competition. That process contains all the intangibles required for a value-filled life: the acquiring of endurance, patience, temperament, anger-control, unselfishness, and curiosity. When competition is the only goal, the process through the trial and error becomes the excuse and the blame. We see this everywhere, not just in AAU or in sports. Consider the case of affluenza that occurred in Texas in 2013 when juvenile Ethan Couch killed four people while under the influence, and then took the defense of affluenza. Couch blamed his accident on his parents who, he claimed, taught him that wealth buys privileges. Couch was given a probation sentence, infuriating people across the country. Although this case is in the extreme, it exacerbates the problem in the United States where standards lose their grit and adults lose their nerve.

PERSPECTIVE FIVE—TRANSFERS

Players and parents, think very carefully about transferring, if things aren't going *your* way. Quite a bit of fools' gold attached to this notion. Instead, develop a plan for improvement to attain the goals you wish. If lack of playing time is a reason for consideration to switch schools, why not investigate and evaluate the reasons for all the bench time? Perhaps your son or daughter is not as good a player as you think.

Player transfers have become far too common. I know of many examples of players deciding, or rather the *parents* deciding, to suddenly leave a school, so that their chances of a college scholarship increase. In one instance at one of my schools, we had a very good freshman who was already attracting college scouts—he had not played a game yet-but the upside was apparent. Unfortunately, that player was ineligible all season due to poor grades. He had size and quickness and would have helped our program a great deal. One college sent an assistant to see him workout at 6 a.m. during the pre-season. We had high hopes for him the following year. Grades had improved and he was participating in summer camps. One day he was at our camp, the next he had transferred to a city high school with a record of state championships. This transfer had followed a conversation between our head coach and the parents who had assured the coach that their son was staying. So much for integrity. In many cases, transferring is not about the player's wish, it is much more about the parents' egos.

What are some possible antidotes for irrational expectations?

1. Athletes should be encouraged to play at least two sports: coaches should be directed by their school administrations to foster this encouragement. Honest, face-to-face communication for all relevant parties is a major step to keeping the interest of the athlete at the forefront. Parents should hear this message at pre-season

meetings in each sport, no matter the season. Although impossible to make a rule about this, if districts and schools desire to develop their athletes and help them experience a wide range of learning situations, those districts must keep that message at the forefront of communication at opportune moments.

2. The *first priority* for inter-scholastic athletes during the summer should be the school's camps and clinics. Parents and coaches might be concerned with exposure for their athletes. If the players do not participate in AAU, the fear is they will not be noticed and lose out on possible scholarships. I believe that if you are a good player, you will be noticed. Coaches have an amazing pipeline within the profession; they do talk with each other. There are scouting services that attend summer high school tournaments and shootouts. High school coaches can make phone calls to potential college suitors. The key is for players to develop the skills and the physical strength for their sport. If they are good, they will be noticed. High school is about physical, mental, intellectual, and social development. Those might be lofty ideas in today's entitled world, but well-grounded families understand the permanence of such foci.

3. Parents, want to watch a confused player who will never play up to his ability? Then, backstab the head coach at every opportunity. Allow your athlete to hear those comments. Around the dinner table, destroy the philosophy, game decisions, or playing time decided by the head coach. Those types of discussions will surely enhance the digestive system.

4. Parents and players, have faith in the coaching staff and let those people do their jobs. Of course, there will be times when parents disagree with the coach. Yes, there will be times when coaches treat players unfairly. How parents handle those moments teach just as much to their children as any free throw does to win or lose a game. When adversity strikes (injury, loss of playing time, a bad game, a tough loss, a glaring mistake by the athlete or coach), welcome that moment as an opportunity for growth for all involved, as difficult as that moment will be. Those moments are the times

for teaching lessons about the foolish notion of entitlement and the expectation of receiving anything that has not been earned. Put faith in the process for improvement, not just in the end result. The process keeps calm temperament in the present; the end result thinks too much about the future.

"If you can't believe, if you can't accept anything on faith, then you're doomed for a life dominated by doubt."
~Kris Kringle, *Miracle on 34th Street*

Learning to Expect Nothing (Memoir)

Tom, you're either getting better or getting worse; you never stay the same.

Ray Meyer, the DePaul University men's basketball coach for 42 years (1942-1984) said those words to me in April of 1968. Having earned All-Area honors as a junior, I attended the *Chicago Sun-Times* All-Area banquet for boys' basketball in the Wrigley Building on Michigan Avenue. Coach Meyer was the guest speaker. To this day those words Meyer said to me and to my parents remain a cornerstone of my life. Professional and personal improvement is part of that cornerstone. People ask me now, "Tom, you enjoying retirement? What are you doing with yourself?" I mention a few things, but believe me, I do not want to be as busy as I was in my teaching-coaching career. On the other hand, I never saw myself in retirement lounging around watching the soaps, drinking mint juleps, gaining weight, and watching the world pass by. There is always something to do worthy of the life one has left on this planet; I just don't have to do anything with the breakneck speed I was accustomed to.

Improvement happens with taking risks, trying unfamiliar things, and/or practicing the correct repetition of skills and good attitude. I am interested in learning the harmonica, learning the Chinese language, writing a book, and traveling. These goals do not just happen. They are the by-products of the foundations for excellence developed in teen and young adult years. One of the foundations is learning to expect nothing; that attitude keeps me humble; humility often discovers pride.

I was an anomaly. This freak of nature began immediately at birth when the nurse attending my mother at St. Anne's Hospital in Chicago said to her, "23.5 inches! He is one of the longest babies I have ever seen!" As time progressed, due to various circumstances and my own effort, I made astronomical gains from age 14 to 18. I grew about five inches from eighth grade through high school. I credit my great-great grandfather, a 6'10"/300 lb. specimen, with this splurge. The physical gains did not come without a price of much blood, sweat, and tears. The mental gains matched the physical through the grind I experienced to gain necessary skills. Those gains reinforced my rising confidence with the game of basketball. Once I fell in love with what I was doing, the rise came quickly. Once Coach Meyer spoke those words to my face, I became obsessed with the idea of improvement. How good could I be? Could I play college basketball? Those two questions drove me relentlessly throughout the summer of 1968. (See also Section 2-B, chapter titled *Dedication*.)

The *Chicago Sun-Times* rated St. George High School in Evanston as one of the top ten teams in the Chicago area in the fall of 1968. Coach Schaefer scheduled them, part of his toughening up process no doubt, so we bussed there in early December to see what we could do. That night turned out to be another essential chapter in my life's basketball book. We upset St. George 49-44 and I had one of my best games. One of the assistants, one of the brightest minds in the game who would later coach college basketball at Creighton and Texas A & M and pro basketball as the head coach of the Memphis Grizzlies, had observed my play. As it turned out, one of his closest coaching friends was Chuck Daly who was taking the head coach position at Boston College. Coaches have a wide and closely knitted pipeline, and that level of relationship later helped me foster incredible coaching friendships I have to this day. That assistant told Daly about me, Daly contacted me, watched some of my game film, and kept in contact. In May of 1969, I visited B.C., but I was also debating among Loyola University, Pepperdine, Wichita State, and Loras College. I had ruled out the Air Force Academy, wondering how I would ever fit into a cockpit, much less be able to get out of one. I ruled out Pepperdine, knowing I would never study there, the campus being far too siren-like. Wichita State was in tornado alley- no way. Loyola was enticing; my family could see me play quite often, but I was enthralled with the idea of distance. After I visited Boston College's campus, my gut told me what to do, and that gut awoke many mornings to the vision of B.C. Boston had a charm all its own, the campus was beautiful, and the challenge of playing Division I basketball was overpowering. Getting *on* the court, however, would be a steep challenge.

In September of 1969, I said good-bye to my parents at O'Hare Airport. Mothers cry at these moments, my mother no exception. My father said good-bye, took me by the arm, and advised, "Son, keep it in your pants." When you receive eloquent advice such as that, how can you not listen? We hugged. I wondered when I would see them again. I disappeared down the corridor to the plane, my mind astir about exactly what I was doing. Here was big ol' Tom Anstett, All-State and All-Area in Illinois boys' basketball on a college scholarship, leaving home to go to school 1,000 miles away, having graduated from an all-boys seminary of 700, having rarely been around a girl, much less dated, and knowing no one there. Talk about taking risks. I was taking a quantum leap into the unknown. I felt at the lowest end of the food chain in terms of expecting anything.

The start of freshman year began as a dark Monday morning in a couple of ways. First, my plane landed in a ferocious rainstorm lasting for eight straight days that could have drowned Noah's ark. Second, the Vietnam War unsettled the beauty of the campus. Sit-in protests and demonstrations over the war heightened tensions among the variety of students. Moreover, rumors about a severe tuition hike the B.C. administration had legislated fomented further unrest. In the spring of 1970, there was talk of a student-strike over the tuition hike, a strike that eventually occurred. Since I could not attend classes where neither the students nor the professor would appear, I practiced whiffle ball, suntans, basketball workouts, women-gazing, and frolics on the campus green. The strike lasted for two weeks and mimicked a visit to a carnival with fun, frisbees, and games dotting the campus. To make matters better, the weather cooperated: sunny skies, warm temps, pleasant conditions were the order each day. Once negotiations finalized and the strike ended, I actually resumed classes. However, due to the lateness in the school calendar, the faculty administration had to come up with creative ways to end the semester while giving academic credit.

Being a late bloomer in basketball, I knew I was behind everyone I competed against. Perhaps that stirred my competitive juices and my desire to improve fast. At one of our first pickup games, I found out how far I had to go. I caught the ball in the low post and turned to shoot, my pet move in high school. One second later the ball was flying out of bounds, having been swatted by my defender with the question, "Got anything else?" One trip down court and I was defending my roommate, a strong 6'6" inside player from Washington D.C. One second he was in front of me, the next he was laying the ball into the basket with as smooth a drop step I had ever seen. I was still standing in the same spot. Two trips down the floor, a matter of thirty seconds, told me all I needed to know. This All-State high school player was now All-*Slate*–slow-footed and devoid of savvy and experience. I sought two years of improvement in two months. But my high school experience had already taught me that trials and difficulties could lead to success after success. B.C. was already paying off.

In 1969-70 freshmen were not allowed by the NCAA to play on the varsity. Freshmen played on their own team with their own schedule. It was a fortunate turn for me because I met Coach Frank Power. Coach had penetrating eyes, a reserved manner, but a serious voice, a voice that could grab the gut and make it stand at attention. He knew basketball. He talked as if he had invented it. He described for me and my teammates the nuances of post play, the pick and roll, transition play, and just about any other aspect we needed. He was as classy an individual as you could meet; he never yelled; he never cursed. He explained and corrected. He wore Patience as his ID tag. When I was out of a game, I sat next to him, wanting to hear what he said, the encyclopedia for hoopsters. I knew I wanted to teach secondary English, but it was the experience with that coach that inspired me to pursue coaching.

Throughout my coaching career and before each season started, I would select eight to ten games out of the 26 my team would play to determine the extent of improvement my team was making, the barometer games I would call them. I think there are certain students in every teacher's class that wear that barometer tag; those certain kids tell you the extent of effectiveness of your instruction. During that freshman season, the game against Harvard was one such game. Harvard had decided to emphasize success in basketball and they had just landed a stellar group of recruits. There was a 6'6" skyrocket from Washington D.C. who could play just about anywhere. He has been the lead for *The NFL Today* on CBS and presently has a similar role for the NFL Network. There was a 6'5" rebounder and inside player who really got annoyed if you tried to screen him off the boards. A third quality player could play inside or out. We played them at Harvard in February and the event captured local interest with *The Boston Globe* highlighting a preview for the game. The game lived up to its hype. Harvard ending up beating us 94-91, but I walked away eager for more. I scored 24 points and had some success defending each player during various stages of the game. I was gaining expertise on defending quick perimeter players, and my offensive moves were also taking shape. Although my overall game still was not varsity level, I would take my next steps under the tutelage of Chuck Daly.

I can capture sophomore year with one brief anecdote. About halfway through the year, I was as down about basketball as I'd ever been. I was not playing at all and Coach Daly was treating me like the proverbial whipping boy. Seniors took turns pulverizing me at practices, and Daly did not miss many turns at making that known to everyone. I couldn't guard one of our forwards who had a jump shot release almost as quick as Stephen Curry of Golden State. I couldn't guard a 6'7" swingman. I couldn't guard one of our post players for two reasons: one, he sweated more than a sauna bath–once your hands got close to him, forget about catching any passes; two, he was just tougher and more temperamental than anyone. One night I called my dad and after some discussion of my current self-imposed depression, he offered to call Coach Daly to talk to him. I answered my dad with one response, "Dad, if you call Daly, I will never speak to you again. I have to figure this out myself." Unlike many contemporary fathers, he backed off. Ironically, that conversation told me I had to stop whining, and start competing. After all, I made the statement and had to back it up. Not sure what made me be so assertive to one of my idols, but the challenge was teaching to expect nothing handed to me and to search for the best way to succeed. Sophomore year gave me a clear idea that my improvement would start from my taking ownership. By the end of the year, I had earned about 7-8 minutes a game off the bench, and earning those precious minutes was the result of increased toughness and skills at practices. Seven minutes here and there don't sound like a lot, but the Villanova game jumpstarted another leap into the *I can do this* phase of my college basketball career.

The final game that year meant our season. Coach Daly told us that with a win, we would receive a bid to the National Invitational Tournament in New York at Madison Square Garden. The N.I.T. in 1971 was no small potatoes. It had all the lure of the N.C.A.A. tournament during those years. Villanova was ranked in the top ten in the nation. They had a 6'7" future NBA pick, a rugged 6'8" postman with a soft shooting touch, and quality guards. At one point in a close game in the second half, I caught a pass at the foul line, pivoted, and shot. One second later the ball was beamed to half court–the NBA player had blocked my shot, appearing as a phantom through the air. The fans screamed and roared. One of his teammates, a 6'6" forward, took the ball and raced for a layup. My embarrassment must have fed my adrenalin. I sprinted down the court and though I could not catch him, I launched myself toward the backboard as he released his layup. Somehow, I managed to pin it against the backboard. No foul or goaltending. One of the seniors told me it was one of the best defensive plays he had ever seen. The crowd roared its approval. I passed the ball to our best player, who scored a bit later. For one moment I was the player in the spotlight; the next moment, I was back on the bench after a slap on the back from Daly. We lost a close game and that finished our season. I relished the chance I would have the next two years to keep improving. Sometimes, it only takes one moment in the sun to keep the pump of motivation primed.

During junior year I strengthened a friendship with one of the seniors, and that experience made me marvel at the depth and meaning of the word *teammate*. Jim, a 6'3" guard and the smartest player in the program, had spent his sophomore and junior years watching from the bench, but he had a good chance to start senior year. We decided to make each practice extra tortuous by playing one-on-one for at least thirty minutes before practice. This time of pre-practice is where I made the biggest jump in my skills, a jump that fortified me for the next twenty years of playing basketball. My footwork, outside shooting, dribbling skills moved another level through the competitive games Jim and I played. The games were nasty, no one gave either an inch. There were no smiles, no soft fouls. We wanted the same thing, meaningful playing time. And that is what we both earned. Our team finished 13-13, but won 7 of the last 10 games. Seniors provided good leadership, and Jim had an excellent year, being named an Academic-All American. He provided outside shooting, great decision-making, and good communication. "Fox" as he was so named, later earned a Ph.D at the University of Chicago, then took his intellectual talents to the English department at The Ohio State University where he has enjoyed a wonderful career as both a distinguished professor and as an author. He served OSU as the department chairman for eight years. I owe him a great deal and am so pleased we are good friends today and keep in regular touch.

Senior year presented an altogether different challenge. The coaches had recruited some star power for the freshmen class. Four of the recruits were fine athletes destined for good things. They had solid skills and toughness.

They seemed programmed to start as freshmen. That anticipation posed a threat. I certainly wanted to win, but I was not ready to wave a white flag or put down a welcome mat for any freshmen. I had to earn things; so too would they. When all was said and done, I started for the majority of games. The freshmen found college basketball tough, but did well overall. We were an average team that year, sometimes fighting each other more than any one opponent. I ended my college career earning the Student-Athlete award, a nice way to finish, despite the fact that I felt my best basketball was ahead of me. I still had the feeling I was behind. Without that feeling, one can grow bored. Always fight boredom.

After college I began my teaching career at Quigley-North, but the strides I made as a teacher throughout the years paralleled the strides I made as a basketball player from 1973 to 1988, the year I stopped playing the game, with the utmost appreciation from my knees and back. I played for the same team throughout post-college competition, making wonderful friends, seeing some of the world, and competing with and against some excellent players. A player named Bob for Elmwood Park High School and I had butted heads in the boys' state regional my senior year in high school. Little did I know that that same Bob would be my manager/coach for my amateur team, Midwest Bank, which he organized in 1973. Bob made it a habit and a passion to find the best players he could and the nucleus for this team remained quite constant for the fifteen years I played for it. We practiced once a week, maybe twice, if we secured a gym, and those practices were just as competitive and hard-nosed as the games; scrimmages involved some brief squabbles when tempers got too high in close games, but friendship and socializing afterward calmed those waters and unified the team. We belonged to the National Amateur Basketball Association (N.A.B.A.), and we earned spots in the national tournament almost every year. The two differences between the N.A.B.A. and the N.B.A. are one letter and millions of dollars. We played in Minnesota, Wisconsin, Indiana, Ohio, Barbados, Kentucky, and Cuba. We sometimes played seven or eight games a week during summers, being in various leagues throughout the Chicago area, traveling to Evanston for a 5:00 game, then hustling to Franklin Park an hour away for a 9 or 10:00 game. There was always time for a few beers to replenish the engines, however, no matter how late the game. All of us had full-time jobs, yet all of us played for the love of the game. Plus, we liked each other. When any team has those two assets working, great things happen. We finished second in the nation in the N.A.B.A. National Tournament one year when we hosted the tournament in Arlington Heights, Illinois. These post-college playing days set the groundwork for the gains I made as a teacher.

Sometimes an extraordinary experience transfers to learning. Such was the case when we had the opportunity to travel to Cuba for a ten-day tournament in May of 1979. Much of this experience diagnosed my sentiment that I was not the center of the universe, thus entitled to every favor and good fortune. Witness:

- Being besieged by young kids after games and during sight-seeing, begging for gum, shorts, shoes, anything they never have possessed...remindful.

- Having our passports taken from us upon landing in Havana and not knowing if and when they would be returned...bewildering and frightening.

- Landing in Havana, we noticed the initial observation—that of an emotionless soldier pointing a machine gun at us...fearful.

- Waiting for our return plane on the final day for ten hours at the Havana airport, passport-less, in one room with no one else around...distraught.

- Realizing later that our return plane's original destination was *not* Havana. The pilot received the call to pick up an American team in Cuba *by accident*...fortunate.

- Thinking I was fast at my ability to run the floor, only to be overpowered and outraced by Cuban, Mexican, and Panamanian players, the tortoise vs. the hares...humbling.

- Seeing the buildings in Cuban cities each needing a new coat of paint, overdue since 1959...appreciating.

- Enjoying the afterglow after beating Russia, a Cold War nemesis we still distrusted...disarming.

- Thinking I could hold my liquor very well until I drank 90-proof Cuban rum with their beer...crippling.

- Being accustomed to stale ham and Swiss cheese sandwiches, until that entity was the whole menu for six straight days…nauseating.

- Thirsting for a good glass of milk until I asked for one at a dinner. The milk placed before me was accidentally tipped over and nary a drop came out of the glass…disgusting.

- Losing our guide and translator, Carlos, for the final three days… alarming.

The Cuban experience was just one of many moments and trials enlightening me to a clearer understanding that if I wanted something good, I would have to earn it. As I progressed as a player and developed more leadership skills on my basketball team, I warmed to the goal of being the best teacher in my department and one of the best coaches in the area, no matter what school. So the desire for improvement, wedded to my love for competition, was a constant in my life. Moreover, I was blessed to be around some of the best teacher/coach-models in the many colleagues I befriended at various schools. I made it a habit to listen much more than talk. I watched good teachers teach. What a plethora of tips and strategies I saw and applied. I attended many basketball camps and clinics. I would attend practices conducted by coaches I knew were maestros.

Every quality method I witnessed involved student engagement; is it no wonder that engagement is all teachers hear today regarding evaluations? I took the drive I exhibited as a player and connected it to the work ethic it takes for a teacher to do a thorough job on a daily basis. Improvement means engagement with life as a learning partner. Engagement involves risk taking, but what rewards will be gained during the process. I have found that the more you expect less, the greater the accomplishment, significance, and satisfaction can be discovered.

YOUR TURN

Use this space to write some reflections for this section.

SECTION 2-A

TEACHERS, BLAME NO ONE.

CONTEXT

BLAMING IS TOUGH TO RESIST and all too easy to accomplish. Pressure is one of its sources. Is pressure a threat or a challenge? The perception and the level of one's acceptance of pressure can be a daunting revelation for people in all walks of life. Pressure lends its back to blame. For example, let's take a look at grades and curriculum. When I was a department chairman, my colleagues and I understood that personal feelings regarding each other do not enhance nor discredit each other's opinions on curriculum. On the other hand, the majority of students are often too indiscriminate to distinguish between a grade they receive and their perception of that particular teacher's opinion about them. While it is optimal for teachers to make students comfortable and safe in their classes and for students to look forward to class, students need to be challenged with the discipline within that teacher's particular style. That combination creates discomfort. Teachers will hear, "Well, Mr. So-and-so just does not like me. That's why I have a poor grade." At times, this outcry can be a personal attack from an immature, emotional student who receives a graded paper, looks at the grade, tears up the paper, and sits like a lump in an all-too-familiar pout. Ever have this happen, or should I ask, *how often* have you had this moment or something like it occur? Stressing to students from the beginning that grades are less of a judgment by the teacher on the student as a person, and more an evaluation of academic performance provides fodder for worthy discussion. This differentiation remains paramount for building nurturing relationships. Many times that lesson poses brick walls for students. Blame runs rampant.

Similarly, teachers have to understand that not every one of their students is going to be a teacher or will enjoy or love the subject of the teacher.

Teachers can tend to see students in one-dimension: the history dimension, the English dimension, the math dimension etc. We catch a few glimpses about their personal lives. Here lies the proverbial two-edged sword. Teachers retain the objectivity needed for a fair academic assessment, but at the same time, lose some rapport. This lesson challenges teachers for within that challenge lie many tense mental battles for staff when they come across likeable students with a 58.9% for the semester grade. The question looms, "Should I just pass this student? Should this kid just get on with his/her life?"

Being an English teacher gave me the open windows to build sturdy relationships with my students mainly through writing assignments. I recall numerous times when students did not agree with my evaluation of their literary analysis or argument. They would question me about the grade or the comments. I always took the paper back and reviewed it, followed that review with a one-on-one conference with the disgruntled one. We discussed the conflict and I explained the grade within the comments I had supplied. These were golden opportunities for learning on both ends. I wanted them to seize the responsibility for their growth or lack of it. When students take on that responsibility, blame diminishes as a crutch. It is unfortunate that the majority of students do not seize opportunities like an individual conference. These conferences can be epiphanies in a teacher's day and incredible door openers for students. Pressure makes diamonds and opens doors to crack the brick walls of blame and mistrust.

FOR THERE IS NOTHING EITHER GOOD OR BAD,
BUT THINKING MAKES IT SO.
~HAMLET; ACT II, SCENE II

ENGAGEMENT

I disliked the end of the school year. There is always one day in early May when I knew that my students were looking right past me to warm beaches, lazy summer days, and family vacations. The sense of entitlement surges; they decide to lower, in some cases stop, their academic focus and energy because they believe they have done enough work. They cringe at more homework with blatant moans. Participation decreases, patience thins, more yawns surface. Now multiply those reactions tenfold if the classes contained seniors. Happened every year. In my first ten years, I took this very personally; I became just as unfocused as they, just in a different way. I did not lose interest, yawn, stare out the window, or ponder my June vacation. I became more irritable, scolded them more, thus losing my own focus. Once I took those actions, what could I expect from teenagers? Even less attention, even less focus, even more resentment.

As my experience increased, I realized that I was the same way as a teen. I was doing to my students what was modeled to me. With the advice of some trusted colleagues at Glenbrook North, I began to reexamine my lessons and to use more collaborative group activities and projects, stimulating students' cooperation and elevating their participation. Focus returned and student empowerment increased. Engagement for all involved became the will to succeed. I was attaining the ability to keep my students in the present tense. One such example of a project was an independent read through a group effort where students chose a book to read and research (same book for each respective group), submit a written analysis, and conduct an oral presentation with a power point. This effort also highlighted more oral skills by students, a proficiency hiding in the closet too often. Even more important, students enjoyed it, most likely due to their ability to make a cooperative decision about book choice. Projects as a norm at the end of the school year decrease boredom and keep the pressure on the students through their engagement for learning. Whether students' own motivation is for the grade or for the learning, no matter. Students need to work through the entire year. One day their bosses will not give them the last two weeks in May as time to relax.

When engagement is a principal fabric in lessons, blame evaporates. There will still be some complaining in classes with high expectations. Consider that moaning a compliment. Students are doing their own empowering. Moreover, the term engagement means two things vital to teacher progress: improvement in evaluations and a mode for learning within each quality lesson.

My best lessons contained high degrees of student engagement. These lessons began with sound preparation, preparation that took considerable time to organize. In these lessons, I handed the keys to the car to the students, and I sat in the back seat. The following list contains four examples of engaging lessons.

1. Any concise reading that employed Socratic Seminar (see 3-A, "Discuss.")

2. I used the following lesson in my AP Language class, so teachers might consider some adaption for a regular track course. Students read the novel *Winesburg, Ohio* by Sherwood Anderson. I assigned each student one chapter for his/her preparation with a schedule for presenting. Goals concerned both close reading and oral presentation skills. Presentations had to cover a minimum of 25 minutes. The entire class had to read the chapter for that day ahead of time. The presenter had to prepare a five-question reading check quiz. There had to be a creative introduction that would segue to that quiz, then, after collection, the presenter would conduct a discussion using any form of appropriate audio-visual device (short video, music, etc.). The focus of discussion might emphasize author's purpose, structure, or tone—usually one of those devices. Students were evaluated on their organization of material, their knowledge and application of the emphasis for the chapter, their speaking skills, and the transitional devices they chose to unify the material. The lesson closed with a brief written learning log or an open discussion about the contribution of that chapter to the novel as a whole. This lesson was done in the second semester, after the students had presented shorter assignments and were more comfortable in front of class. Moreover, this novel was one of the more popular from the entire list we read.

3. In my first year at Lincoln-Way in 1999, I was teaching three sections of English 3, College Prep (a chronological study of American literature). As I prepared for a formal observation, I decided to employ the Norman Rockwell painting, *The Problem We All Live With*.

Rockwell, Norman. *The Problem We All Live With*. 1964,
Norman Rockwell Museum.

Students read the nonfiction piece by Frederick Douglass, *The Battle with Mr. Covey*. In this reading, they were to annotate for the moment of epiphany for Douglass—which by some strange coincidence did not occur until the end. To hook the class, I showed them Rockwell's painting, and immediately asked them to complete a five-minute quick-write for first impressions, striking details, etc. I asked them to title the painting. I grouped them into pods of three, or if you have established learning partners, you can direct students to find those people, or even have them do this task as they enter class. They shared ideas for two or three minutes. At that point I opened the class for reactions and did not hesitate to call on the quiet ones since they had some feedback from their pod. At that point I introduced the learning targets for the lesson and unveiled the actual title. This title I used to segue into the reading with one of the targets: *Students will apply their thinking about the painting to the Douglass piece for defining the writer's purpose.* The students returned to their pods or partners and discussed what they considered Douglass's epiphany, connecting that point in the narrative to the author's purpose. They had to find two pieces of text evidence for these findings, another learning target. I tried to allow at least fifteen minutes for class discussion, and concluded with a connection to *Huckleberry Finn*, the next novel. Students did the work.

D. First, we must acknowledge that there is a huge difference between *assigning* writing and *instructing* it, just as there are huge differences between mediocre and superior teachers. That being said, writing lessons should contain variety. Modeling must be one of the key factors for writing instruction. In the lesson described, students came to class with a rough draft argument. My initial step directed students to reread their own essay. Then, I presented the goal for the day: *Students can apply the revision steps in order to improve their next draft*. We then briefly discussed the purpose of each column. Then, students had to highlight each of the verbs in the essay; after completing that step, they wrote down each verb in the second column. The entire revision chart is framed below, courtesy of *Stack the Deck*.

Sentence # (organize)	First Four Words (sentence interest)	Verb(s) (repetition & tone)	Word Count (the "short & long" rhythm)

With their learning partners, students exchanged essays to check on the thoroughness of the second column. They then reviewed the highlighted material and provided each other with corrections and comments.

Each student's partner completed the third and fourth columns for his/her partner's essay. Discussion followed. I allowed about eight minutes for each of the three columns. With about ten minutes remaining, I asked students to read the comments, reread their essays, and write down a minimum of two emphases they would apply to the next draft.

A version of this starter for the same lesson is to for the teacher to model an AP essay, using the four columns, but also asking students to supply the reason for each column. Then, the students will have a clear idea of the steps to follow.

I hope that these four brief descriptions of lesson plans for increasing student engagement give you some ideas as well as more responsibility for the growth of your students.

Communication

Poor example of communication: In 1977 I was in the second year of my first varsity basketball head coaching position at Immaculate Conception in Elmhurst. My team was mediocre; we had poor skills, although we played hard. Even that last asset, however, had diminishing returns. Losing ebbs the momentum of a team, momentum being simply *attitude*. In February, I detected lack of effort from the five seniors. Being a raw, impatient, inexperienced head coach, I decided to take action after a blowout loss at St. Edward High School in Elgin, a team we had beaten earlier in the year. The loss gnawed at me all the way home; fortunately, our bus driver—me—kept cool enough to avoid steering the entire program into oblivion. After we returned to school, I told the seniors that they were being cut from the team for lack of effort. In reality, the lack of effort was mine. I did not communicate my frustrations, did not enlist their help, either or both of which would have led to better efforts from all involved. I made the decision in the heat of emotion and at night. Many times, delaying judgment is the best recourse.

On Sunday, I received a call from my athletic director who wanted an explanation for my action. He had received calls from the players' upset parents. I was naïve enough to think that my decision would have little consequence. After all, I was the coach and what the coach says, goes. Throughout the following week, I met a plethora of protest: I sat in the principal's office, the athletic director's office. Even my own classroom chair had become hotter as the days progressed: my students would not cooperate with any discussion or activity. Word gets around fast, especially conflict. I guess I should be thankful this event was before Facebook, Twitter, and text messaging. I was pressured from various camps to reinstate the boys. I refused. I was pressured again by the principal, by the school's chaplain, by the students, by the janitor, by some of my own colleagues, by the school newspaper, and by my garbage man. I met with the seniors, but they felt betrayed and would not consider returning. As one said, "Why should we come back and play for someone who doesn't want us?"

We finished the season with some sophomores, players who started winning the next year. One of those sophomores as a senior remarked to me, "Coach, you sent us a message when you cut those seniors. You would never accept quitting." In a cruel bit of irony, the program advanced through the younger players, understanding that quitting was/is a poor choice of action. As much as the aforementioned sentiments should have made me feel more satisfied about that memorable night, they did not. I had created unnecessary conflict, conflict that did create communication, albeit in the more undesired context. As an inexperienced head coach, I lacked the patience to wait until the fires smoldering in my brain cleared. The administration, mainly the athletic director, supported me, but I would never forget that experience which I handled the incorrect way. In many ways we grow more from the defeats than the victories.

Down the road at other schools, I had a few more losing teams. I never coached at any school where pure talent flowed through the door every year. I believe I managed those groups and communicated far better with relevant parties. As teachers and coaches, we cannot be afraid of conflicts, whether we start them or not, but we need not search for them either. They can turn out healthy for all involved. Obviously, the aforementioned incident was not one of my shining moments as a coach. Far from it. I hurt those boys and I regret my rash choice to this day. A sign I saw at Lincoln-Way, *Kids will forget what you say; they will never forget how you made them feel,* has always reminded me of that particular incident.

Coaches can relay their essential messages without being idiots. They must see objectively where the reason for failure lies and, accepting that reason, find the cure and apply that remedy.

Good Example for Communication

As my career continued, I became more invested with parents. Becoming a parent myself assisted this improvement. I did not go out of my way to speak with them, but when they called with a concern or a question, I relished those opportunities. Who knows what damage–or good–a community person or parent can do to you in the aisles of grocery stores, at the library, at a fitness center, or around the water cooler? The answer is plenty of both. Word-of-mouth flies faster than Usain Bolt in the 100-yard dash at an Olympics. Thus, as a department chair and as a teacher, I experienced situations that cost me plenty of agony and time and effort, but the vast majority of those discussions ended well. Why? You treat those situations as the most important one in the world; in the parents' world, it has that place! In your world, it is a priority.

When I was the department chairman at Lincoln-Way Central in 2001, a conflict developed between the parents of their young daughter who did not receive the lead role in the school play and the faculty director of the play. You would have thought that that teacher had committed bodily harm to the child. "You are destroying my child's future as an actress!! This is her career path!! She is the most talented actress in the district!!" lamented and protested those parents. Needless to say, via phone call or email, everyone received these protests: the superintendent, principal, assistant principals, and yours truly. The teacher in question was besieged daily by hurtful messages; she finally came to me in tears, requesting my presence at a meeting with the principal and the parents.

The English teacher in question rarely had a bad day. She was the epitome of class and positive energy with everyone. Her students loved her. So did I. However, I rarely saw anyone more nervous than that teacher the morning of the meeting. My outside kept reassuring her that all would be ok; my inside was doing handstands. The principal ran the meeting. I said nothing until the end. One of my principle axioms in dealing with parents is to give them the time to vent; my role is to listen while taking notes. Listening helps in two ways: one, it makes the parent feel welcomed in a calm, understanding environment; two, it allows me the time to see if their story corresponds to the teacher's, a story for which I had done my research. As Bill Russell, the champion Boston Celtic, wrote in his book *Russell Rules*, "Listening is never casual" (67). So, the parents vented and eventually began to personally attack the teacher. The principal stepped in, much to my relief and approval. After a good 45 minutes of some pointed discussion, the principal asked me what I thought. I took a few breaths, then asked, "Mr. and Mrs. —, what is the role of our high school?"

The mother responded, "My child needs an education."

"Yes, of course, that is it," I replied. "That vision is what we seem to be missing here. Can we think of the big picture? Is your child receiving a quality education here? Is she happy here, the current event notwithstanding?"

I received an affirmative to these questions.

"Then, what are we talking about? In the best judgment of Mrs. —, your child did not show the expertise needed to land the role. She will show her talents in another capacity in this production. Second, this is one part of her education; she is not majoring in theater here, correct?" Nodding heads. "This is part of the whole. She will make a good contribution to this play. I believe in Mrs. —. Her love for kids and her ability to produce great play after great play are legendary. So should you; your daughter is in great hands. When your daughter goes to college, she can focus on a career. For now, she is receiving what you have said she has to receive, a quality education. As you know, not everything goes our way; we do not always get what we want. I have full confidence that your daughter will prosper from this, don't you?" More nods. Conference over. Blame rose from its seat and vacated the premises.

After the parents left, the teacher cried on my shoulder in both relief and appreciation. My principal complimented me, "Tom, your response was perfect." The conflict created the communication. In the end, the communication retained the dignity of all involved.

What did I learn? Be as proactive as possible communicating with parents. Meet conflict head on, but do the research. Find out where the real problem hides and what the underlying reasons and stories might be because there are two sides to every conflict. Be polite and honest. Avoid excessive emails; use the phone, if necessary. Then after it is resolved, go have a drink and reflect... unless you have class to teach.

Conflicts will occur. Blame will run rampant. Treat them as valuable commodities. Teachers earn or lose respect through them.

SUCK IT UP

When I was a dean at Quigley-North in 1974 and 1975, my supervisor, the most feared and mean priest on God's green planet, told me one of my responsibilities was to occasionally venture to the McDonald's in Water Tower Place on Michigan Avenue, about one block to the east, to spy. At times some of the students who were majoring in effrontery would wander over there for lunch, a definite crime against humanity. If I caught them, they would be waterboarded, starved, flogged-oh, wait, that is the C.I.A. Those violators would receive a minimum of ten demerits. I caught a couple of those rascals a few times, but this task required dropping what I was doing, sprinting over to the McDonald's, hanging out innocuously (try that if you are 6'7"), and waiting. Most of the time, the trip was fruitless and the waterboarding would have to wait.

I relate that short narrative to explain that the first time I was told to go over there, I explained that I had too much to do, some reports to write for dean responsibilities, etc. Father Jake just looked at me and responded with his steely blue eyes and riveting voice, "Tom, many times you just have to suck it up." More true words have never been spoken.

Personal discovery and application of grinding one's way to an achievement became all too real for me when I was a teacher at a good high school within the North Shore culture. That phrase does not mean too much to the teachers or readers who live elsewhere, but to anyone who makes a living in that area, that phrase resounds challenge and pressure. Parents give new meaning to *helicopter*, but the majority mean well. Students are despondent with B's. Teachers feel constant pressure from administration to push students to ever-higher grade point averages and state testing records. And while these mandates were ongoing, I was head basketball coach of a floundering program and also decided to enter graduate school to earn my Masters degree. That quest took five years because I could not take classes in the winter due to coaching. The courses I studied required constant reading and writing since my goal was a Masters in Arts in Literature. Whenever I was not teaching or preparing classes, I was doing my own homework. Whenever I was not coaching, I was reading or writing assignments. I was in never-ending flux between the study of writers such as Pynchon, Faulkner, Eliot, Chaucer, Hemingway, and Bellow and the drive for honing the perfect practice plan amid the onslaught of student essay after student essay. It was a merciless grind. Luckily, I was single during those years. Sucking it up, not sucking, became my mental bumper sticker. Throughout all the self-defeat, the whining or blaming, most people find a way to get the job done...once they decide to focus and to take the pressure with a smile

Adults and children alike need to hear those words. *Just suck it up* would make a more insightful car adornment than the *I have an Honors student at Entitled School.* Life gives us very little control. The curveballs thrown at us require faith, diligence, and some guts. William Faulkner, one of America's greatest and toughest authors, maintained in his Nobel Prize acceptance speech in 1950 that *without courage, no other virtues are attainable.* That statement supplies relevance for AP and Honors students. Many times those students must multi-task. At one point in my Advanced Placement Language class, the juniors had an argument to write, a project to research and prepare, a speech to research and prepare, and a novel to read and annotate. During this particular academic siege one day, I read the faces of my class. I knew they felt the pressure. I asked, "What's the matter?" after receiving no enthusiasm or participation at the start of that day's lesson. Blank stares and grumpy looks ruled.

"Mr. Anstett, do your realize what we have to do????? There is too much work. Why do we have all this at once????!!!" Blame had entered the room.

One of my responses was, "Oh, my, I thought something was *wrong*. Did someone die? Anyone have cancer?" Silence.

"What if you get all A's on these assignments; would you still feel the same way?" Shake of the heads.

"Then, go to it. Organize your time. You can do this."

After a bit more exchange, I got to my point of sucking it up, relating it to my experiences as a father-chairman-teacher-coach-husband-friend role. Although the students were never completely satisfied and were not quite ready to nominate me for Teacher of the Year, they understood and, more importantly, they felt that I took the time to let them vent. Blame left the room, pouting.

Pressure makes diamonds.

Letter to Parents:

Dear Parent,

Greetings. First, realize that I am a parent, my wife and I having put two boys through sixteen years of education. We know the angst, the decisions, the joy and the anguish of this hard journey. When conflicts arise, emotion always chimes, "Blood is thicker than water."

Reason the counter replies, "Yes, blood is thicker, but there are always two sides. Before jumping headlong into any fracas and assigning blame, ask, 'Am I receiving all the facts?' "

Irrationality responds, "Yes, I know, but this is my child. I have to be sure I speak for him or he won't get a fair shake. I have to defend him to that teacher, even if I don't have both sides of a story." And kids can spin terrific stories. In many cases, what the teacher actually said is not what the students actually heard.

When I became a parent, I resolved to do all I could to defend their teachers, even at the expense of my child. I knew the difficulties of teaching. So, *make no excuses* became a lifelong mantra for both my parenting and my coaching. Frankly, no one cares about illness or a bad day, a lack of sleep the previous night, teasing at school, lost or stolen notes, misplacement of a phone, ad infinitum. No one cares about a car's bumper posting a sticker about a child having achieved honors status at the school, probably for things he or she should be doing anyway. Being a teacher and coach was a major factor in my disposition toward raising my children, so I realize that those of you reading this argument who are not teachers might have a difficult time understanding this explanation. When my child came home complaining about a teacher, I said, "Sit down with your teacher and explain your questions, do not attack the person" or "How much study time are you devoting to that course? Are you bringing the book home every night? Let's see it; let's read together. How committed are you to that class, whether you like it or not? Liking a class, or a teacher for that matter, has little to do with being successful."

As my wife and I continued to demand this attitude from our boys, more resiliency and toughness were manifested in their growth. We could see it as they moved up grades. They began to take harder courses. I already mentioned that my older son John rose from a 21 to a 28 on his ACT, but not without his sound preparation and a lack of alibis. My younger boy Timothy decided to take a couple AP courses as he rose through the high school ranks. At times, he questioned all the work and would moan about the reading and his grade. We reminded him that the choice was his to take the course. We reminded him that the course tests his own level of grit and determination and would promote his learning. If he gave maximum effort, did all his work, and participated in class, we would be satisfied with his grade. Only one question remained, "Tim, will *you* be satisfied?" We tried to clarify who truly owned the responsibility.

More ideas:

- Discuss your child's goals—a great conversation for a Sunday evening each week.

- *Look at* your student's homework; ask your child to explain it to you.

- Is your child writing down all assignments in his/her planner? *Look at* that planner. Discuss expectations.

- Eat dinner together whenever possible and discuss school, the highs and the lows.

- Attend parent conference nights, especially if your student isn't passing or is struggling. Many times on these nights, most teachers only conference with the students who are doing well. Makes me wonder!

- Do not rely too heavily on emails as a form of communication with a teacher; they can often be misunderstood. Use the phone.

- Stay positive about your child's teachers. Your kids will lean a great deal on your attitude.

I hope you can see what I am communicating: put the onus for learning on your kids. They will develop the inner toughness and independence necessary to survive and achieve in a rather unforgiving world, a world where you as the parent will not always be at their sides. Parenting is a very tough, uncertain responsibility that arrives without a manual, so it is a natural outcome that parents want what is best for their kids. At the top of that list should be discipline, the best form of love. The more clear the discipline, the less the blame and the whining. When the particular discipline is communicated, even better.

I wish you the very best.

Regards,
Mr. Anstett

Summer-ize

Probably just me, but I always felt a gigantic letdown in late May as the number of remaining classes diminished. I felt I did not accomplish much through nine months. What have they learned? What might they retain? Will those students even remember they had me as a teacher? Have I had *any* positive influence? These questions can linger and chink one's morale, creating confusion about all the energy, late nights, etc., that a teacher experiences. Conversely, these questions can also spark new creativity, increase motivation for next year, and decrease any move toward staleness for veteran staff. After more contemplation, I chose the second route. I would not take it personally if some students chose to limit their learning in my class, chose to relax too much before school actually ended, chose to limit their own potential and use of time. When summer takes its grip and teachers have some time to decompress, they reflect and realize they did a lot of good. The frustration lies in the ones we think we failed; those can stick for a long time, one of the chief mental challenges of teaching. Yes, I always felt unfulfilled in June, but as time progressed my own frame of mind eased the inner tensions.

For all teachers, June, July, and August represent three venerable words, near the top of any faculty's vocabulary list. Less pressure, and more fun; fewer dresses and dress shirts, more sandals and shorts. Teachers need this time to both decompress and to progress. However, for many teachers, that is where the comparisons stop. Want a salary increase? Attend nine hours of classes. Have to get a Masters degree or a doctorate? Research, write, and present a thesis after attending a myriad of classes. Have a new prep? Start reading the novels or textbooks and writing lesson plans. Have a curriculum change or review? Get to school and spend the hours in committee work.

After Boston College gave me my official exit paper and released me to the outside world in 1973, I received a phone call from Quigley North asking me if I would like a teaching job in the fall. I beamed back a yes. They informed me that I would have to attend and pass six more hours of Spanish; they needed a Spanish teacher and I had hours at Boston College. Spanish, you say? *Spanish*?? Needless to say, I attended two classes at Northeastern Illinois University where I could barely understand the professors. (If you really want to know the inferiority of such an experience, read David Sedaris's essay *Me Talk Pretty One Day.*). In the fall, instead of staying one step ahead of those students in my Spanish 1 course, I tried to stay one minute ahead. I did have three English classes as well, but the Spanish kept me up at night. That schedule began my teaching career; I am sure that many teachers have had similar experiences.

Besides, all teachers know that in reality, teachers have roughly sixty days to unwind, as opposed to three months. August 1 means one thing: summer is nearing an end and the thoughts wander from beaches and trips to books and bells. With that transition comes an increased heart rate, excursions to school to make copies, classroom preparation, textbook searches, computer hunts for rosters, and classroom supply purchases with most of that money coming directly from teachers' already barren pockets.

I am not complaining or blaming, mind you. *I chose* the teaching profession. Those features are all parts of a teacher career. I am clarifying to the general public who tend to criticize a teacher's professional experience by maintaining how *easy* it must be to be a teacher because of the summer months. Summers are enjoyable times for teachers, but they are not all fun and games, at least not for teachers who want to establish themselves, improve themselves, or keep the internal fire alive for the important work they do.

For teachers, summertime's leisure and proper preparation transfer to wintertime's victories. Moreover, a personal choice for a life to lead diminishes the foible of finding blame when that grass turns out to be less than green on the other side of the fence.

SHARE

Having taught in five different high schools, I heard plenty of horror stories from teachers about sharing materials. Teachers can be very private about sharing their own materials or lessons with colleagues. In one of my previous stops before Lincoln-Way, a few teachers would keep their materials under lock and key. In one instance, I fielded complaints from one teacher about a colleague's stealing the former's essay prompt. Those same teachers were the first to complain about the lack of professional development in their district, failing to realize that one of the best resources for their development lies right within a department-the sharing of materials and techniques. Robert Fulghum's *All I Really Need To Know I Learned in Kindergarten* promotes sharing as one of life's prime guidelines. This virtue fosters camaraderie and promotes communication among levels and individual staff. During my tenure as department chairman, sharing materials was one of our many excellent team traits. People gave credit where credit was due, a basic maxim of any quality organization or team. That maxim is similar to giving compliments to people when praise has been earned; the giving far outweighs the value of receiving a compliment, although both are worthy actions. At a few department meetings, we shared one new idea for a lesson or activity with each other in small groups by grade levels. At other times after having observed a quality activity, I would ask that teacher to present the steps of that activity to the entire department. Due to activities like that and also due to my position as an evaluator where I could witness wonderful lessons firsthand, I learned so much from my English teachers in so many areas. If they are on your staff, they have talents. A department chair or leader has to prime that pump for collective and individual growth.

If a certain teacher is reluctant to share, I would suggest that you meet him/her one-on-one to discuss what he/she feels is a good technique. Ask if you can try it in your class. Most likely you will receive permission. After you use it, if it is successful (or maybe even if it isn't), meet again with that teacher to acknowledge and praise. Ask permission to relate it to the staff at the next department meeting. The teacher can either relay the information, or you can. Agree to that. I would go out of my way to praise the technique, and through that distinction, praise the teacher. Many times that strategy would soften the iron will against sharing, and every teacher starts to play nice with others. Sharing takes a major step to insure that whoever deserves credit, receives it. Moreover, the health of any department or team qualifies the concept that no one cares who gets the credit as long as the caravan improves: hence, another area where coaching influences teaching.

Sharing sure takes first place over blaming, would you not agree?

YOUR TURN

Use this space to write some reflections for this section.

SECTION 2-B

COACHES, BLAME NO ONE.

STEER

IN 2003, I WROTE A letter titled *Coaching is About Kids, not Money* to the *Chicago Tribune* and the newspaper published it. In this letter I countered a statement by a college basketball coach from Auburn, "I don't understand why _____ lost his job. High school coaching is supposed to be about helping kids get a scholarship." The main point in my article was that high school coaching should be about three things:

1. Steering kids correctly in their studies and classwork

2. Teaching players sound fundamentals, unselfish team play, and good sportsmanship

3. Preparing them for life's unfair challenges

See anything about *winning*? You should since winning is embedded in all three premises. If a coach has the talent and knows what to do with it, winning will occur. Coaches are first teachers; their classrooms are those courts, swimming pools, football fields, and locker rooms. When I read a statement like the above from that college coach, I read another example of delusional spoon-feeding to young people by irresponsible adults. Excessive ego quickly embraces the world of blame.

True leadership blends adequate ego with the humble ability to steer athletes in the right directions. Refusing to point fingers is an essence of leadership. Leadership can be learned if humility is the foundation. You as a coach cannot be afraid of taking a few humiliations along the way, as uncomfortable as those events can be.

In 1983 I attended the NCAA Men's Basketball Tournament Final Four in Albuquerque, New Mexico. I did not know, nor did few others, that that Final Four would create one of the most memorable moments in tournament history. Jim Valvano was the head coach at North Carolina State, one of the final four and a team few expected to make it that far. North Carolina State won the national title with a 54–52 victory in the final game over Houston, coached by Guy Lewis. The ending of the final is one of the most famous in college basketball history, with a buzzer-beating dunk by Lorenzo Charles, off a high arching air ball from 30 feet by Derek Whittenburg providing the final margin. This ending contributed to the nickname given to North Carolina State, the *Cardiac Pack*, a reference to their close games that came down to the wire. In fact, the team won 7 of its last 9 games after trailing with a minute left in the game. Both Charles's dunk and Valvano's running around the court in celebration immediately after the game have been staples of NCAA tournament coverage ever since. North Carolina State's victory has often been considered one of the greatest upsets in college basketball history and is the fourth biggest point-spread upset in championship game lore. On a personal note, the dunk left my mouth agape and my mind questioning what I had just witnessed. My buddies knocked me back into reality, hitting my arms and screaming. I had seen a miracle within an inspirational college basketball championship game.

Coach Valvano was a fantastic leader because most every word he uttered bled humility. Ten years later, Valvano was presented with the Arthur Ashe Most Courageous Award at the 1993 ESPY's. Upon receiving that award, he gave the world another memorable moment, with his stirring, humble acceptance remarks. He had to be helped up the stairs to the podium since adenocarcinoma/glandular cancer had spread throughout his body. I invite you to watch that speech at your convenience; I guarantee it will give you plenty to ponder. Among the many moments of inspiration, Valvano said:

> *To me, there are three things we all should do every day. We should do these every day of our lives. Number one is laugh. You should laugh every day. Number two is think. You should spend some time in thought. And number three is, you should have your emotions moved to tears, could be happiness or joy. But think about it. If you laugh, you think, and you cry, that's a full day. That's a heck of a day. You do that seven days a week, you're going to have something special.*

In that speech alone, not to mention the ways he lived his life, Valvano gave us something to do-support the *Jimmy V Foundation for Cancer Research*, which he initiated that very evening, something to hope for, something to dream, and something/someone to love. In a final bit of magic that rivals his team's astounding victory in 1983, Valvano was so optimistic despite his illness that he never lost his hair, contrary to his doctors' predictions, despite the excruciating periods of pain and exhausting bouts of chemotherapy. He died two months after his ESPN speech (https://youtu.be/HuoVM9nm42E).

Valvano's leadership echo the words of Lao-Tzu, Chinese philosopher:

> *In the leader's desire to be at the front of people,*
> *he must in his person be behind them.*
> *In his desire to be above the principles,*
> *he must in his speech be below them.*
> *Sincere words are not showy,*
> *showy words are not sincere.*
> *Those who know do not say;*
> *Those who say do not know.*

Excellent models of leadership are probably right next to you. My personal list touts an all-star group, a *who's who* for basketball and classroom acumen and talent, and each one left an indelible impression on my English teaching and basketball coaching. Those impressions I identify. Each impression profiles an aspect of a professional leader at work. Each person revealed a high level of conviction in what he/she was doing or attaining; conviction is a prime energy source. Each person let subordinates or students know when there was disagreement, without robbing those people of their dignity; each role model applied the maxim, "It is not what you say, but what they hear." Each coach was a fine teacher; each coach blended adequate ego with the ability to foster values in his/her athletes. *Leaders must be able to teach.* A teacher-coach organizes, prepares well, knows the details of his or her craft, understands his people, can communicate those details in refreshing and accurate ways to the charges, turns conflicts into advantages, and, most importantly, does all these assets every day.

Coaching is a rough profession with many issues that the average fan will never experience or be able to understand. As Abe Lincoln once said, "As soon as you make a decision, 50% of the people are against it." Lou Holtz offered, "Problems exist: 50% don't care about your problems and the other 50% are glad you have them." Blaming others for problems only increases the anxiety, delaying clear thinking about solving the problems. Of course, there are many times when blaming becomes a handy defense mechanism: the car dented in the parking lot when you shopped inside the store, the doctor informing you of a sudden illness, etc. Everyone has some of those moments. The best coaches I have known were above blaming others for their issues. They each coached their sports with a sense of dignity, calm, and detail. Their humility embellished their inner pride in their work. They love(d) their athletes. I learned from each of them.

EXEMPLARY COACHING LEADERS WHO TOOK RESPONSIBILITY IN THEIR OWN SPECIAL WAYS:

MY MOTHER AND FATHER
(Keating Ave., Dickens St., and Roscoe St. in Chicago; Des Plaines IL)
~work ethic, loyalty, commitment~

COACH ED MOLITOR
(DePaul Academy, Marist High School, Palatine High School, retired)
~modeling and nurturing player enthusiasm…if one ever observed the players on his bench during any game, great enthusiasm and teammate support was evident and those players played with that enthusiasm~

COACH TOM MCCORMACK
(St. Scholastica Grade School, Immaculate Conception High School, Conant High School, retired)
~building a program and sustaining it with the right blend of discipline, ability, and demeanor~

COACH WILL REY
(Gordon Tech High School, Crete-Monee High School, Fenwick High School, Evansville University, Loyola University, St. Mary's University-Minnesota, Wright State University, Northridge Prep)
~unafraid of change for the good of the team~

Coach Pat Sullivan
(Providence High School, University of St. Francis, retired)
~continuing knowledge of the game and the evolving methods
for teaching it with the constant willingness to share his ideas~

(the late) Coach Bill Gleason
(Loyola Academy, Oak Park-River Forest High School, Chicago Hustle,
University of Tennessee-Chattanooga)
~love of the game with a great sense of humor~

Coach Steve Little
(head boys basketball coach, Lincoln-Way High School, retired)
~the ability to enjoy the game while meeting the pressures of
the expectations of exceptional talent~

(the late) Coach Rick Majerus
(Marquette University, University of Utah)
~the unselfish generosity of time to high school coaches, usually
at a restaurant with the greatest fondness for food I ever witnessed!
Rick could also dissect two minutes of any game with an astounding
amount of accurate detail~

(the late) Coach Bill Schaefer
(Quigley Seminary North, Fenton High School, Rosary College)
~foresight by advocating and using strategies no one else had
thought of or witnessed~

Coach Hubie Brown
(Atlanta Hawks and New York Knicks, present ESPN color analyst for the NBA)
~ability to spend hours talking about basketball and lecturing at clinics
and camps…I *always* learned from Hubie. I once traveled to Atlanta
when Hubie was head coach of the NBA-Hawks and watched
his rookie camp for three days. This instruction was unparalleled
for its discipline, detail, and teamwork~

(the late) Coach Frank Power
(my freshman coach at Boston College)
~belief in the fundamentals~

(THE LATE) CHUCK DALY
(Boston College, Penn, Cleveland Cavaliers, Detroit Pistons)
**~best dresser ever…sound practice planner who
let you know the honest truth~**

(THE LATE) COACH AL MCGUIRE
(Marquette University)
**~enjoying the game…probably the precursor to today's Joe Maddon
(Cubs manager) by** *not letting the pressure overcome the pleasure~*

COACH MIKE KOLZE
(Highland Park High School, retired)
~excellence at adjustments, especially after timeouts~

(THE LATE) JACK TOSH
(DeKalb High School, Evanston High School,
York High School as athletic director)
~teaching five classes and coaching two sports is the best job in America~

COACH BOB WILLIAMS
(Palatine High School, Schaumburg High School, Niles West High School)
**~the ability and self-belief to defy the odds, demonstrated by his
Schaumburg team's state title over favored Thornwood in 2001~**

COACH GENE PINGATORE
(St. Joseph High School) and
JIM TRACY
(DeLaSalle High School, Reavis High School, St. Laurence High School)
~the endurance required to coach~

COACH RICH KOLIMAS
(Gordon Tech High School, Lincoln-Way East High School)
~the steady hand at the helm underscored by the inner faith in his ability~

DR. PAUL PRYMA
(St. Patrick High School, Evanston High School, St. Ignatius High School,
Glenbrook North High School as principal, retired)
~ability to articulate the virtues and values within the game~

COACH GORDON KERKMAN
(West Aurora High School, retired)
~the ability to coach all kinds of players and allow their talents to blossom~

COACH DICK FLAIZ
(Quigley Seminary South, Downers Grove South, retired)
~the utter drive and competitiveness, always with class and dignity~

(THE LATE) COACH STEVE PAPPAS
(Gordon Tech High School, Deerfield High School)
~the Ernest Hemingway trait of *grace under pressure...* you can read about him in Dr. Pryma's book *Coaches of Chicago*~

What are more ways to learn leadership? Read about people in leadership roles. In the back of this book I have a list of *brain food* for readers with the curiosity to explore and improve leadership skills. Read the following example, an excerpt from the biography *Ronald Reagan* by Dinesh D'Souza:

> From the time that he delivered his national television address for Barry Goldwater in 1964 until he won the presidency in 1980, Reagan faced a serious problem. How does a man who believes in principles that are out of touch with the prevailing public ethos get elected? The ordinary politician has an easy solution: modify principles to suit the regnant mood. The leader, however, is not interested in just getting elected. He seeks public office in order to vindicate his principles and realize his policy objectives. Thus, the option of accommodation to the fashions of the moment is not open to him.
>
> Fortunately, there is a second option. The leader can remain true to his principles, refusing to yield even when the elites and the people are against him. This does mean he is condemned to virtuous defeat. It does mean he must be wily and opportunistic in finding issues that allow him to neutralize

his strongest opposition and enable him to find the greatest common ground with his popular constituency. He must be patient when circumstances are difficult, self-disciplined in staying focused on his goals, and creative in his selection and presentation of issues, until the moment of opportunity presents itself. Reagan's political career from 1964-1980 illustrates this higher path (57).

Now read a personal example of poor leadership.

In 1996 I came home from York High School after basketball practice and my wife gave me a long look. I was unsure of the reason; she told me, "Sit down, it's not good." Evidently, one of my basketball parents with whom I had been at odds had distributed a letter to other parents with a petition asking for signatures demanding my removal as basketball coach. Susan had a copy of the letter and the petition. I read both. We discussed a plan for action. What we decided was to do nothing. I felt support from the principal, but the weeks ahead were loaded with pressure, distraction, and uneasiness at practice. The player in question, a junior, had good talent, but was as headstrong as his coach. When those two collided, there were bound to be sparks. I liked the young man; doesn't every coach like a player who has valuable skills? I tried to convince him to play with more discipline on the court, but he was not a reliable practice player. I was a coach who demanded and stressed strong practice habits on a daily basis. That combination was a storm in the making. I dismissed him from one practice for lazy effort during the week we were preparing for a game against Proviso West. Proviso was a big rival and a conference foe and York had not beaten them for 75 games in a row. We played them at their gym and the player in question was playing very wildly, taking contested shots, and not running our offenses. In one trip he drove on three guys, threw up a wild shot, and was hit hard, falling to the court. My heart sank. I could feel trouble ahead. As I hovered over the player, his dad stood next to me. He did not say a word, but I could feel the wrath. This moment tipped the scales as far as the parent was concerned.

The following morning I drove to the player's home to see how he was doing. Dad was not home. I surprised his mother; she let me in, but her distant look told me I was not welcome. Mom informed me that her son was asleep;

she told me he had broken his elbow. I told her I felt bad and offered my assistance in any way. I left, feeling that darker mood I spoke of earlier. The next week the petition surfaced.

All in all, the petition garnered a total of three negative letters as opposed to over fifty positive ones. My principal and I discussed the matter a few times. He said it was a dead issue. I felt relieved, but still at a loss for what to do. As coaches we often have that combined feeling of dread, confusion, and uncertainty. Those difficult moments in any career make a good attitude a strenuous task. The York example is a bit extreme, but serves as one that surfaces whenever a parent or an administrator begins to believe that Mr. or Mrs./ Coach So-and-So just doesn't have what it takes. I took some comfort in Hubie Brown's words, the NBA radio analyst for ESPN, "Dogs bark, but the caravan moves on."

The player came back after eight weeks of mending and rehab. The following year we beat Proviso West at home, ending that horrendous losing streak, and that player was a part of that victory. We would not have won that game without him. That victory was one of the most fulfilling I experienced throughout my time as a head coach, but great events come at a cost and with untold sacrifices. Although I never quite had the relationship I wanted with that player—more my fault than his—we had a far better understanding from that incident. I respect him to this day. He reminded me of Derrick Rose in a way, not insofar as his physical talent is concerned. It was more the player's willingness to play the game and come back from serious injury. If he reads this, I hope he feels he accomplished the ability to respond to adversity from his high school career.

I can supply many more examples of adhesive moments more suitable for a night out with a group of friends/coaches at a local establishment. Each tale would run a gamut of emotional highs and lows. Suffice to say, frame of mind remains a barometer of the mettle of each coach. We enter the doors of school each day uncertain of what awaits, but prepared and confident about our abilities. We don't always leave school or an athletic contest that way, but players and students always surprise and challenge us with their resiliency or their out of sight-out of mind outlooks. Those transitions buoy our development of the required toughness and relentlessness for overcoming the odds, accepting and conquering challenges, and improving our ability to foster sustained relationships with the players.

In the above instance, however, I realized I had not been a real leader with this player. Right or wrong, I did not blame anyone except myself for the situation. You readers might say, "I don't see how you can blame yourself for this injury or situation." I did because I had not built trust. My communication skills were not as earnest or as open as they needed to be; many times my communication was as about as clear as a doctor's signature. I was still relying too much on yelling, rather than explaining or calmly analyzing. I expected a lot from this player, as I did from everyone, and as coaching goes, when the expectation falls short of reality, coaches look for personal straitjackets. Here lies the conundrum and the challenge-*the ability to blame yourself even when fault lies elsewhere.* That lesson is harsh and quite unfair, but I believe it constitutes a form of humility, cultivates the objectivity required within chaos, and discovers the optimism in the self. Good coaches will always seek a better way for future applications. Coaches must learn the patience to succeed. That reward comes only through accepting and learning through failures. Failures avoid blaming. Failures do not mean that one *is* a failure. Failures are the roads to self-discovery.

DEDICATION DISCOVERS AND DETERMINES ABILITY (MEMOIR) 1965-67

Speaking of failures, I have often wondered through the trails of tears and tribulations that constitute teaching and coaching-and any worthwhile career for that matter-why so many are born with so much, but achieve so little; and why so many who are born with so little, achieve so much. I guess I was a combination of the two, born with so much, didn't know it, yet somehow achieved some good things. I was fortunate to have a teacher who would not let me settle on simple ability or shortchange myself, even though it took me quite a while to develop any confidence for any ability in anything.

Many people might not believe that a broken bone would be a fortunate turn of events. In my case, I believe it was. On the very first night of my high school life, I broke my left wrist by sliding into home plate at an evening softball neighborhood game. Sliding would ordinarily not be an issue, but when I slid headfirst on parking lot asphalt, serious consequences developed. I went to my second day of high school with a white cast on my wrist.

Mr. Bill Schaefer was undeterred. Mr. Schaefer, my future high school basketball coach and personal savior, saw something in me that I, a raw 14-year old at Quigley Seminary North, did not know existed. Personal saviors possess that particular acumen. He wanted me for Quigley's varsity basketball team. For quite a while I felt like an escaped con evading the authorities. I tried to ignore the man by avoiding him when I saw him coming down the hall. Hiding in bathroom stalls, diverting down empty hallways, even hiding once in a confessional, or pretending to have other things to do were also various forms of stealth. If I had had the wherewithal and the tools to build a tunnel or escape hatch, I would have done so. During my freshman year, Schaefer became that annoying gnat in my ear, the mosquito I could not kill.

"Tom, play basketball."

"That cast won't be on forever; come to basketball and watch."

"Tom, you got to try out!"

"Anstett, come out for the team. We need your height. I'll work with you. You'll like it. You'll be great."

Great? At basketball? I didn't even like the sport, had never really played it. I was an awkward 6'3," about as motivated for hoops as I was for math, and generally reserved. I had spent my grammar school years playing softball and fast-pitch, running bases, playing tag, mowing lawns, serving Mass and saying Mass (you read correctly) in the basement of my bungalows on Dickens and Roscoe streets, watching *The Three Stooges*, and annoying my older sister. Riding a CTA bus fifteen miles down Addison Street back and forth and passing beloved Wrigley Field every day was a long enough day. I wanted no part of basketball and mentioned that when Schaefer had me in his gym class. Unfortunately, there were only so many places I could hide, and little did I know, the seed had been planted.

Schaefer was persistent. When he learned how I broke my wrist, he chuckled a bit, but kept the pressure on me. Perhaps that headfirst slide into home plate translated into a latent drive, the butterfly waiting its emergence in its cocoon that I had not yet appreciated or used to my advantage. To me, winning a softball game meant the world. After a loss I was at best a very sore loser, pouting, yelling, storming away, throwing bats, if necessary. Couple that fire with the gentle push from my dad who urged me just to try basketball to see if I liked it, I came out for the team in sophomore year, an inch taller but nonetheless fearful of what lay ahead.

I had no concept of what world I was entering in October of 1966: three foot blisters, two destroyed lungs, and a bruised ego were just some of the repercussions from the first three hour workout. I dropped more passes than I caught; seniors laughed at me; Schaefer did his best Hitler imitation propelling me to run and run and run. No such thing as starting slowly and breaking me in. That was all before the three hours of homework that awaited me at home. Day one was a microcosm of the rest of my high school career. The major difference between that day and the rest of the journey was the dedication that proved both the trial and the savior. First, though, I had to learn what becoming good at something involved. Dedication was a decision to be made at a later date. Survival was my first concern.

Sophomore year in basketball became a marathon. Not only did I play four quarters of the preliminary game, but also once that game ended, I had to zip into the locker room, change into a varsity uniform, and play all four quarters of the varsity game. Note that I *had to*, under orders from the great dictator Schaefer. I did not want to. More dropped passes, more angry stares from the seniors, the few rebounds I got dropped into my hands with the help of God. I was turning flatfooted rebounding into an art form. There was no such thing as scoring the basketball. It was difficult to score when I rarely touched the ball or could secure an offensive rebound. One skill I was learning well was getting in the way of my teammates' drives and moves. A definitive high point of sophomore year was a pre-season scrimmage between Weber High School and Quigley. Weber was an all-boys school on the northwest side of Chicago. Their basketball team played in the fearsome Catholic League, a conference known for its toughness, athleticism, and skilled players. Of course, I had no idea again of what I was heading to while the seniors were excited about competing against those giants. On scrimmage day Weber's guard tandem consisted of Mike Krzyzewski (yes, *that* Coach K. of Duke University) and Tom Kleinschmidt, a tough player who became a fine Chicago-area referee. They battered us with their speed and finesse. Does that give you any idea where I stood? I felt like the 110-pound weakling who goes to the beach and gets sand kicked into his face. At one point in the scrimmage, I actually scored one basket after a fairly vicious rebound. The only problem was I put the ball into *Weber's* basket. It was actually a nice play on my part. One of the seniors came over to me after that inspirational move and threatened my entire family if I ever did that again. Imagine that statement from a seminarian.

An avalanche of sprints, screams, sarcasm, and scares covered the rest of sophomore year. Schaefer never let up. We had a great senior guard, a smooth scorer with a dagger for a jump shot. That player showed me some kindness by rarely giving me the ball. He instructed me to screen for him. I obeyed. From him I learned what a great player looked like and the level of competitiveness one player can possess. He was relentless in his offensive skills as our leader, scoring 53 points in a single 32-minute game. After high school, he attended Wichita State University as a scholarship player.

I stuck out the season and started to see some light in my game. By January, I could catch the ball while being guarded, jump as if I was not landlocked, and shoot. Schaefer classified those actions as the new wonders of the world. He then escalated the drills, akin to what the government was doing in Southeast Asia at the time. He would have me come to the gym during lunch hour and shoot free throws and jumpers in my stocking feet. He would make me stay after practice for extra work. I jumped rope; I complained. I ran the floor after inbounding the ball to get layups; I complained less. I practiced rebounding while Coach held a small mat to contest me; it felt more like boxing but I complained even less, actually wanted him to hit me harder. Things were improving because of the Schaefer belief system. I was even receiving some compliments from the seniors. "Anstett, run faster and you can get some scores." "Anstett, get out of the way quicker." "Anstett, set harder picks!" "Anstett, would you mind getting some rebounds?" Yes, those were compliments. I had yet to earn the normal type, but the seniors were paying attention to me. Confidence comes in small doses, the receiver unaware of its silent arrivals.

During the summer of 1967, I shot hoops on my own at a local park. Dad bought me some free weights for the basement and I started to bench press and curl. However, one of the key moments in my development came via a Fenwick senior hoopster by the name of Bill. I was playing in a summer league at St. Catherine of Siena in Oak Park, Illinois. This required a 35-minute bus ride down Austin Avenue, time enough to wonder if I would make it home alive or in one piece. At the first game of the summer, I met Bill. It was a rather sudden meeting: in the first few minutes of the game, he laid me out, swept me under his rug when he decided to swoop for his first offensive rebound of the night. I had made little attempt to block him out, so he took that evasiveness as an open invitation to crush me. Bill was 6'5" and about 230 lbs. He had a quick first step, powerful jump, and an obnoxious personality on the court. I was 6'4" and about 170 lbs. I played with knees straight, with little jump, and with little edge. That pairing is called a mismatch. After Bill's first smack, he stepped on my chest and smirked. I cried a bit to the ref, got up, started to breath, and continued play. That was the first of many collisions Bill decided to enforce that game; he knew a lemon when he saw it.

In the last few minutes, wondering how many imprints of Bill's foot, elbow, or head would be permanently engraved on my body, I caught a pass in the low post, turned, shot, and scored. Bill actually tried to block the shot, but somehow I managed to pull it off. Some mental inspiration settled in my brain. I realized I could do something with that man-child. He came down the court, posted me up, took a shot, and I blocked it out of bounds. "Lucky, man," he groused, as he peered over his shoulder at me. Lucky or not, I had done something at both ends. My turnaround jump shot became a staple; my blocked shot the first of many. After the game, he approached. I was afraid he was going to let me have it. He shook my hand and said, "You played hard and did a good job. You were tough. You're only a junior? Keep playing. You can be good." Those words elevated my mind to places unknown. Praise from a senior who would become *Chicago Sun-Times* All-Area after the season and All-State?

The game started to be fun as confidence made a token introduction that steamy summer night in Oak Park. Perhaps dedication was born that night as well. Playing against an experienced, talented player gave me a view of how a player can be Mr. Nasty for 32 minutes, and afterward, be Mr. Classy. We all need good models; I had found one that would perk me up when I needed a mental push.

1967-68

I walked into Quigley for my junior year at 6'6" and 185 lbs. It had been a productive summer, well before the constant presence of AAU and summer leagues. Players had to find the competition at local parks and pickup games. Many times that competition would be players of all sizes, skills, and ages. I had spent a good portion of the three months working at my dad's place during the days and shooting hoops and lifting in the evening. Softball now became a respite from the basketball workouts. I was replacing an enjoyment with a passion. However, it is one thing to shoot and dream without actual competition; it is another to gauge the actual improvement. Could I score against good players? Could I rebound in a crowd and actually hold onto the ball? These questions needed answers. I discovered those answers with the help of three seniors and a sophomore gymnast.

Dedication needs personal enthusiasm to be effective. Greatness requires a discipline for the moment, ignoring consequences. I had put in a good amount of work during the previous summer, but mainly as an individual. I felt stronger, but would I be able to use it effectively? I felt I could shoot pretty well, both from inside and from 20 feet. Official practice began on October 1. That meant at least six weeks of Schaefer before we saw anyone from another school. The three seniors were headstrong, tough, and disciplined leaders of the *TNS* society (Take No Shit). I looked at all three with equal admiration. Mike was a heady guard who could score and defend. He played with an edge, enough of one for the entire team. He was another example to me of what dedication could do; Mike prepared in the offseason as well as anyone; and everyone saw it. Ken and Ron would have made great bouncers at any nightclub. Both were not true basketball players: translation-both had little talent for basketball. Neither could score well, pass, or dribble. Ken was a stocky 5'11" lefty, a terrific baseball pitcher. Ron's red hair symbolized his fire. He coupled toughness around the basket with a determination for winning. I felt safe around those guys, and all three embraced me as one of them. I think they knew–or maybe Schaefer got into their ears–that I was to be a key component to the team. First, though, I had to show them I could play. All players have that challenge at the start of the year, no matter what accolades they might have earned in the past. Every team develops a respective chemistry and a degree of confidence in each other.

Practices became contests of will between Schaefer and the seniors. They tested each other. I was just trying to improve and staying out of the seniors' way. They would argue with Coach Schaefer, never hesitating to show their annoyance at the repetition of drills, the challenges of the coach, the long practices. One of the more exhausting episodes was Schaefer's races at the end of practices. "OK, you guys, everyone on the baseline. Down and back. First guy to finish is out of the running." Imagine being the last two guys in Schaefer's version of the Toilet Bowl. That meant you already had lost roughly 10-12 races, depending on the number of players that day. There was even a worse side. The *last* words you wanted to hear from Coach Schaefer were, "Tie. Run again!!" If the race was close, that yell boomed off the walls. Ron and Ken were two of the slower guys, especially if they had lost those ten in a row. They nearly started fighting after a few ties. What they never did, though, was play soft. That included me. If I was tiptoeing instead of playing, shying away from contact, or dropping passes, I heard from Schaefer, yes, but was bombarded by the three amigos. Ron would scream at me; Ken would push me and mutter something under his breath; Mike would just stare at me. I understood all three messages. We played a tough schedule for a seminary of 300 boys, and I was scoring in double figures. During that season, though, no one event showed me more how far I still had to improve than my game against DeLaSalle High School and its future number one NBA draft pick, the day I became *Superflop* in the eyes of my coach.

DeLaSalle's center was a 6'8" senior who was predicted to be one of the premier players in Chicago. Schaefer thought it a great test for my progress. He could think whatever he wanted. I was scared to death and played that way. The player made me miss before I ever thought about shooting. He did what he wanted with me. I scored eight meaningless points. After the game Schaefer glowered at us, but targeted his angst toward me, heralding me as *Superflop*. The name stuck for much of the season when teammates and coach reminded me if I played poorly or spineless. From that game I continued to spiral; I grew meaner on the boards and on defense. That game against DeLaSalle, as poor as it was, had lit a bonfire from the feeble embers of my personal expectations. I had thought I was a good player, but I realized I had to raise the dedication, and raise it immediately. We ended this year at 15-9, but I knew much more would be expected of me in the year to come. I do know that without those three seniors, my senior year would never had exceeded the 27 points per game I averaged as a junior or set a baseline for what I could be as a player.

My parents had opposite reactions to the change of fortune for their middle child. My name was appearing in newspapers. Quigley-North, that little seminary, had a budding star and a good team. My dad thought Coach Schaefer walked on water. I was rather hoping at times he would drown in his holy waters, most often during the killer sprints or races at the end of practices. Schaefer was convinced I could play college basketball, a vision I slowly adopted. He mentioned this to my parents. So, sympathy for the wounded was out of the question. When I came home with a face looking like stagnant algae, Dad conveyed, "Good for you—just do what he says. You'll be fine." My mother was just worried I would be injured. "Are you ok? Are you hurt?" Those questions loomed after games as well. I am not sure how my mother knew to ask those questions since she watched most of the games with her hands over her eyes, especially when I was slammed to the floor, dove on a loose ball, or took a hard charge. "Are you ok? Are you hurt?"

"I'm ok, Mom. By the way, did you like the game, the win?"

"Not sure. Are you ok? Are you hurt? Some of those boys play too rough." That was the extent of Mom's basketball IQ.

As it turned out, I needed one more push for any future excellence. Enter Mike T. Mike was a 5'9" sturdy sophomore and a devoted gymnast. I ran into him after school in the spring, and he asked me a favor. 'Tom, could you count the number of dips I can do? I want to test myself."

"Sure, Mike. Will do."

I counted every dip, deep and full and slow. Once he got to 75, I thought he was done. He stopped to "rest" with elbows locked, looked at me, and said, "Now it's winning time."

Twenty-eight more with some screams and curses seasoning the final ten. He dropped off the parallel bars, yearning to get to 104. I felt like puking just watching him.

103 dips. 103.

All I could do was stare. I could do about 20. Did it take great ability to set a goal and drive it to fruition? What was more important for personal success? What comes first, ability or dedication? How much ability did I actually possess? The dips image locked in my mind as I decided then and there to push myself physically as I never had done, fall in love with dips and pushups, and thus define and conquer what winning time meant to me.

1968-69

On the covers of Wheaties' boxes during these years, Bob Richards was an Olympic champion in the decathlon. I used to listen to him give speeches and had some of those speeches on tapes. He once said, "An Olympic champion is in the best shape of his life for four consecutive years."

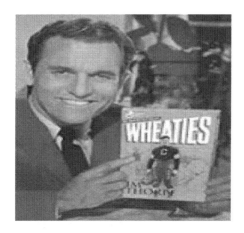

I was just trying to cover four months, June-September of 1968. That shape began to manifest on a 92-degree day in June when Coach Schaefer took the returning players to Lake Shore Park after the last day of school. He began, "Boys, we can be really good next year. So let's start getting into shape to win. You are to run 40 laps, 10 miles, and finish in 2:30. Oh, and keep those ankle weights on. Ready?"

We looked at each other. Now being considered the leader of the team, I asked Coach, "Did you say 40 or fourteen laps?"

"You heard me, Superflop!" That stung a bit. "40. Ready??"

You have heard the saying, "You don't know what you can do until you try"? Every time I watch *The Outlaw Josey Wales* and get to the part where the old woman is tied to a wagon, being towed relentlessly after being captured by mercenaries, I squirm in my seat. Painful reminder. Despite the omnipresent sun, the deathwatch from Schaefer, and the warnings from our bodies, everyone made the time. Pushing each other was a must and probably what Schaefer wanted the most. Being in the 1960s, coach received no parent complaints, no phone calls, no arguments for mental and physical abuse. I don't even remember talking about it, much less complaining, with my parents.

"How was school?" Mom asked upon my struggle through the back door.

"Fine. Nothing unusual. Last day, we ran a little at the park after school." My legs were protesting at this point, but my ankle weights were still on.

"Now that school is over, you can start at the shop with Dad tomorrow morning."

No breather, no days off. I mumbled my assent and welcomed a well-earned hot shower.

We assembled the next day to play basketball, despite the soreness and frustration. I had put in eight hours of work. I did not listen to my body which can think up some pretty good lies when convenient. Sure, some of the guys thought up new curses, lobbied for death threats and mailbox bombs for Coach, but we bonded. We decided to be a good team; we voted for dedication. None of us was a track athlete; we loathed cross country; none of us had ever run that far at one time. We took the road poet Robert Frost spoke of when he noticed two roads diverging into the wood, "I took the one less traveled by, and that has made all the difference."

That road paved my way throughout the summer. Each day I biked the sixteen miles round-trip to Dad's factory. Each day I ate in twenty minutes, then ran or biked to Notre Dame High School for girls seven blocks away from home to workout. Many nights I spent alone, shooting and dribbling up and down the court, imagining the end of close games against Little Flower or Quigley South, two of the formidable conference foes next year. It did not matter if peers were there to scrimmage or not; I felt I improved every time I left that gym. Hundreds of shots. Left hand and right. Up and down the court. Layups, jump shots from all distances. Game winners and losers. Imagination was my opponent within an empty gym; I pictured my opponents and practiced ways to beat them. I watched NBA games on Sundays and planted pictures in my mind of inside moves I admired, and then tried those moves out at the gym. I was a testament to the adage from Dick Butkus, the Hall of Fame Chicago Bear: "Be the first one at practice and the last one to leave." The basketball ended around 9; I went home and lifted weights in the basement and did dips between chairs. I was beginning to like what I saw and felt. I was my own boss. I determined the boundaries for my dedication. I alone was in charge; I was both teacher and the pupil in the Tom Anstett Basketball Camp, far ahead of its time.

I walked into Quigley in September of 1968, 6'7" and 200 lbs., and ready to lead a team, not just play. I had learned the lessons from my predecessors. At the start of the season, practices were grueling and long. Schaefer knew we had the grit and teamwork, and enough talent, to be a very good team, although Niles-Notre Dame routed us in our road opener by about twenty-five points. It was in that game that I met a future post-college teammate, who torched our junior guards with excellent one-on-one moves that created space for his killer jumper. That game set a tone for accomplishment;

it gave us a barometer of what we needed to improve. Practices intensified, if that mode was even possible. As the season progressed, we played many large schools in tournaments and held our own. The conference season was a dogfight: we beat Little Flower twice, Quigley South lost to Little Flower twice, Quigley South beat us twice. Providence Catholic in New Lenox gave teams headaches as well. Providence had a 6'9" center who had good skills but never was in top shape. In our home game against the Celtics, he scored 35 points, mostly on my porous defense. I responded with 44, so we were able to pull out a win. We also beat them at Providence 47-46. My main frustration that season was losing to Quigley South in the title game. I sat numb in the locker room. I admit that I could not stop the tears. Athletes prepare for those big moments for month after month in their respective sports with the risk of loss or injury sitting at their elbows. Part of life, but hard to accept for an eighteen-year old. By the end of the season, we finished 13-10 and in second place in the South-Central prep League. Overall, I averaged 31 points per game with a personal high of 51. I had one game with 27 rebounds and ten blocks. All those heights I earned from the previous summer. Personal stats aside, my teammates were men of the highest caliber of character and selflessness, Tom the most. Tom was a 6'3" wingman who looked for me every trip down the floor. He had a good shot, but used it sparingly. He supplied the glue for the team, the unsung teammate every coach desires. We were not that talented, but in the face of Quigley's toughest schedule ever, we were satisfied with what we accomplished, even though we bowed out of the state tournament in the opener, being upset by Walther Lutheran, a team we should have beaten. In that game I discovered the value of a post player's ability to pass well out of a triple-team, the defense I faced every time I touched the ball. Later in May of 1969, my dedication and relentless training and vision earned a four-year scholarship to Boston College, saving my parents $30,000, a huge amount in the late 1960s. Playing college basketball required more ruthless dedication, a story for another time.

Dedication makes all the difference to whatever walk of life a person chooses. In case you have not paid attention, dedication *is* more important than ability. Dedication discovers and determines ability. True dedication eliminates blaming and whining.

HOME PLATE

Now read about Coach John Scolinos who tells a tale underscoring the essence of dedication and through that essence, describes ways to conquer blame and entitlement. The following article is retold from the voice of Chris Sperry, a baseball consultant who develops players and amateur coaches, assists professional scouts, and counsels families of prospective college-bound student-athletes.

In Nashville, Tennessee, during the first week of January, 1996, more than 4,000 baseball coaches descended upon the Opryland Hotel for the 52nd annual ABCA convention.

While I waited in line to register with the hotel staff, I heard other more veteran coaches rumbling about the lineup of speakers scheduled to present during the weekend. One name, in particular, kept resurfacing, always with the same sentiment—"John Scolinos is here? Oh man, worth every penny of my airfare."

Who the hell is John Scolinos, I wondered. No matter, I was just happy to be there. In 1996, Coach Scolinos was 78 years old and five years retired from a college coaching career that began in 1948. He shuffled to the stage to an impressive standing ovation, wearing dark polyester pants, a light blue shirt, and a string around his neck from which home plate hung—a full-sized, stark-white home plate.

Seriously, I wondered, who in the hell is this guy?

After speaking for twenty-five minutes, not once mentioning the prop hanging around his neck, Coach Scolinos appeared to notice the snickering among some of the coaches. Even those who knew Coach Scolinos had to wonder exactly where he was going with this, or if he had simply forgotten about home plate since he'd gotten on stage.

Then, finally…

'You're probably all wondering why I'm wearing home plate around my neck. Or maybe you think I escaped from Camarillo

State Hospital," he said, his voice growing irascible. I laughed along with the others, acknowledging the possibility. "No," he continued, "I may be old, but I'm not crazy. The reason I stand before you today is to share with you baseball people what I've learned in my life, what I've learned about home plate in my 78 years.'

Several hands went up when Scolinos asked how many Little League coaches were in the room. "Do you know how wide home plate is in Little League?" After a pause, someone offered,

'Seventeen inches,' more question than answer.

'That's right,' he said. 'How about in Babe Ruth? Any Babe Ruth coaches in the house?'

Another long pause.

'Seventeen inches?' came a guess from another reluctant coach.

'That's right,' said Scolinos. 'Now, how many high school coaches do we have in the room?' Hundreds of hands shot up, as the pattern began to appear. 'How wide is home plate in high school baseball?'

'Seventeen inches,' they said, sounding more confident.

'You're right!' Scolinos barked. 'And you college coaches, how wide is home plate in college?'

'Seventeen inches!' we said, in unison.

'Any Minor League coaches here? How wide is home plate in pro ball?'

'Seventeen inches!'

'RIGHT! And in the Major Leagues, how wide home plate is in the Major Leagues?'

'Seventeen inches!'

'SEV-EN-TEEN INCHES!' he confirmed, his voice bellowing off the walls. 'And what do they do with a Big League pitcher who can't throw the ball over seventeen inches?' Pause. 'They send him to Pocatello!' he hollered, drawing raucous laughter.

'What they don't do is this: they don't say, 'Ah, that's okay, Jimmy. You can't hit a seventeen-inch target? We'll make it eighteen inches, or nineteen inches. We'll make it twenty inches so you have a better chance of hitting it. If you can't hit that, let us know so we can make it wider still, say twenty-five inches.' ...what do we do when our best player shows up late to practice? When our team rules forbid facial hair and a guy shows up unshaven? What if he gets caught drinking? Do we hold him accountable? Or do we change the rules to fit him, do we widen home plate?

The chuckles gradually faded as four thousand coaches grew quiet, the fog lifting as the old coach's message began to unfold. He turned the plate toward himself and, using a Sharpie, began to draw something. When he turned it toward the crowd, point up, a house was revealed, complete with a freshly drawn door and two windows. "This is the problem in our homes today. With our marriages, with the way we parent our kids. With our discipline. We don't teach accountability to our kids, and there is no consequence for failing to meet standards. We widen the plate!"

Pause. Then, to the point at the top of the house he added a small American flag.

'This is the problem in our schools today. The quality of our education is going downhill fast and teachers have been stripped of the tools they need to be successful, and to educate and discipline our young people. We are allowing others to widen home plate! Where is that getting us?'"

Silence. He replaced the flag with a cross.

'And this is the problem in the Church, where powerful people in positions of authority have taken advantage of young children, only to have such an atrocity swept under the rug for years. Our church leaders are widening home plate!'

I was amazed. At a baseball convention where I expected to learn something about curveballs and bunting and how to run better practices, I had learned something far more valuable. From an old man with home plate strung around his neck, I had learned something about life, about myself, about my own weaknesses and about my responsibilities as a leader. I had to hold myself and others accountable to that which I knew to be right, lest our families, our faith, and our society continue down an undesirable path.

'If I am lucky,' Coach Scolinos concluded, 'you will remember one thing from this old coach today. It is this: if we fail to hold ourselves to a higher standard, a standard of what we know to be right; if we fail to hold our spouses and our children to the same standards, if we are unwilling or unable to provide a consequence when they do not meet the standard; and if our schools and churches and our government fail to hold themselves accountable to those they serve, there is but one thing to look forward to...'

With that, he held home plate in front of his chest, turned it around, and revealed its dark black backside, 'dark days ahead.'

Coach Scolinos died in 2009 at the age of 91, but not before touching the lives of hundreds of players and coaches, including mine. Meeting him at my first ABCA convention kept me returning year after year, looking for similar wisdom and inspiration from other coaches. He is the best clinic speaker the ABCA has ever known because he was so much more than a baseball coach.

His message was clear: "Coaches, keep your players-no matter how good they are-your own children, and most of all, keep yourself at seventeen inches.

(http://www.sperrybaseballlife.com/stay-at-17-inches/)

YOUR TURN

Use this space to write some reflections for this section.

SECTION 3-A

TEACHERS, DO SOMETHING.

CONTEXT

GREAT PEOPLE ARE WORKING WHILE EVERYONE ELSE IS SLEEPING.
THIS STATEMENT SEEMS MOST APPROPRIATE HERE,
SO TEACHERS, LET'S WAKE UP AND DO SOME THINGS!

THE FOLLOWING SECTIONS BLEND THEORY, pedagogy, research, and personal experience in the classroom. Each part has the potential to bolster what you already do well in your instruction, no matter the discipline. Each part focuses on self-action. Each part encourages with an action verb; people who initiate, who *do*, are action people. They are the most *patient-impatient* doers on the planet. These hardy souls cannot wait to arrive at school or work; they anticipate great things happening every day. For the vegetation crowd, the non-doers, whining and blaming hinder goals, make those people too lazy to face and/or conquer their own weaknesses, and, most significantly, provide brick walls to the road to significance, the end result detailed later in this book.

For starters, I offer eleven ways teachers can instill and excite dedication to their charges:

1. Discuss the word *dedication*. Ask people or students what that concept means to them. Set individual and team goals from those teaching points.

2. Have great bad days. The tough days usually begin immediately: Your kid decided to throw up at 2 a.m.; thus, you had three hours of sleep. The coffee spilled in the car. Upon arriving at school, you heard two nasty voicemails. There was a note in your mailbox to see the principal upon arrival (marked *urgent*). You started

printing the copies you forgot to do for first period, and the Xerox broke. *Note*: all of these events occurred *before* first period.

3. How do you turn this horrible day around? Compliment three deserving people to drown your self-pity. Find two struggling students to see what you can do for them. Start each class with a song or music that applies to the lesson. Do your best teaching in your final period of the day. In short, shine your spotlight on others who might need the pat on the back more than you.

4. First one arriving, last one leaving. This feat is not always possible, of course, but my motivation increased when I entered my school's hallways as a teacher and they were silent, vacant. That serenity, if only for a few minutes, pushed me to imagine the course of my day and my involvement with my students with positive anticipation and outcome.

5. Promise, then deliver. If you cannot deliver, explain the reason.

6. If you don't know the answer, find it out for the *next day*.

7. Offer your time more than your knowledge.

8. Reread the books you teach, no matter the repetition.

9. Make no excuses.

10. Expect nothing handed to you.

11. Do something.

Discuss

They just wait you out, don't they?

The "they" = the students. The "you" = the teacher. Through little fault of their own, but rather more the fault of the system, many teachers nurture the dominant feeling of learned helplessness to their students. The kids wait the teacher out. They know the bell has to ring sometime. Most know when that time is to the very second; unfortunately, so might the teacher. In the last few minutes of a discussion, or worse, the lecture, teachers will give up and tell students the answer(s) they desire. Let's take a drive and specify typical scenarios.

A discussion-centered lesson takes one of two roads. Route 1, the *Learned Helplessness Expressway*, contains little traffic, quick speeds, and direct routes. The teacher prepares some material and structure for discussion. The teacher provides some questions, most of them literal. The teacher knows the answers he/she wants. Throughout the discussion, the same students, the overachievers, the ones who actually read the material, and the ones the rest of the class count on to provide comments, supply the responses. These students are those who must encase their arms in ice after school. There are no five-car pileups on this expressway, no debates or inquiry; the eager ones supply the answers the teacher wants, the weather is fair and sunny. Teachers determine their discussions a success: the classes are orderly, students cooperate, the majority of them are silent pacifists. Two-thirds of the class take a few notes, doze occasionally, think about the weekend, rarely ponder the questions or stay on task. The teacher does the driving. The bell marks the exit ramp. The Learned Helplessness Expressway does its job. The lesson is handed to the students at no charge. Students continue to understand that the less they do, the less will be expected. There is comfort there. From this route it is easy to blame the teacher for a bad grade.

Route 2 is an uneven, two-lane road, marked by weather-beaten holes, products of vast in-depth thought on the part of the passengers and drivers. Traffic ebbs and flows; occasionally there is an unexpected detour that can result in some impatience and anxiety. In this classroom, students drive to the destination of inquiry, but not without challenges and obstacles. The teacher prepares for a debate/argument and the questions scaffold from the main idea (what the text says) to inference (what the text means). Teachers sit in the back seat and anticipate, but rarely know, the pace students will drive. (*Hint*: Knowing teenagers, expect speed because they want the lesson done.) The structure for this lesson engages all students; each has a responsibility for the lesson's purpose. Debate surfaces with argument, counter-argument, evidence riding the bumps in the road. The room is noisy at times. The students don't wait the teacher out; the teacher does the waiting. There might not be an exit ramp for this lesson; the journey might continue tomorrow or at a later date. Students leave with more questions than answers, unsure of the exact exit. The lesson retains student curiosity for more inquiry. Route 2, the *Help Yourself to*

Learning Highway, can be hard to see on a map. In this route, little is handed to the students. Students are expected to be prepared and know that they will be in charge of their education. Sound teachers will build further inquiry on lessons that take detours, even seem incomplete. The old saying, *The bell will tell* becomes more, *The bell will swell* (student curiosity).

YOUR TURN

Language arts teacher Esther Wu states, "Whoever is doing the talking is doing the learning." Can you evaluate the role this statement plays in your own classroom discussions? What would we observe happening in a good discussion? Think about her statement and those questions for a couple of minutes. Yes, write down your reactions before continuing:

Creating an environment for good discussion *and* sustaining a good discussion takes patience, trial and error, fresh approaches, and less teacher control. Here are some terms and road markers for Route 2:

IRE (Initiation–Response–Evaluation)

Teachers *prescript* both questions and answers, control topics, only *evaluate* student answers rather than responding to them. Students are *vessels to fill with knowledge.* Teachable moments missed, student voices unheard.

As opposed to…

Authenticity

Teachers ask questions that respond to student voices, that get information, that convey teacher interest in students' values, that have little prescription, that place a priority on thinking, not just remembering, and that build upon previous responses. (Nystrand, 1997)

Metacommentary

Making a point of explaining what was already said or written ("What I meant to say was…") or telling an audience how to interpret what was already said or what will be said. This is a way of commenting on a claim and telling others how to think–or not to think–about it. (Graff, *TSIS*, 2012)

Interactive Discourse

- Student responses are sustained.
- Understanding and retention are promoted by opportunities for self-generated elaborations–information is chunked rather than unrelated
- Encourages students to digest what *they do not yet know* in terms of the familiar
- A minimum of teacher talk with students self-promoting or selecting others

- Authentic questions, journals, drafts, learning logs
- There is a quality to the classroom talk–the "language of learning" (Cazden 1988).
- A "responsive-collaborative script" (Gutierrez 1993) as opposed to an IRE pattern with correct answers as the only goal.

Text-dependent questions

Look for teachers to be...

- asking students questions that require reference to the text in order to respond in both spoken and written word
- teaching students strategies for citing evidence from text
- crafting questions for students that are text dependent the *majority* of the time
- asking students questions that require them to *cite textual evidence*, infer, and respond to questions that are at higher levels of thinking
- building in increased processing time for students to respond to text—dependent questions

Look for students to be...

- citing text both orally and in writing when responding to questions and supporting arguments
- becoming accustomed to responding to questions based in evidence from the text (literally/inferentially)
- responding to questions at both the lower and upper levels of thinking with consistent reference to text
- engaging in close reading activities that require rereading, developing stamina for task completion

Dialogic vs. Monologic

DIALOGIC	MONOLOGIC
Discussion as conversation	**Discussion teacher-controlled**
Students piggyback	Students take turns
Tension-structured	Responses compliant to right answers
Responses are thinking devices	Rote memory, answers short, tentative
Teacher monitors & probes	Teacher keeps order, evaluates
Teacher & students expand on answers	Teacher fills students with what's left

(Nystrand, 1997)

YOUR TURN

After reading that terminology, reflect where your preparation for classroom discussion falls. Write a few notes, considering for some moments which of those strategies you do or which would you find provocative to implement for your classes.

The following are some strategies to consider implementing classroom engagement and interaction within any discussions. Each aligns to the Common Core and to teacher evaluations.

- *UPTAKE* (Marshall, Smagorinsky, and Smith 1995)
  Alternative to *IRE*–turn student responses into statement or question to encourage further elaboration

- *PADEIA*
  Open seminar, arena classroom, questions on screen, students volunteer responses

- *THE CLASSROOM ENTRANCE*
  Each student receives a question as he/she enters the classroom; students prepare an answer; students begin discussion by calling on others or asking for volunteers (questions mix recall with inferential and evaluative).

- *SMALL-TEAM REPORT FORMAT*
  Small groups assigned as students enter room; they have some time to discuss responses; each student must say something to whole class discussion; listeners take notes and add oral comments (a form of UPTAKE)

- *SILENT DISCUSSION*
  All students sit in a circle, each with a blank sheet of paper. Each student writes one recall and one inferential question about the text under discussion. Students pass paper to the right and students write one answer to one of the questions, then add another question. They pass the paper to the right again. Ask students to read everything on paper and pose an argument agreeing or disagreeing with one of the answers. Students can take as many turns as teacher feels feasible. At conclusion of turns, students report one pertinent idea or concept from the paper they have in their hands.

Three-Index Card Strategy

OPENING ACTIVITY

Each of you has three index cards. We will consider the *Pledge of Allegiance* as the document for discussion.

Ponder the following questions:

1. What are the two or three principal words in the pledge?
2. Why do you choose those?
3. How relevant is the pledge today?

DIRECTIONS:

After recall of the pledge, you will form circles of four. For each turn you take speaking in discussion, you are to throw one of your cards into the center of your circle. You must use all three cards; once your three cards are in the center, you are finished. You have 12 minutes. (Wilhelm, Baker, and Dube, 2001)

News Reports

Teacher divides students into small TV news teams. Students choose a relevant theme from current reading and prepare a news show based on that theme (include weather, sports, features, special reports, etc. if possible). Students present to class and the class rates each show.

Poll Everywhere

This website will have students use their cellphones to answer questions. Answers are anonymous. This method can also be used for a course evaluation or for any formative assessment ("Where Am I Now" Chappuis).

SOCRATIC SEMINAR

During my tenure at York High School in Elmhurst, Illinois, English chairman Dominic Belmonte and fellow English colleague Judy Jackson were very influential. Mr. Belmonte showed me the ability students exhibit if you plan for them to have more control within lessons. He urged teacher creativity to engage students in lessons. I marveled at his skills to engender rapport, provide seamless lessons, and facilitate student empowerment, all while maintaining a warm, yet steely calm. Dominic is now overseeing the training of new teachers at the Golden Apple Foundation in Chicago. Ms. Jackson approached me with a form of student-led discussion called Socratic Seminar in the mid-1990's. I was so intrigued by this format that I studied and watched it, then ran with it. Throughout the following years, I watched it develop into a technique students enjoyed, one where I took a backseat, and students did the driving on Route 2. When I came to Lincoln-Way in 1999, no one in the English department had ever heard of this approach, much less tried it. I introduced it there and am proud to say that numerous teachers use it to this day, and in various disciplines. Before I say anything more, just a warning. This technique is not made for you teacher control-freaks; however, I recommend that such teachers take the plunge and try this method. On the other hand, if the control freaks want to continue to do most of the work in their classes, continue to answer their own questions, and leave bored everyday contemplating trite lessons, do not try it.

This technique should be modeled in an actual practice. *The Pledge of Allegiance* is a very good piece to use for such a model to the students (See Three Index Card strategy in previous section.) The concept of Socratic Seminar is a modified approach championed by Mortimer Adler and Dennis Gray. Students are given a short reading passage. Choose fiction or nonfiction, poetry or prose. Distribute the passage one day in advance and ask students to mark their questions (read Doug Buehl's book mentioned earlier about self-questioning) and comments about the passage. It is best to Xerox the passage, ask the students to annotate, and also request those students to type three questions and/or comments from their annotations. I collected those papers as a part of their evaluation. Once in class, students divided into two groups, and they moved their chairs or desks to form an inner and an outer circle. Someone read the passage aloud; I preferred passages that could be read a minimum of two times. Discussion then began. The teacher asked an introductory question, especially when doing this for the first time, but the goal was to have the students of the inner circle do all the questioning and commentary. Students controlled the direction of the discussion. The outer circle took notes; I asked those students to write down a minimum of three comments the inner circle provided that helped the outer circle to understand the passage. The outer circle noted the interaction among the participants, main points of discussion, points of clarification, strategies the inner circle uses, and new questions surfacing from comments (Belmonte 46). The teacher put the tape over his/her mouth and allowed the students to take charge of their discussion. No law against taking your own notes, teacher. My notes consisted of at least one striking comment each participant stated, my own questions that surfaced from their comments, and the degree of courtesy by the participants. I also noted the number of times each student talked; some liked to dominate discussion; this domination must be discouraged. Note also that this method can be used as either a formative or a summative assessment, and the teacher can direct two inner circles during one class period or have the students in the outer circle on the first day be the inner circle the next day. Allow time for reflection and feedback from students after the entire class has had an opportunity to participate.

What are the ADVANTAGES of this method?
There are plenty.

- How often have you heard the shifts in the Common Core State Standards of "Extract and Employ Evidence" or "Engage in Complex Texts"? This method supports both shifts. If you haven't heard of these shifts, consider yourself behind the times. Socratic Seminar emphasizes and develops students' skill to examine a key part of a novel or a short story/essay with close analysis and focus. Trying to teach novels or longer pieces of literature can result in very general instruction where the teacher is doing most of the talking. By directing students to the adhesive moments within a text, students have much to gain. Dr. Douglas Fisher of the University of San Diego refers to the skill of close reading as having students read the same portion of text for multiple purposes: tone, theme, author's purpose, syntax, etc. Can you not see how Socratic Seminar can assist this? A bit later I will refer to my article in NCTE's *NotesPlus* from January, 2003, *Scrambling the Socratic Seminar,* for more ways to use this seminar.

- In a monologic, non-interactive discussion, many teachers will depend upon the same gifted students to supply answers. I found myself doing that dullness before my enlightenment about the Socratic Seminar. I erroneously called that method "teaching," leading to many nights of frustration. Those quiet students, those reluctant learners just watched the world pass, knowing that Mr. Anstett would eventually turn to the smart ones for answers. In Socratic Seminars, no one can hide. Once students feel comfortable with this method, miracles occur. I can recall many reserved students slowly developing more confidence in their abilities, more openness in their personalities after some success in inner circles. Furthermore, some of the comments from students who rarely spoke in the past astounded the rest of the brains. These turnarounds do *not* happen quickly. They are the result of teacher patience and short conversations with some of those quiet citizens after class when I would compliment them on their comment.

- Increased courtesy and respect among your classmates. My guidelines for Socratic Seminars included no interruptions, addressing each student by name, no side conversations, good eye contact, sufficient volume, and no domination of discussion.

- Students learn the value of close reading. One rule I insist upon is that every answer needs *concrete textual evidence*. In this way, students begin to notice the various impacts one passage can contain. With some teacher modeling and motivating, students will begin to develop more insights in areas of argument, analysis, synthesis, and evaluation.

- Students develop acute questioning skills, learning to think more quickly to ask impromptu, yet relevant, questions from a peer's comments. Question stems and Bloom's taxonomy are useful models to give to students so they understand what constitutes a good question. Yes and no questions are prohibited, as are questions that lead to one-word answers. Questions that ask for personal opinion are also verboten. Modeling is very essential. If you stay with the method without overuse, you will see the growth in the types of questions students create.

- Discussions will have more depth; students are now more engaged in your class. Students will look forward to this activity, especially if the teacher sets it up well.

- Sometimes students are stunned at the amount of control you are giving to them by this method. The vast majority of students are very appreciative for this control. You will know this fact when they ask, "When are we doing Socratic again??"

- Students will discover parallels between what they have previously read, whether in your class or elsewhere. Cross-curricular connections create thoughtful discussions.

- Students can see there is more than one *right* answer.

- Speaking skills improve. There are no answers acceptable such as: *Everyone does it* or *No one cares*. Students learn to avoid hasty generalizations, anathema to sound arguments.

What are the DISADVANTAGES?
Here are the main ones; each has a remedy.

- TEACHER DERAILMENT
  Students move into areas unrelated to the topic and the teacher promptly interrupts. This detour can occur in the early stages of applying this method. The teacher should let students do the talking and avoid unnecessary comments.

- STUDENT RELUCTANCE
  Students may be reluctant to first speak or to speak at all. Some will view their comments as useless or less intellectual. Others will retreat into the backward view of themselves as a student who cannot speak well or rely on their perceptions as to who the smart kids are. These beliefs will diminish in time, if the method is used regularly, but never quite disappear.

- THE GARRULOUS ONE
  Beware of the students who like to talk and say very little. This habit needs to be addressed at an opportune moment, out of the earshot of peers.

- OUTER CIRCLE IN OUTER SPACE
  Students in this role should be listening well and writing periodically. They cannot speak.

As I mentioned previously, I wrote an article in NCTE's *NotesPlus* from January, 2003, titled *Scrambling the Socratic Seminar*. This article describes a variety of approaches a teacher could use to maintain the basic ingredients of the Socratic, but to also offer some variety. I would not use any of these variations until students feel comfortable with the basic format. I also would advise that inner circles do not number more than twelve whenever possible, eight is ideal. Moreover, teachers should consider the clientele, the strengths of the class, and the personalities when they ponder which of the following approaches might work best.

Method One

Form three inner circles in the same class period. Each inner circle has ten to fifteen minutes of discussion time. Each group can discuss a separate passage or the same passage. If each group has a different passage, the entire class should have read the three passages. They should walk into class not knowing which passage they will discuss. One person from each group reports to rest of class on main ideas.

Method Two

This method forms four inner circles of six to eight students apiece. Passages can vary or be the same for each group. This method has one distinct advantage of encouraging the very shy student to participate. Students will feel less pressure to speak. This development can also work against the prime purpose of seminars; once again, teachers should determine what might work best for the type of students they have.

A disadvantage of this method is that it is more difficult for the teacher to monitor discussion. For example, I used this method a few years ago when my English 3 students read *The Grapes of Wrath*. The passage focused on Jim Casy's retirement from preaching. One group began discussing the level of morality exhibited by the Roman Catholic Church in the wake of sexual abuse cases by its priests. Certainly there is a contemporary connection, but students moved too far into personal opinions and too far away from the text. The text is key. If you try this method, teachers need to circulate among all the circles and be ready to rein in discussion. Teachers can also appoint roles for students to maintain focus.

Method Three

Students form one inner circle with a prepared passage and a specific purpose for reading. I ask for volunteers. If Socratic is a regular at this point, getting volunteers is not an issue. For instance, when I taught *The Great Gatsby*, I assigned the opening two paragraphs of the novel and asked the inner circle to concentrate on Fitzgerald's characterization of Nick Carraway. Identification and development of tone, traits, and point-of-view for establishment of Nick's persona were additional tools for students to examine. Students had one night to prepare. Discussion lasted a maximum of thirty minutes.

Here was the twist: after discussion, each inner circle student paired with an outer circle student for feedback. I had surreptitiously arranged this beforehand, so each outer circle student focused on his/her partner. The interview setup often proved helpful.

Method Four

For this method, I extended the time for discussion to 35-40 minutes, out of a fifty-minute class period. Once students are very comfortable with the seminar, this method can be insightful. The passage is assigned the previous day with a focus and results in a quick-write. Every student in class completes a quick-write and the question might be-*Identify one concept you feel you understand better after the discussion. Provide some evidence from the inner circle discussion that support your reasons.* This technique reinforces students' ability to take quality notes. A more critical thinking question might be: *What is the most important line in the passage?* This question might have been discussed or might not have been; it would be up to the student to synthesize an answer. With the emphasis today on differentiated instruction, providing a variety of choice for the quick-write would be prudent. The quick-write could be used as a formative assessment, helping the instructor weigh the effectiveness of the seminar.

Method Five

I give students an article written by the author or by a secondary critic about the novel in question. I prefer doing this at the end of the book because it can provide a fitting conclusion and/or a lively debate to that reading and dovetail to the next reading in the curriculum.

At the end of *The Grapes of Wrath*, I distributed an article by Steinbeck from the February 1998 issue of *Literary Cavalcade* titled *America and Americans: Is the American Dream Even Possible?* Students read the article three times and annotated it for author's purpose. Students were also to compare the article's purpose to the novel's. The following day we formed four inner circles and students had twenty minutes for discussion.

A persuasive essay followed where I asked students to argue which character in the novel is the *best* representation of Steinbeck's view of the American Dream. In the essay, students used both the article and the novel for evidence. Research was controlled. Writing becomes a partner to the discussion. Some type of writing should follow any discussion.

One bedrock of any method for Socratic Seminar is the fundamental of Extract and Employ Evidence (Shift #2 in the CCSS). Students *must* refer to the text for reference and evidence of close reading as part of their oral and written comments. This requirement challenges students to read a passage multiple times. As they become more familiar with the words, they become more comfortable comprehending an author's meaning on multiple levels and expressing their ideas. Gradually, the hope is that students will become more articulate people when they read and think about what they read.

Give Socratic Seminar more than a try, no matter what subject you teach. Give the method your commitment. Wu's statement bears repeating: "Whoever is *doing* the talking is *doing* the learning."

By the teacher and student expecting nothing, students start at ground zero. Each within his or her role has to climb the mountain toward achievement. No one can expect any reward unless the participation is provided. No one can blame anyone else for a lack of participation; the onus falls on the shoulders of each participant. Each has to *do something*.

YOUR TURN

What *big* ideas do I gain from this section? Identify three strategies you will implement into your lessons. How will the described methods decrease the issue of entitlement and increase student empowerment?

The Three Rs

What do you do the first few days of school in each of your classes? Read syllabi? Check attendance? Distribute textbooks? Explain your classroom rules and policies?

If you have been the dutiful teacher, you answered yes to all those questions. I would invite you to throw all that out and take the – er off the word teacher. Begin to teach. The first two or three days, begin to build *Relationships*, the first of the three R's. Curriculum can wait until your students are at home because you have given them readings to pique their curiosity about the curriculum, and to initiate reading with the right amount of rigor. You begin to establish your humanity, your persona, your class's persona, and the atmosphere conducive to learning. You find out their perspectives about school and your particular discipline. Hopefully, you have a laugh or two along the way, but students leave class knowing they have some homework for which you will hold them accountable in a couple of days, and also understand that this particular class will be different. Different and demanding.

I found that building good relationships and some form of identity for each class bought me credibility during vacation weeks when students are less focused, especially in the month of May. Here are some ideas for the first few days:

Day 1

I greet them at the door every day. I am always glad to see them-whether I am or not. On day one, I shake each one's hand, introduce myself, and ask each for his/her full name. I smile. If you cannot smile on Day 1, find a new career. Usually, I have already put each student's name on an index card and on one desk, so students have to find their desks.

Begin class with a personal story that has some tension or some humor to reveal your skill as a storyteller. I tried to tell a short narrative about my school days that can have some personal association to the everyday student. This narrative should connect or support the intended lesson. For example, I once began a class with the story of my father's introduction to World War II, D-Day on Omaha Beach. I expressed my gratitude that the Germans missed him or that he was just lucky to survive. I extended that story to the lack of gratitude the government reveals through its treatment of veterans. I was introducing the concept of anecdote/personal example as a method of argumentative evidence. The argument centered on the need for a revamp of the support system for veterans in the V.A. I ended class with the fight my father experienced getting the necessary medical help when he was fighting cancer instead of the Nazis. Personal story formed the nucleus for the lesson itself, and in the first couple of days, I was beginning to communicate the curriculum.

Bridge that to a quick-write, a five-minute writing for students to write their thoughts about your discipline. This will be their exit slip. Ask for complete sentences and neatness. You might already have put a sheet of loose leaf on each student's desk before they entered class, in case a few (there are always a few!) who just come empty handed or headed.

I mention the skill of introductions and the shaking of hands, one chance to make a good first impression. Depending on the size of your school, it is unlikely that all your students know each other. So, I ask students to rise and introduce themselves to as many people as they can in three minutes with their name, good handshake, and good eye contact/smiles. This breaks some tension and gets them talking. It lessens the tension/pressure of public speaking, or at least the angst of standing in front of the class. Any time students are doing the talking buys some time for the teachers to catch their breath and anticipate where to go next. The next step can be unpredictable in contrast to what your pencil jotted down the night before.

Next I put myself on their radar. I ask them to write or discuss the necessary qualities for a good teacher. I might group the students randomly into sets of three or four and give them ten minutes to discuss. After ten minutes, they receive two more minutes to determine their two most essential qualities. After that task has been accomplished, I ask for one spokesperson from each group and use chart paper to record main ideas. I explain that this is *our* class, not mine. I try to build a sense of community with this teacher being a good listener who values students' ideas.

Those activities fill day one, but they do not leave without a reading. Many years I used Joyce Carol Oates's essay *Journey*, a metaphor about personal growth. No syllabus. It is *online* and I direct students to read the syllabus tonight with their parents. I suggest a follow-up the next day to inquire from the students what they learned or predict about the class from reading and discussing the syllabus.

Day 2

I greet at the door and address each student by name. If you don't remember, ask for it, which is a far better model of a social skill than ignoring the student or mumbling your guess.

The target today is to extend the empowerment of your students. By doing so you extend some core relationships that bolster the curriculum. We discuss the following topics:

- What makes a good classroom?

- What makes a good writer?

- What makes a good reader?

- What makes a good student?

I can either have each student complete an independent quick-write for each question, allowing about twelve minutes, or put students into groups and form carousals which time discussion on each question with rotation to the next station. I prefer the quick-writes; I want my students becoming accustomed to writing every day. Students will soon discover that writing would be the primary tool for their assessment and learning in my class. We then open discussion to answers with my tabulating the key points. I continue to emphasize to students that they are the ones in control of this classroom; they are making the rules even though they have an online syllabus, complete with classroom procedures. Some of the guidelines, of course, students do not cover: late work policy, etc. Each year students refresh the atmosphere with incisive comments and answers to these questions. I will collate and prioritize their responses and they will stay on our walls for the rest of the year. When students forget their place for various reasons, I simply point to these guidelines. That direction usually suffices.

Before class ends (or at the start of class, a better time for assignments), I ask students to *reread* the essay from day 1, a prime component for sustained learning, but this time for a different purpose. They are to bring it to class tomorrow with detailed annotation.

Day 3

Students discuss the essay and write a formative response with a choice of question. This is homework. I might introduce a Padeia format today. Whatever I choose, I want to see if students can extend discussion for an entire period. I ask text-dependent questions, non-evaluative, without praise or criticism. The writing sample must be typed and will give me a sample of diagnostic writing. Writing becomes a prime dynamic for a sound teacher-student relationship.

At the start of this period, I will have laid out a textbook for each student. I do not waste valuable class time by distributing books; I try to make this tedious task as innocuous as possible. There is a reading assignment from the book with a template for a page of notes in each book. There are also directions for a one-minute speech for students to prepare as an introduction of themselves to the class. I give them two or three days to prepare this speech and will model one about myself in two days. Each of these directions is on paper with the textbook. Waste no time.

This outline of the first few days is just a suggestion, of course. However, the emphasis on relationships sustains teachers over hard days. Sound relationships build rapport. "It's not what you gather, but what you scatter that tells what kind of life you have lived." (Helen Walton)

Rapport, the second of the three R's, is the day-to-day karma students anticipate for your class. If I recall the alphabet, the letter p comes before the letter s. *Person* before *Student*-the individual relationships a teacher develops with each student surfaces in a group rapport. All teachers know how much kids will talk about their teachers outside of teacher earshot. This talk transfers to the level of commitment students will have for their teacher, a commitment first revealed by the teacher. I have employed two favorite techniques: check-ins/outs and 2-minute interventions. Checkins came on Monday and started class. Each student had a few seconds to provide the class with some interesting, exciting personal fact or event. These provided some humor, some pathos and gained momentum as weeks progressed. They help to develop rapport. I would include myself in this collection of data. Some true identities of students would surface as the year unfolded: the class humorist, the class poet, the class social humanist, etc. On Friday, I tried to set aside the last five minutes for checkouts with the same format.

Two-minute interventions consist of two-minute conversations with individual students. If a student completed an assignment early, I would try to sit with that person and just dialogue, asking him or her how things were going, what I could do to help, how English was progressing, what was new in his or her life, etc. It is an informal two minutes and I would record the date I intervened with each student so that I could keep track of whom I might have missed at the end of a quarter. These interventions casually let students know I was noticing them and was interested in their lives. Building rapport is a constant responsibility and the more you can build early in the year, the greater the level of trust and respect develops throughout the year.

Another way rapport can be developed is a teacher's attendance at students' extra-curricular events. Easier said, than done. In the film *Mr. Holland's Opus* (a must-see for any teacher), Richard Dreyfuss, who portrays Mr. Holland, a music teacher, takes to teaching so he can "write beautiful music in his *spare time.*" As he soon discovers, spare time is pure fantasy. When I taught AP Language, many of my students were very musically talented, in band or choir or madrigals. Very little else warms students' hearts more than seeing their teachers at their events. Just one appearance can build sturdy bridges. I attended Madrigals, concerts, school plays, badminton matches, baseball games, ad infinitum. Advertising these events in class also helps communication; students will even refer to their own specialties during checkins or checkouts in a particular week. Public birthday notices where I would ask the class to give a two-on-two group clap for the celebrant is another small, yet effective bridge-builder. I also had a ritual of *High-Five Friday* where students could not enter my room on each Friday without giving me a high-five with a *Happy Friday* greeting. At the end of each quarter, I would have a Smartie candy on everyone's desk. Why that candy? One of my favorite expressions is to keep pounding into students' heads, "One day you will be paid for being smart," thus a Smartie was the only candy for this teacher and his students. I would try every means possible to end each quarter on a high note.

Remember, however, no method or gimmick replaces a warm smile and greeting at the entrance of each student. Through all the gimmicks work ethic also bolsters the rapport between teacher and student. Once real rapport is established, students will work hard for that teacher.

Rigor represents the third R and this word can mean many things to any one teacher, sometimes a threatening, very misunderstood concept within our self-created, at times mandated, pedagogical universe. I know what this concept does *not* mean. It does not mean the amount of work you assign to your students, or the number of failures in classes. If that definition defines your modus operandi, I would wager that your classroom lacks sound relationships with an uncomfortable rapport.

So, what is *rigor*? To me, rigor is the relentless incorporation of the necessary skills and standards in a discipline that plans a high level of student engagement. That engagement balances *difficulty* (work load) *with complexity* (levels of thinking) (qtd. from Fisher & Frey). It requires an examination of not only what is taught, but also *how* the material is taught. Critical thinking, the student application of the top three levels of Bloom's Taxonomy (analysis, synthesis, and evaluation), is the central ingredient that elevates a curriculum from the mediocre to the rigorous. Critical thinking requires less teacher control, more lessons in inquiry, and increased reading and writing in curricula. Rigor requires an embracing of the Common Core State Standards in a school-wide sense; students do not become independent thinkers without all staff cooperating in that venture. Clinical psychologist and author Sarah Fine remarks in *Education Week* (2010):

> *What we need is to infuse the work around the common core with an element of visionary thinking. The standards themselves do not confine teaching to the realm of the scripted or undemocratic, but without serious reflection and rethinking, they will. The balance depends on our collective ability to come to terms with the standards and to use them as an opportunity for reflection and growth. Let us hope that we can muster the courage and energy to do so.*

Fine's comments reveal a progression for my career as a teacher. When I started my career in 1973 I taught by the worksheet, not knowing any other way. After all, taking classroom and education theory in college filled in the schedule, but accomplished very little in terms of the reality of a teacher life. I assigned a good amount of writing, but compared to writing pedagogy today, my methods lacked real substance. I even remember receiving written feedback from my high school English teachers. The feedback contained a few general comments, but there were few specific suggestions about organization, development, or overall integration. Most of the red ink centered on grammar flaws for which we received a healthy diet of drill work. I do not lay culpability at my teachers' feet. They did not know any better either. In any case, for whatever reason, I enjoyed writing.

As my English instruction progressed, I was fortunate to coexist with some excellent writing teachers. At Immaculate Conception, my English chairman was an original. His classes were founded on humor, fine instruction, and rigor. Rigor in those days was the amount of work a teacher could pile onto his students, and unfortunately, is still the mantra of many teachers. He worked his students hard, but to my everlasting amazement, his students typically left his class in high spirits. One of his many salient gifts was his penchant for writing a column for the school newspaper titled *The Coalition*. He would have given the late Mike Royko or John Kass, two model *Chicago Tribune* columnists, a run for their money. That chairman's column contained humorous and relevant insights, methods of satire, and prolific moments of creativity. From this teacher I learned that even serious topics could be delivered with pointed humor, a trait I used on my Masters exam years later. His talent to combine rigor with good relationships inspired me.

When I entered Northeastern Illinois University in 1984 for my Masters program, I had the pleasure of meeting Dr. Jerel Howard, my professor for the course Southern Writers. Howard was ahead of his time. He took the word *integration* and marched to his own beat. The course was literature-based, but Howard found moments to instruct his students in specific lessons in writing. Many of those lessons he devised from the literature, then transitioned to the actual assignment. He was fascinating. Every part of a lesson made sense and built on the previous ingredient. Much of his mantra preached the value of students' writing for authentic audiences, not just bland prosaic for a teacher. If only teachers in all disciplines could have seen him work a lesson. Modeling a variety of brainstorming for student use, Howard kept the assignments short and the focus and tone very specific. He started slow, but moved with a brisk pace to larger pieces. He made an indelible imprint on me regarding authentic lesson design and writing methodology. He was *Common Core* well before those standards came alive. As you might ascertain, Sarah Fine's words were becoming more realistic with the more people I met and the more methods I learned and began to apply.

Speaking of the Common Core Standards, listen to what noted author Mrs. Carol Jago (*Classics in the Classroom, With Rigor for All*) says:

The most important thing for teachers to understand about the Common Core is that it is a clarion call to accelerate learning in our classrooms. More is more when it comes to reading and writing. At the moment there is still too much filling out of worksheets going on in classrooms. Just calling the page a "graphic organizer" doesn't make it less of a fill-in-the-blanks task.

Jago has never been afraid of speaking her mind and her position has always been clear: all students, no matter their ability level, need to read and write in abundance. No matter what type of college entrance or proficiency test might be administered, more writing and reading will push students into the higher levels of Bloom and the areas of critical thinking and inquiry. Rigor as it is intended will be established and sustained. Thus, the actual look of lesson design has to change to charge students with greater ownership for their learning, and charge teachers with finding ways to engage students. Here are five questions teachers should ask regarding their lesson designs:

- Are *all* the students engaged and thinking, or only those who answer a question?

- What kinds of questions is the teacher asking? True or false? Recollection of facts? Or are students asked to recall something they already know and use it to solve a new problem?

- Are students given time to think through answers? If they don't have the answer immediately, does the teacher move on to someone else? Are students talking and sharing information appropriately, or is there total silence?

- Are teachers asking students to reread texts in acceptable doses for a variety of purposes and inquiry? (Fisher, Frye, Buehl).

- Are students aware of the end goal and the type of assessment they will encounter in terms of the learning targets?

School districts should conduct a detailed scrutiny into the instructional methods used by their faculty in their schools. Embracing the C.C.S.S. as a *unified* district/school is a good first step. Those standards are the best ones ever created and for now, the *only* ones. The push for critical thinking and student inquiry as the curriculum's fundamentals would elevate student achievement and confidence to a college-ready level.

Immediately on day one teachers set the tone for student engagement and individual responsibility. I would instill the mantra within the activities so that students hear the words, *Expect Nothing, Blame No One, Do Something.* These concepts can be the basis of the classroom rules or replace the titles of the aforementioned suggestions under Day 2.

YOUR TURN

Identify areas of interest for your own application in your classrooms. Also consider methods you would use to sustain the classroom atmosphere you desire throughout the year.

WRITE

I entered my first English class as the main man in the fall of 1973, beginning writing instruction with no real idea of what I was communicating or how I needed to communicate it. Boston College, my alma mater, is a terrific institution and I enjoyed my four years there, but the educational theory classes I took paled in comparison to the actual experience of student teaching. So, as a real teacher with live students teetering on my every word, I gave my thoughts and ideas from personal experience, a nebulous textbook about unity and coherence, and a lot of hunches. Feedback was a foreign language; rubrics were disguised by teacher red slashes and marks. Student conferences? Hardly. A mentor? Really?

As I slogged through 41 years of essay upon essay (and my classes wrote enough to satisfy Leo Tolstoy and Edgar Allan Poe), I gained the necessary data, experience, training, trial and error, and partnership to teach authentic writing instruction. Through all of this journey, and especially in the last ten years, I realize all the more how closely writing supports good reading, and vice versa. With the Common Core State Standards and the continued inspiration of colleagues, writing has the potential to be a valid assessment within every discipline in both formative and summative formats. The CCSS give all the ingredients and reasons to encourage and promote more challenge and rigor to subjects: audience, purpose, genre, media design, and stance.

If any school district is serious about evaluating and increasing its students' cognitive abilities, writing has to be at the forefront. Arthur Applebee states in his article *The Common Core Standards: The Promise and the Peril in a National Palimpsest*, "The CCSS elevate writing to a central place, not only giving it the same number of individual standards as reading, but also making writing the central way in which content knowledge is developed and shared" (*English Journal* 2013). Good teaching takes time, correct practices, trial and error, good modeling, patience, and administrative support. Class size can discourage some teachers from assigning too much writing, but will not discourage the *best* teachers. When every department plays a role in developing student writing ability, the confidence and readiness of all students will rise with a more complete student emerging. Carol Jago in *With Rigor For All* discusses the value of written assignments as "discovering the relationship students had developed with the text" (102), *text* being a key fundamental in the Common Core. This discovery not only promotes additional challenge and enhanced skills for students, but also assists teachers' reflection about the quality of their instruction and "the commitment of students as readers and writers" (102). A unity to establish writing as a baseline for assessments in *all* disciplines among a school's faculty would validate curriculum, make a quality curriculum even better, and provide a common language within a school. Within any college-entrance exam, students have to exhibit improvement as readers and writers and be able to apply the upper echelons of Bloom's taxonomy with higher application. Are not examination and comprehension of texts primary fundamentals for students? How do teachers know that students can apply or synthesize essential concepts without a project or written piece? Providing students with assignments via pen in hand for practical experience bolsters students' thinking. With the onus today on differentiated instruction, how much more differentiation can we get than a choice of writing assignments with a teacher-student writing conference appropriate to the text under study?

Furthermore, the application of language and methods from the Common Core delivers increased ownership by the students for development and sharing. Most students have heard of the political response, "Oh, that's just rhetoric." How many, however, can define, apply, and discuss what rhetoric means? High school teachers at Joliet Township High School in Illinois, Sean Hackney and Brian Newman advocate using the rhetorical situation as the school-wide rubric (*English Journal* 60). They encourage the use of genre, purpose, design, audience, and stance as the measuring sticks for all rubrics in all disciplines. This supports the conversation Gerald Graff, distinguished professor at the University of Illinois-Chicago, promotes in the text *They Say, I Say*, co-authored with his wife Cathy Birkenstein. In this text, Graff places argument as the primary learning method. With these functions in place, teachers can design more relevant writing assignments; students have the opportunities to develop more powerful voices for a variety of audience, thus enlarging the playing field for student partnership. This approach enhances what the standards are trying to achieve: writing standards across three modes of narration, exposition, and argument reveal outcomes such as *Produce clear and coherent writing in which the development, organization, and style are appropriate to task, audience, and purpose* (W.11-12.4), *anticipate the audience's knowledge level, concerns, values, and possible biases* (W.11-12.1 argument), *use precise language, domain-specific vocabulary* (W.11-12.2 exposition), *and engage and orient the reader* (W.11-12.3 narration). Newer writing instructional programs for teachers such as *Writing Matters* and *Writing to Read* reinforce such goals.

As an example of writing across the curriculum in 2007, there was an initiative at Lincoln-Way District 210 for the entire faculty to embrace writing as a means of assessment for every discipline. This movement would be supported with the inception of a writing center for students. As the department chair at Lincoln-Way Central and I presented this plan at a faculty institute, we were greeted about as enthusiastically as an oncoming flashflood. I remember some of the looks on the faces in the audience. "You want me to do what?" "Teach writing?" "I'm a P.E. teacher, not English." "I'm a math teacher, that is your job." We gave the faculty rationale for this curriculum innovation, a template for a rubric all departments to use or tailor, and details about the new writing center.

As with anything new, time helps to allay the initial fears. The social science and science teachers began implementing new writing features. The art department, family and consumer education, music, and world languages started to embolden their curricula with student reflections and short writing assessments for unit tests and final exams. The writing center moved from its infancy, an untrusted stage, to a productive, energetic home where writers received individual help. The center was especially helpful with the struggling student, the low-achievers, and the students who feared writing. As the years unfolded, attendance at the writing center grew by 25% every year. Student tutors gained experience playing the role of a teacher. Staff rarely had enough time within a lunch period to handle the influx of students requesting individual help with their papers. Moreover, teachers were requesting writing center staff to visit their classes to instruct students on assignments germane to that particular discipline. All gratifying. The growth of the center stands as a tribute to the leadership and teamwork of the English departments at each school, plus the willing attitude of the Lincoln-Way staff.

Here are some examples of prompts for each discipline in a school where writing is the backbone for student learning and thinking:

- Social Science—Write a justification for a major historical decision discussed in the first semester. Audience is one of the personae involved in the decision. Decide on a specific tone for the writing. Genre can be a letter or professional document.

- Drivers' Education—Research a current driving law that needs change or modification and argue for that change to an actual state official.

- Science—Write a formula and evaluate its effectiveness in an experiment/lab report. Audience is the portion of the general public who would be affected.

- Math—Assess your improvement in math in a formal letter to your teacher. Develop your evaluation in chronological order with examples from the various lessons.

- World Language—Write a class note using an informal tone to a peer in the language you are studying. Then write another with the same content but with a more formal tone to your teacher.

- Health—Prioritize two improvements to your personal health throughout the course. Compose an advertisement for a product that would support one of those gains.

- Physical Education—In narrative form, assess your physical development throughout a semester or a quarter. Create a chart with data to evaluate progress. This assignment stems from the goals you set at the start of the course.

- Reading—Compare or contrast the thesis and the style for a nonfiction article and a recent reading. Supply appropriate text evidence from both choices.

- Art—Write an analysis of a famous painting in a letter to the artist or to another art lover.

- Special Education—Write a letter of at least 500 words to your parents about the achievements of your goals on your IEP or 504 plan. Supply evidence from your folder or portfolio. Employ a tone of _____.

- Music—Argue the benefits of studying contemporary (or another mode) music in a Letter-to-the-Editor for the local paper. The purpose is to establish a course for student study.

- Business—Compose a resume summarizing in correct form the qualities for employment. Compose a cover letter to an audience for a current job opening.

Hopefully writing gets to the point in a school similar to putting on that comfortable pair of broken-in blue jeans, so smooth and familiar.

Speaking of writing, do you as the teacher try to write the prompts *yourself* before assigning them to students? Come on, really, Anstett. You think I have the time to write essays in addition to grading all of them? I know.

This request is asking a lot. I liken this suggestion to the kitchen. I often marveled at the culinary talents of my mother who could weave delicious masterpieces day after day. Whether it was her Hungarian recipe of chicken and rice, her beef stroganoff, or her famous red cabbage, Mom ruled supreme in the kitchen. Never in my dreams would I have attempted to cook those delicacies. However, if I would have made the attempt, I might have had a better appreciation of the skills necessary to complete the final product, or for that matter, to even begin the task. Besides, Mom always conducted her own taste test, based on her very lofty standards. If the test failed, she added what was necessary.

The same can be said for writing assignments, even projects. I do not suggest every assignment, but for formal papers, an occasional teacher-written draft reveals the relevance and clarity for the assigner and the assignment. This clarity would be very insightful for the actual prompt; many times, prompts for written assignments or projects are muddled, containing far too many directions and nebulous targets and steps.

Speaking of prompts, here is a "David Letterman Top Ten List" about writing prompts I gave to my department:

1. Consider: What have I desired the students to learn? What skills are appropriate for this prompt?

2. Consider a fake-out day where students come into class knowing they have to write an essay. They receive the prompt and start. The teacher stops them after ten minutes. The teacher and students dialogue about the methods they used to understand the prompt and to pre-write. This activity can assist students who have trouble starting their writing engines.

3. Write *one* question. Avoid an overabundance of questions; student confusion will follow.

4. Consider the verb for a desired response. For example, do you want students to *explain* or to *evaluate*? To *justify* or *describe*? Students should know the differences. These differences should also be a core for a variety of questions in discussions so that students understand and can apply those nuances.

5. Along with the question, list relevant writing strategies (figurative language, style, argument devices, etc.) for students to include for evidence in their essay.

6. Consider writing prompts with two prongs: one for more able students (more analytical or evaluative) and the other a bit more literal for less-able students.

7. Consider writing prompts that take students through the process.

8. Consider writing in response to your prompt. Can *you* do it? Can your students? You can model this activity as a hook to students' performing the task.

9. Consider giving and/or discussing the rubric for evaluation of the essay when you inform students about the assignment.

10. Consider one of the Essential Questions as the prompt from the unit.

Teachers can fall into monstrous ruts. They can use the same prompts every year, falling victim to the malaise from a lack of reflection and self-evaluation. When teachers attempt to complete, or at least begin, the actual assignment, clearer alignment will follow. With the continuing Common Core, evaluation of assignments is a necessity. Whatever teachers have been using will require a thorough cleansing. If they want to keep any one prompt, give it the acid test: write it and then evaluate. Chances are you will not finish the piece; you will already have thrown it out. In my retirement I have been tutoring six high school students each week in English skills. Some of the assignments and assessments these students are being asked to complete have little to no credibility in the areas of thinking. True and False? Questions that rely on simple recall/literal answers? If we desire students to be able to think, teachers, rethink assessments and their purposes and their formats. Have the courage to rewrite lessons and activities so that assessments are relevant. Getting the time to do this thinking and these tasks requires cooperation from your administration, but the best teachers find that time.

Many of these tips deal with some form for self-examination. If you have stayed with this book thus far, try this activity. In both my AP and college prep classes, I assigned the following excerpt from Henry David Thoreau's journal,

Walden, to help students assess their present abilities and skills, all with the codicil that those skills and abilities can alter throughout the next ten years, and some hidden talents will suddenly appear through a myriad of circumstances. I asked students if they could surmise or predict any latent abilities that could surface in the future. High school students lack confidence, part of the maturation process, so I discovered that this exercise boosted some of the low confidence levels in the class. I found this excerpt uplifting and optimistic and excellent discussion material. The student writing produced profound and genuine ideas and feelings. As you read it, see if you can detect the message Thoreau is providing through his metaphor:

> *Every one has heard the story which has gone the rounds of New England, of a strong and beautiful bug which came out of the dry leaf of an old table of apple-tree wood, which had stood in a farmer's kitchen for sixty years, first in Connecticut, and afterward in Massachusetts—from an egg deposited in the living tree many years earlier still, as appeared by counting the annual layers beyond it; which was heard gnawing out for several weeks, hatched perchance by the heat of an urn. Who does not feel his faith in a resurrection and immortality strengthened by hearing of this? Who knows what beautiful and winged life, whose egg has been buried for ages under many concentric layers of woodenness in the dead dry life of society, deposited at first in the alburnum of the green and living tree, which has been gradually converted into the semblance of its well-seasoned tomb—heard perchance gnawing out now for years by the astonished family of man, as they sat round the festive board—may unexpectedly come forth from amidst society's most trivial and handselled furniture, to enjoy its perfect summer life at last!*

At this point, I take out my education coin and flip it to the reverse side from the writing and find writing's blood brother, reading. Plenty of research exists connecting students' ability to read with their ability to write. Methodology for each skill, however, does not retain too many similarities. I can attest from teaching English to thousands of high school students that the better the students comprehended what they read, the better writers they became. The better readers thought about what they read, battled with strange vocabulary or nebulous paragraphs, showed the patience to reread, and annotated well. Through this interplay, they were subconsciously studying models for good writing. In any event, I present here information and teaching suggestions about reading, another form of *doing* for teachers.

For my personal introduction to reading, meet Miss Ryan, my fifth grade teacher at St. Philomena Grade School in Chicago in 1961. Miss Ryan was a combination of Dracula, Brian Urlacher, and Frank McCourt. There was the teacher in her of Irish descent, there was the blood-sucking workaholic who would seek every breath of her relentless demands out of her students, and there was the physical dominator who could have competed for an inside linebacker position on any National Football League team. Needless to say we were all timid around Miss Ryan and God help us if we neglected our reading homework. This last item befell me in the late fall.

Reading was as important to this teacher as the very breath she took. Thus, she told her students that she expected plenty of outside reading, akin to at least eight extra books in one semester. On the last day of the month, she would orally collate the books read by each student, her version of a showcase. This exhibition more resembled *The Green Mile*. Miss Ryan strolled down each row and asked each student to tell her the number of books he or she had read, along with titles. There were no tests, no papers, just old-fashioned reading for which each student was on his/her honor. Yes, we read for fun. We picked any book of choice, but Miss Ryan never allowed that choice as an excuse for not completing our regular assignments. This was Miss Ryan's version of a reading program, and it worked. However, on a final day in a month I cannot remember, not that I want to, Miss Ryan called on me and asked me how many books I had read.

I responded, "3."

Ever hear or experience the calm before the storm? Two seats ahead of me, Brian Moriarity turned around, gazing at me as if giving me last rites. Every girl in class who secretly wanted to date me glumly looked down, knowing their chances would have passed them by, my immediate death being in just a few minutes. My breathing began to halt. Paralysis was setting in.

Miss Ryan stood up, took a deep breath while the rest of the students sat lifeless, and peered at me. Utter silence blanketed the room. I stopped gazing at Mary Ann Gilbert's pigtails, and froze.

"MR. ANSTETT, did I hear correctly?? 3 books??"

"Yes, Miss Ryan."

"You are trying to tell me that you only read three books this past month? Why the audacity, the complete effrontery to be that irresponsible! What do you have to say?"

Since I did not know what audacity or effrontery meant, and really had no idea that vocabulary in context actually existed, I simply sighed and replied, "Only 3, Miss Ryan." After all, what did words mean at this point? I had seen my teacher stuff two small lads into one locker a couple months ago for disrespect to a girl.

I had no idea I had the innate ability to read more than two library books in thirty days, but Miss Ryan's expectation showed the way. That standard is what she demanded; that amount is what she got. Sure, I whined and complained; what else do people do when they are besieged by problems? However, I received discipline and conscience in return. After school I walked straight to the library. I did not leave empty-handed, empty-headed perhaps, but not empty–handed. Francis Marion and Robert Louis Stevenson escorted me home.

How or when do students actually realize the lessons in grit and responsibility that teachers bestow?

Miss Ryan had a reading program; it was called *Read A Lot*. Today there are various forms of reading assistance and instruction, whose criteria are concise and detailed. Lincoln-Way District 210 instituted a reading course for freshmen in the fall of 2005. The superintendent directed his curriculum people to develop this program, underscored by the term *SubSearch*. Each letter described a particular skill for reading comprehension:

S = SKIM, SCAN, SURVEY
(preview the text, set purpose, general sense of text)

U = UNDERLINE
(important ideas connected to purpose, main idea, and a brief margin note)

B = BRACKET
(whole chunks of important text)

*The **SUB** phase of SubSearch is the quick first draft reading focusing on the big picture or main idea of the text.*

S = SYMBOLS
(stars for important quotes, question marks for understanding are examples of symbols)

E = ENUMERATION
(Lists of facts, details, names and dates are clues an author gives readers— must be relevant to the text)

A = ABBREVIATION
(whenever possible—students do this well being masters at text messaging)

R = REACT

C = CONNECT
(This phase is essential. Students write personal notes and/or emotional reactions. Here I would go a step further: each connection must be linked to the specific text that inspired the connection. Thus, close reading remains a constant emphasis.)

Please note:
The CCSS are most relevant when reactions and connections deal with evidence or elaboration that reinforces and supports an author's purpose or theme. Personal reaction is not the focus.
By reacting and connecting to author's purpose, intellectual inquiry and subsequent commentary are the goals.

H = HIGHLIGHT
(This can be teacher-directed for essential passages in a text, so that students can write paraphrases or summaries that serve as evidence for accurate comprehension and interpretation of a reading.)

You might be thinking…all that for students for each book or passage they are assigned? Yes, these steps are demanding tasks to complete efficiently. Students were hounded about annotation of texts, especially in English classes. Notetaking became a science for students who could not write annotations in state-owned texts. As students became more proficient at subsearching, I would ease the load a bit and focus on a few of those requirements. I would always assign the react and connect pieces. The last thing teachers want is for this method to turn off students to reading.

There were plenty of advantages. One plus side is that students had to reread texts. That one demand alone meant higher understanding of texts; this rereading led to deeper discussions under the guidance of skilled teachers. It also wore on teachers since grading novel after novel becomes quite tedious and highly subjective. I probably had more arguments over grades I handed out for booknoting than for written work. Students invariably compare. One plus side for me was that I found some original, intellectual points for class discussions from student comments. Booknoting also was another way for the silent, non-participatory students to engage in a book.

As the program took shape, one of the main ingredients for its subsequent success was the adoption of its application to all courses, not only for the actual reading course or for English. All faculty were enlisted to use that methodology for their respective curriculum and texts. That cooperation made the system work; everyone stood shoulder-to-shoulder to help students improve reading skills. Initially, the freshmen who were enrolled in English 1 Honors due to high placement scores were not required to take that course; that changed in 2011 when the superintendent decided to have all freshmen take the course, Honors or not. The program is still improving student abilities today at Lincoln-Way's three high schools.

No matter what type of strategy of motivation districts might implement regarding improved reading skills for students, Miss Ryan still had one indelible key, reading choice.

Still another key…**rereading**. After I retired in 2014, one of my principal goals was to avoid dreaded Brain-Dead Syndrome for as long as possible. I decided to teach two classes of Rhetoric at Joliet Junior College, begin a small tutoring service, and see if I could assist teacher development. I joined the Joliet Professional Development Alliance as a consultant. Through a series of trainings, I have presented workshops such as "The Shifts in the Common Core,"

"Content Literacy," "Close Reading," "Writing to Sources," "Socratic Seminar," and "Academic Vocabulary." I rediscovered the familiar feeling teachers have from time to time, especially the veterans of, *If I only knew then what I know now.* This new knowledge I have learned applies most directly to reading instruction. One particular moment carries special relevance. In the midst of preparing a four-hour workshop for grades 5-8 teachers at Newark District 66 in Illinois in 2015, I read Doug Buehl's book *Developing Readers in Academic Disciplines* (2011). Within that text, Buehl describes methods for instruction to enhance student engagement and comprehension in their reading of subjects across the entire curriculum. Included within these methods are links to the Common Core Standards. These discoveries returned me to my own classroom instruction as I pondered the higher degree of excellence in reading my students might have achieved had I used just a few of Buehl's strategies. The following list contains some samples, but these items do not reflect the entire scope in this book. For the rationale and specifics, you will just have to read his book…and I encourage you to do just that, no matter what subject you teach.

For Frontloading:

- Quick-writes
- Meaningful Associations
- Knowledge Ladders
- Confirm-to-Extend Grid (I like this one!)
- Prediction Guides
- Thumbs Up–Thumbs Down
- Vocabulary-infused Predictions

Reading as Inquiry:

- Essential Questions
- Self-questioning (for each discipline)
- Questioning the Author
- Think-alouds

If you are motivated or mandated to improve your students' reading abilities, especially in terms of your respective discipline, I recommend this book as a gift for your next birthday. It would not be placed in the leisure category, but for professionals' instructional development, this book belongs in the forefront. For an even further understanding of disciplinary literacy, read articles on that topic by Timothy and Cynthia Shanahan from the University of Illinois-Chicago. Remember Frank McCourt's words, *If you're teaching and not really learning, you're not really teaching.*

FACILITATE

There was once a man traveling by train. He took that train with such regularity that the ticket taker knew him well. During one trip the ticket taker came to the man and asked for his ticket. The man reached into one pocket, then the other. He paused. The search became more frantic. First an inside pocket, then his satchel, once more to the outside pockets. He even looked into the inside brim of his velvet fedora. Nothing. He looked at the ticket taker.

"Don't worry. It must be there somewhere. I know you all too well; you have always bought and had a ticket. Take your time," soothed the ticket taker.

The traveler continued to search as the ticket taker resumed his examination of other passengers. After a short while, the ticket taker returned to the traveler who by this time was flustered, having searched every part of his clothing and possessions he could.

The ticket taker said, "If you haven't found it, it is ok. Next time, be sure you have one."

The traveler responded, "You might not need to see it, but I do. I don't know where I am going."

Most students, unlike this traveler, have some idea where they are going, as nebulous as that vision can be for a teenager. The classroom teachers, like engineers, drive the students to completion of their respective diploma-destinations, but what makes those journeys complete, fulfilling, and engaging? How can teachers help students know who they are and where they might be headed? What tools does a teacher try to provide for their students? These questions can be answered with *student* control.

A fine example of student control is Student Council. Notice the term is *student* council, as opposed to teacher council, teacher council being the gripe session for teachers to an administration. I was privileged to witness many student councils in action, mainly at Lincoln-Way East, moderated by two talented teachers, both named Laura. They supplied the background guidance; the students thought their officers and electorate ran an efficient council. The officers directed the action and the activities, and supplied the ideas. One of the more excellent examples of what they did was a framing dinner when the members nominated their most influential teacher, wrote a speech about that nominee, and gave the speech at the dinner. Frames supplied the invite to the respective teachers and those frames were eventually filled with picture of the teacher and his/her nominator. I was present at three of those dinners and they were wonderful events with students running the entire show. Refreshing it is to watch students follow through with their ideas. Why is not the same model used to some degree in the classroom?

The concept of student control scares many teachers, so some parameters are in order. First, teachers do not lose control. They *share* it so that students can engage in the lessons. There is an interaction that unfolds within student control. That interaction combines the factors of the Common Core State Standards, student responsibility and accountability, teachers' individual interaction with students, and project-based learning. Allow me to explain the combustion of all these factors in my experience with my English 3 classes a few years ago. Perhaps teachers can use this as motivation to see how the Common Core can light latent fires for improved teaching. Note how each of the aforementioned factors appear in the following episode.

Throughout the initial ten-year span of my experience at Lincoln-Way District 210, English 3 teachers at Lincoln-Way assigned a literary analysis for the junior research paper in the late winter to early spring. Most of the teachers used a novel from the curriculum (*The Great Gatsby* or *The Grapes of Wrath*) as the basis for that research. Students might be assigned a theme from one of those novels to research, formulate a thesis, and garner secondary sources for support. In some cases, teachers would compose a short list of fiction for students' independent reading as the basis for that paper. I had chosen the latter, but also included poets and short story writers. It was unbearable for me to sit and evaluate with the objectivity needed, 125 to 150 research papers about one certain novel. Talk about brain-dead. That process made me reconsider the actual novel, much less stay awake throughout all those essays. At times I scolded myself for even becoming an English teacher! Student choice was basically limited; dull writing was the result for the majority of the papers. There had to be a better method.

In the fall of 2009 I attended a conference at Chicago-Loyola University titled, *News Literacy and Digital Initiative*, a title that intimidated this computer-illiterate. The purpose was a dialogue between high school teachers and university professors about the readiness of high school students to implement a plethora of research beyond the print sources. The mode of writing would be argument instead of literary analysis. Argument was (and is today) the desire of colleges for their future students. Moreover, students' ability to blend various media, political cartoons, charts, graphs, videos, etc., formulates what colleges see as a basic skill for incoming freshmen to possess. I walked away from this event inspired to revise my upcoming junior research paper. Not only does argument require a variety of evidence, but it also demands student engagement in the research and the skill of synthesis to write a thorough argument.. Furthermore, students would be delving into the world of nonfiction, a world that the Common Core would soon be advocating. Off I went.

After a phone call to my district's superintendent for curriculum and instruction for permission to pilot such an adventurous alteration to the curriculum, permission I received after my enthusiastic recommendation and rationale, I first reviewed my reading list, adding nonfiction previously read and subtracting most of the fiction. I had plenty to prepare: reading the more enticing unfamiliar nonfiction on the list, revising my lesson plans to include a new unit plan, learning the structure of argumentative writing, recognizing credible websites (see The Ohio State University's webpage for this–http:// liblearn.osu.edu/tutor/les/1), and instructing models for the types of evidence students could employ. The amount of work was low compared to my excitement. After all, we were the guinea pigs; moreover, I had to sell this to my students. After that sales-pitch was accepted, I made students keep a journal each week, recording the highs and lows of their work. This was a formative assessment, a term from a foreign land at that time. I applied periodic checks for understanding throughout lessons that were accomplished through peer conversations or written reviews. Each student prepared his/her own reading schedule with everyone having the same due date. Students collaborated to have verbal discussions about the process and about their findings regarding their research. These discussions also whetted the appetites of their peers who, after listening to the contents of a certain book, would vow to add that to their own list for future reading. My lessons contained tight verticality; the next day's information and activities depended on the preceding days. The learning was palpable.

The results were gratifying. For one, the papers were far more authentic than literary analyses. Teaching the students methods for argument and persuading them on the merits of learning such methods for future projects, seeing students enjoying their reading choice, evaluating the types of research students discovered to support their claims were just a few of the thrills I experienced. Second, the excitement from the labor by the students was a sign that argument synthesizing various types of media for nonfiction holds high credibility for both student engagement and student readiness for the next tier of education. Little did I know how much I was preparing myself for the advancement and subsequent alignment of the Common Core; little did I know the level of enthusiasm and interaction my students would reveal; little did I know the amount of individual accountability I would have to organize so that students would appreciate their toil in this endeavor and feel they were evaluated fairly. When students were asked to ponder the elements of authentic writing (stance/tone, media design, genre, audience, and purpose), then synthesize those elements, their confidence levels rose. I kept telling them they were doing what AP students have to do, and although that scared a few, most felt the challenge well worth the effort. I did relay sufficient feedback to my assistant superintendent, and eventually presented the entire rationale to my department's junior English teachers for next year. Read some feedback from a few English 3 students upon the project's completion, and before they knew their grades:

Drew read *The Things They Carried*, "The whole argument process was a good learning experience. Writing the essay seemed easy because we really went over what the structure should look like in class. The next time I have to write an argument with research I will know what to do better."

Sara read *1,000 Splendid Suns* and wrote, "I feel comfortable with how I expressed my feelings toward my topic, the subject of oppression. I hope my paper inspires readers to help make a difference. This paper helped me grow my knowledge about writing."

After reading John McCain's autobiography, Cameron responded, "The one thing I could change about the paper is inserting a personal experience as a source of elaboration to show a connection between my life and McCain's. Overall, though, I understand argument better and I enjoyed this paper."

Emily (*The Immortal Life of Henrietta Lacks*) wrote, "I had the determination like none other doing this assignment. I have become a better writer and a better student from doing this."

Four comments a majority do not supply; however, this research project dovetailed into all the necessary aspects for student ownership in the classroom. With the right amount of teacher risk, preparation, and ingenuity, students' confidence will grow, as will their grades. That growth is the dominant feeling running through many seniors upon graduation. The more *we are willing to assess kids in contexts where they're really solving problems and we're looking not so much at the answer but the process by which they solve those problems* (quoted from *Change Agent*, Will Richardson), the better teachers will embrace standards by means of their own creativity, and the more students will embrace control of their learning.

Unlike that train traveler, students will acquire a more lucid picture of where they are going with appropriate teacher facilitation and through the discovery of their own talent-another form of doing in the empowered classroom.

MOTIVATE

MAXIM:
CORRECT IT OR ACCEPT IT.

This statement came from a basketball speaker at the University of Illinois-Chicago basketball clinic and that sentence stopped my active pencil for a moment of clarity when I knew I had something that made the trip worthwhile. I have since applied this precept as a parent and as a teacher-coach. There was a time when I thought that ignoring an ill-chosen behavior would dissolve that person's willingness to show it. How naïve I was. Ignoring only prompted more of it. Then at another teacher institute, I heard three questions that helped diffuse poor behavior. These questions both informed the target that I was noticing and also put the pressure on that target to own the problem. The irony within this scenario and questioning is that the student being cross-examined will be completely honest.

What are you doing?

Student replies, "I am talking to my neighbor out of turn."

What are you supposed to be doing?

Student replies, "I should be taking notes and listening."

What are you going to do now?

"I will take some notes and be quiet."

Thank you.

These questions often solved the issue-each one asked in a calm voice.

MAXIM:
USE NON-VERBAL TO CORRECT BEHAVIOR;
USE VOICE TO PROJECT ENTHUSIASM.

This concept comes from the head boys' basketball coach at Lincoln-Way East, teacher of excellence and good friend. His patience is a marvel; he is expert at delaying judgment with his infamous pregnant pauses that enlist everyone's attention in class, putting students on edge as they waited for this teacher's next move. The non-verbal stare, the walk to proximity, and/or the facial expression revived a recalcitrant learner's focus. These techniques also provided humor. The vocal comments stirred the ambition of those reluctant people. These comments are neither criticism nor extreme praise; they retain a bit of neutrality, yet massage delicate egos. He states each comment with the right amount of volume and inflection. Questions or statements with follow-up questions that push the student's thinking surface. Some examples:

"I see you are putting your trust in Mr. Steinbeck, Mark."

"Why not give (that) a try and see how it works out?"

"Good idea...where else in the text can we support Martha's comment?"

"Where have you been hiding, Joe? That idea has some promise!"

I wish I had known and applied this concept as a beginning parent.

MAXIM:
MOTIVATE VIA PROXIMITY.

I cannot remember where I read this, but I liked it as soon as I saw it. Typical motivation is attempted in face-to-face conferences, the teacher in one corner vs. the student in the other. In his plays, Shakespeare employed the stage convention of the *aside*. In this technique, an actor recites some inner thoughts within other characters' earshot, but with only the audience actually hearing the words; the proximate actors play a deaf ear to those inner thoughts. Think of this type of motivation the same way. Two parents praise their child's recent work aloud to each other, but feign ignorance that the child is within earshot of that praise. The key here is that the parents *know* that their child *can hear* their praise. This action can work wonders, maybe leading to miraculous changes. Teachers can use this method as they might praise aloud an unnamed student in front of the entire class, or talk to two teachers about his/her student when that student is conveniently nearby. Think about trying this tactic and observe the results.

It might take decades to realize new techniques, but only seconds to be inspired by one. Be open to improvement and suggestions.

LEAD

Francis Cardinal George, the late Archbishop of Chicago, once stated, "The only thing we take away in death is what we have given away in life."

A leader's words. What do we "give away" as teachers or as leaders, as coaches or as parents, as administrators or as CEOs? Let's take a look at four concepts of sound leadership, concepts that exemplify the personal and necessary giving away to children of all ages. Teacher-Leaders will inspire their students and colleagues to:

1. Have something to do,
2. Have something to hope for,
3. Have something to dream,
4. Have something or someone to love.

You did not know that those guidelines are a part of your curriculum or your organization? Surely they are. Let's see why.

Teacher-Leaders will try to show the path toward achieving those ideals. Giving people under your charge something to do establishes and sustains the relevance and example of hard work. Physical actions relay to observers the care amid the details, the pride workers have in themselves. Something to do keeps people in the present, focuses one's concentration on what is necessary at the moment, and develops skills. As a parallel, teachers need to give their students something to do most every night. Currently, I tutor six students each week for one hour a week in English skills. Two of these students had no reading or homework of any consequence for the first two weeks after the semester began. What? Really? What is happening in that classroom? I find that particular example disturbing. Perhaps it is no wonder that many students today can earn a high school diploma without the necessary acquisition of a work ethic, a work ethic accomplished through a plethora of assignments, projects, and nightly inquiry into problems and readings. Teachers who feel they would be too hard on their students or lack the backbone to establish the rigor appropriate for thinkers help pave a path toward entitlement: "It's the weekend; why should be get any homework?" "That other class never gets homework, why should we?" "I couldn't figure it out so I didn't do it." Excuses are easy; challenges shape the person. The vast majority of students will do what the teacher demands.

Teacher-Leaders will provide their tutelage something to hope for, something to look forward to. People who live by the seat of their pants without goals and ambitions have little focus. Perhaps they find no meaning in their work; teacher-leaders will provide some of that vision. In my AP classes or in my individual dealings with my students, I always asked about their goals for class both a grade and a level of learning, for example, what did they desire to improve about their English skills the most? The ends of quarters or semesters are good times for students to consider their goals and their hopes. The next section in this book considers the importance of evaluating progress. Formative assessments can also provide feedback for the level of student readiness or mastery of a certain skill, another form of evaluation.

Teacher-Leaders give their people something to dream. This can unify an organization, providing its members with a common goal. When I was explaining the format of the AP Language test in the spring to my classes, I would mention that I did not believe in 2's for any scores on the spring AP test.

A score of 3, 4, or 5 was the common goal. My basketball teams would discuss team goals; where did we see ourselves in one, two, three, or four months? Dreaming considers the big picture.

Teacher-Leaders give something or someone to love. The best example I can think of concerning this concept is the teacher. With what passion do we teach on a daily basis? What persona do we project in our body language, our speech, or level of encouragement or interest in our students on a daily basis? Everyone is a hero for the first week of school, but students will detect an uncommitted teacher within a few weeks, even days. They will know each teacher's level of commitment as their year progresses; teachers cannot hide this. We can parlay that passion into conveying to students the hope for each of them that they find something to love for a career, someone to love for a lifetime.

The irony of all the giving within the four concepts is the receiving. Teacher-leaders realize a deep satisfaction, at times unknown in other professions. It is no wonder how often I would meet ex-business people who desired a new career in teaching, feeling that their former line of work had left them unfulfilled.

REFLECT (MEMOIR)

Kayos and *The Chicago Sun-Times*. I herald from a simpler and in some ways a harsher time, the 1950s and 60s. Growing up from infancy to about fourth grade in a second-story flat on Keating Avenue on the northwest side of Chicago, I looked forward to Saturday nights. Dad and I would saunter a few blocks to Cicero Avenue in the early evening to Pop's general store. You could fit about a thirty of that teapot into one Jewel today, not to mention the Home Depots or the Walmarts. Pop was a grizzled denizen who knew everyone by name. He owned a fascinating Coca-Cola machine caressing my treasured Kayos. For those of you running to Google, Kayo is a chocolate-flavored drink, an elixir from the gods, best cold. Yoo-Hoos are Kayo-wannabes, sort of like looking at pictures rather than actually taking them. When I find Kayos today, I stop and buy, no questions asked. Pop's machine had a cover to lift. The bottles would stand at attention in rows, looking up, pleading to be released.

Dad and I walked there most every Saturday night, just talking about nothing in particular, except for maybe the Cubs. We returned with the Sunday *Sun-Times*, Dad holding the newspaper, I holding my treasure. This was my time with my dad. I knew of no other time when we walked. I was frozen in space, an oddity for the future. On many of these walks we smiled and laughed, even after the day I broke a window by plastering a sixteen-inch softball through a third story apartment window. Little did I know then that these walks were blazing some future. Instead of walks to a small general store, my sons and I walked through the woods or forest preserves some fifty years later. I chased them as the monster, or we played hide-and-seek while we marveled at Nature's wisdom and grace: the awkward, yet smooth curve of a shattered tree trunk serving as a rest stop; the playful cha-cha of the leaves in autumn; the towering old oak protecting its little fella next to it trying to be as big as its dad; the duck family sailing its own ocean blue in a rivulet. On those walks we smiled and laughed. I could not offer them Kayos, but afterwards, we sometimes stopped for ice cream at the Frankfort Creamery.

Memory always has a Jeckyl & Hyde persona, but reflection has a personality all its own. My walks with my dad are a bit of both. The memory revives the love for my dad and my youth; the reflection in it carries its own reward. After all, what would life be without memories? The good parts I learned as a youth I carried to my own sons. After all, what how-to manual is given when one becomes a parent? We have to rely on what we have experienced and found relevant and inspiring. So too does reflection, an awareness of the present and an anticipation of the future, play an ever-essential role in fostering our youth's learning.

Reflection was clearly a part of professional golfer Curtis Strange's career, now a current golf analyst and the first professional golfer to earn one million dollars in one tour season. His heyday rose in the 80s when he won the U.S. Open twice in the 80s. Strange once said, "If you don't stop to evaluate, you don't care," a statement I took to heart as a teacher and as a coach, as a father and as a husband. Consistent self-evaluation and reflection is a core piece to any sustained improvement as a teacher, a coach, an employer, or a head of an organization. Let's not neglect constructive criticism from colleagues and superiors. Classroom teachers should collect data from their students once per quarter about their teaching skills, the level of rapport, the amount of learning, etc. No matter the form, teachers always find good ideas from their students. Here are some methods for that data collection:

Index Card

Students fill out one index card and answer two or three questions such as:

1. "What is Mr. Anstett doing well?"

2. "What could he do better?"

3. "What suggestions do you have for increased participation and/or engagement in the class (activities, etc.)?"

Narrative

Write a letter to your teacher describing your learning experience in the semester. Include the best part of class, the worst part, suggestions for the future, and an evaluation of the teacher. Try to separate your feelings from your grade, no matter what it is. You must sign your name.

Checklist

You can find these online or from colleagues. There are columns in survey form where students can be anonymous.

Polleverywhere

This is an online website that polls groups of people. As a teacher, you create and filter the questions. Students use their phones in class to answer the questions; the teacher receives instant feedback. One large advantage to this device is that students remain anonymous, so it is more likely the teacher will receive honest data. I have also used this device to measure students' opinions about some of the novels we read.

I wonder about the frequency reflection is done in the business world? How about parenting? When their kids are old enough to understand, do parents ask them how they are doing as parents? I know from personal experience that I never gave my two sons a survey or a checklist for their evaluation of my parenting skills. I typically learned after making an egregious error in judgment or opening my big mouth far too quickly without deliberation. Parents can usually decipher their effectiveness through the day-to-day dealings with their kids. Many times the evaluation surfaces through conflicts. This topic makes for good dinner conversation.

Reflection requires ACTION. Reflection requires DOING. Reflection requires CARE.

RESPOND

"If we learn from our mistakes, shouldn't I make as many mistakes as possible?"

Brad Faxon, a professional golfer, was always at or near the top in putting accuracy. A reporter once asked Faxon why he was such a great putter. His reply? "I'm not afraid to miss."

Throughout my career, various students asked me why they had to revise their papers so often. I responded that I enjoyed seeing the effort and subsequent improvement that blossomed from initial errors. I further explained that just because writers make mistakes does not mean that those persons are poor writers. Similarly, I encouraged players who made physical mistakes to respond with greater vigor immediately afterwards. Mental mistakes were far worse than physical ones, I would preach, and mistakes just notified players what they needed to improve. In both cases, the feeling of letdown and discouragement emitting from mistakes takes all the attention from the many things a student or a player is doing well. All the focus dwells on the errors, as if those particular shortcomings display all the character flaws of the transgressor. Such faulty thinking.

Thus, in some ways, the American culture has become, *Go ahead. Beat yourself up for your mistakes.* Despite that notion or perhaps because of it, classrooms, businesses, organizations, and families pass or fail on the fundamentals of two concepts. One is the brain food people give themselves when encountering their errors. Most of that diet is negative. The second essential is sound relationships; the ways mistakes are perceived and responded to, no matter who makes the error, is essential to sturdy relationships and trust. So many moments of brilliance or enlightenment are lost in the classroom because teachers fail to capitalize on incorrect responses. Students have to recognize that teachers treasure wrong answers; those answers lead to breakouts from otherwise recalcitrant students, students who fear being wrong, and students who think the right answer is the only path for peer recognition and acceptance. *I have to be right* is a worthy goal and can motivate learners, but teachers can promote healthier relationships, rapport, inquiry, rigor, and intellectual stimulation by soothing the fears of students who give wrong answers. How can teachers do that? Positive body language by the teacher is one way; encouraging verbal responses in a soothing voice is another. Patience by the teacher remains the key. Teachers must stay with those particular students and inquire further, coaxing those students to strive for the more accurate or complete answer. Incorrect answers also invite skillful targeted *rereading* so that the expectation and inclusion of text evidence is the norm for insightful discussion.

Example:

> TEACHER: As we explore the transformation of Hester (*The Scarlet Letter*), what factors are the more critical ones in this change?
>
> STUDENT: Hester just changes because that's the way the author wrote it.
>
> TEACHER: That's a start and the author is certainly in charge of his text. Why would he write it that way, Mike? Would you read from the top of page 165? Let's think about one factor that would motivate Hester to change.
>
> STUDENT: (reads aloud)
>
> TEACHER: Everyone read that again silently and focus on the question. Mike, decide on the factor involved in those paragraphs and be ready to read the part of that text that supports your response. Haley, would you please examine that part of the text for author's purpose? In that way we will detect how one technique supports the other.

The above being just one brief example, there are numerous ways a teacher can stay with errors and push a student to think beyond a superficial response. Students won't like it too much; most would rather have the teacher call on the smart one to clarify an answer. Teachers reveal care and commitment to students when they decide to help students find a way through the maze that confuses them. Notice the above example includes either questions or prompts for further action by the students. After all, didn't the teacher pass this course a long time ago? It is the students' turn to show what they can do, and when they can't, it is up to the teacher to show them the advantages of trial and error. Teachers have to put gentle and consistent pressure on the students in order to see any growth.

No matter what the situation, teachers should consistently explain to students about the opportunity for learning from wrong answers. This explanation opens relationships and supplies distinct windows for *critical thinking* through inquiry, not just dull recall answers requiring little mental acumen from both teachers and students. The planning and in-class skills of the teacher to guide students through difficult texts and to worthy discussions will also promote evaluation and creation of more accurate assessments.

> IF YOU PUT A WALL UP IN FRONT OF YOU,
> YOU CAN ONLY SEE A SHORT DISTANCE
> AND YOU'LL HAVE A VERY SHORT PATH TO WALK.

DIFFERENTIATE

In my first fifteen years of teaching, I dominated, even intimidated the students in classes just by being 6'7." So, getting my students' attention by standing up or by increasing my volume was never too difficult. During those years, my physical stature, not my teaching skills, was even a part of some evaluators' comments for my good classroom discipline. Being the head basketball coach did not hurt either. Being a coach buys some credibility in students' eyes.

Although size can help, just being a rather large person does not guarantee students learn anything. Fortunately, I discovered that teaching meant much more than students being afraid of me. Teaching at Glenbrook North, at York, and finally at Lincoln-Way opened my eyes to a variety of strategies for student learning and engagement which made my size less of a factor and helped me become a far better teacher. Those strategies promoted research and study into differentiation, a prominent factor in today's classrooms.

The area of differentiation, not only meeting the needs of your students through lesson variation and variety of assessment, but also knowing how each student works to his/her best ability, has become a major emphasis for teacher evaluation. The basis for any differentiation strategy is still the rapport and relationships teachers develop with their students. No strategies work as well as they might if students and teacher are not pulling the oars in the same direction. Consequently, the better a class and its teacher can work as a team, the greater chance of amazing amounts of learning and smiles. This oar pulling is reminiscent of the scene in the film *Mr. Holland's Opus* when Holland, played by Richard Dreyfuss, is debating with the gym teacher about a student in Holland's music class. As they play chess one evening, the debate becomes an argument. The gym teacher wants the student, one of his wrestlers, to pass Holland's class. In order to pass, that student has to learn to play an instrument. The small problem for Holland? The young man cannot play anything. The coach coaxes Holland, "Just teach him some instrument," to which Holland responds, "He can't learn the music." The gym teacher retorts, "You mean to tell me you can't teach a willing kid to play something? Then you're a lousy teacher." From that point, after bruised feelings simmer, Holland devises various ways to teach that pupil. He finally succeeds. Such is the challenge and the hope within differentiating instruction. A host of teachers at each school I worked showed me a variety of instructional methodologies that assist this area of emphasis. The following list contains just a few.

- *Think-Pair-Share* is just what it sounds like. Students think about a question, write for some time about it, then find a partner and share findings. This discussion makes it easier for the teacher to call on reluctant students who typically are unprepared to answer an impromptu question. With some previous thinking, students will be more prepared and will build confidence.

- *Hotseat* emphasizes student readiness to respond with the skill of response to quick questions. Select a student to sit in the designated hotseat at the front of the classroom for a certain length of time.

- Journal writing can be employed a number of ways. One prominent target for this method is for students to write daily. 80% of the topics targeted to the curriculum and the day-to-day lessons. This is a formative assessment, but periodically, I assigned students to select their favorite essay from the collection of journals they have compiled. They would edit and revise, and then turn the journal in for a summative.

- Group Schema became a way for teachers to give students more ownership of the curriculum. In the past I lectured about a unit's necessary background and ask students to take notes. In Group Schema students in a group researched one part of a unit's background, an example being "Fads in the Roaring 20s" for *The Great Gatsby*. They reported to the class. A choice of graphic organizers for student note taking was supplied.

- Cycle Instruction for Novels or Thematic Units retains a distinctive flavor for differentiated instruction and, I believe, aligns to PARCC more effectively for junior high staff. For a given unit teachers prepare the novel, film clips, appropriate poetry, a couple of critical essays, a couple of complimentary essays, all with the goal of synthesis within a summative project, paper, or inquiry-based assignment.

- The task of oral readings has gone the way of the Edsel; I can say the same for cursive handwriting. In fifth grade I had to provide an oral reading of the poem *The Highwayman*. I had to read expressively, pronounce every word correctly, and read with sufficient volume. Nerve-wracking, but unforgettable, I discovered more poise. When I heard Dr. Douglas Fisher from San Diego State University speak at an IATE conference years ago, he made one remark that shook my foundations, "Be sure to read every day to your students, no matter what the discipline. It does not have to be long, just read to them." Oral readings and speeches require practice and target students toward the more neglected Common Core State Standard of Language (listening and speaking).

- We have Bloom or Webb; let's use them. Consider the verbs from the taxonomy as the vocabulary for daily learning targets. More on this taxonomy later.

- Consider changing writing prompts according to Bloom's taxonomy so that each student feels challenged, yet confident to master that writing. See Appendix B for an example.

- Two excellent English teachers I worked with at York High School mastered media to excite student learning. One possessed an entire library of CDs at his home and used them in conjunction with opening units and as prompts for lessons. The other master created a film course that seniors enjoyed. In the present culture this type of course is commonplace, but in the 1990s it was bending the rules. Those students studied the nuances of film *after* reading the literature by studying the special effects, camera angles, cinematography, etc., and their effects on audiences. His course was rigorous, yet students flocked to it.

- Another effective use of differentiation is the set-up of *learning partners.* I used this method in various high school classes, even in my previous Rhetoric classes at Joliet Junior College, and I found it very effective. The method encouraged cooperation and participation among students. It decreased pressure on reluctant students who might feel more at ease talking with a peer. I tried to pair up a good student with a struggling one. One might argue that the struggler gained all the advantage. However, the better student learned how to communicate understood material in various ways, and appreciated the role and responsibility of a teacher.

Differentiation supplies subtle, yet powerful, advantages in other areas. One lies in problem solving. Within thematically structured courses (see Appendix A, #1), students strive to tackle issues and concepts that push their efforts to the higher orders of Bloom and critical thinking, instead of muddling their way through a chronology-ordered anthology. Another advantage is the motivation to plan with extra care and commitment, so that both a variety of texts are offered to students and independent readings are encouraged by teachers. Planning for differentiation will light continuous fires in the competitive teacher who strives to make his/her course the best one available. A third positive for differentiation helps veteran teachers avoid the dreaded staleness that can emerge after years of teaching the same course(s). Writing instruction will also blossom.

Recent research also verifies the importance of differentiation:

The document Assessment and Accountability, published by the Illinois State Board of Education in 2015, outlines criteria for sound differentiation. Classroom assessment practices should be appropriately differentiated to meet the specific educational needs of all students.

> *Students with disabilities receive special educational services to meet their learning needs. These students include those who have an Individualized Education Program (IEP) or have a Section 504 Plan. Assessment practices may need to be adjusted or differentiated to allow these students to best demonstrate their learning. Options include accommodations, modifications, and alternate assessments. Accommodations refer to changes in the way a student accesses the assessment. Modifications refer to changes to*

the instrument or evaluation procedure. An alternate assessment is used when students cannot participate in the regular assessment process. Typically, alternate assessments are appropriate for students whose instruction is adapted from grade-level content and reduced in depth, breadth, and complexity.

Differentiating the assessment process should also address those students who are gifted and talented. These students may require assessments that are intended to measure learning outcomes that are different from their grade-level peers in order to sufficiently challenge them and meet their learning needs.

GUIDELINES

1. *Use assessment accommodations, modifications, or alternate assessments that comply with local, state, and federal policies.*

2. *Provide accommodations, modifications, or alternate assessments that are most appropriate for the student with special needs on a regular basis for all types of classroom assessments.*

3. *Provide appropriate accommodations, modifications, and support for English learners (e.g., word banks, access to a dictionary, modeling instructions).*

4. *Use formative, interim, and summative assessment practices that target the appropriate learning expectations for students with special needs.*

5. *Work with support staff to provide appropriate assessments for students who have a need for differentiation of assessments.*

6. *Modify grading procedures as needed for students with special needs so that it accurately reflects these students' individual education plans.*

7. *Involve each student and their parents/guardians, whenever possible, in decisions about what accommodations/modifications work best for the student.*

For appropriate differentiation a final note might be: be the guide on the side, not the sage on the stage. The more students feel empowered, the less blaming and finger-pointing will occur when conflicts emerge. Applying differentiation at appropriate points promotes trust between teacher and students. With increased attention to differentiation, teachers will enlarge their ability for teaching.

EMBRACE

Did you realize you work with some certifiable *saints* in your building? Some of their names are St. Secretary, St. Custodian, St. Buildings and Grounds, St. Transportation, and St. Cafeteria Worker. As you put the pertinent faces with those names, consider the ways those people make your mission of teaching easier.

I cannot overvalue what a positive environment does to promote students' learning and teachers' eagerness to teach. The cleanliness after a pep rally, the preparation of school after a snowstorm or for cookies for an evening event do not just appear. People who work under the radar and behind the scenes are the unsung heroes in any school district. I had the privilege of knowing many of these heroes at each school. Some repaired what was broken; others kept the place spotless; still others worked in the Griffins' cafeteria at East-where else could I be addressed as *Cupcake* or *Sweetheart*? These workers, like so many others, went out of their way to make things better, and did so cheerfully without much recognition. Sure, they are paid employees, but it was the positive attitude of all these people that helped make teaching less stressful and more enjoyable. Moreover, one of the best parts about establishing a good relationship with these co-workers is that, as a coach, when our teams won, they felt great. They were often the first to say, "Congratulations, Coach!" Cafeteria ladies wore basketball t-shirts or football jerseys on game days. Even further, many became great listeners. One particular individual at Immaculate Conception High School knew basketball very well and never missed a home game. He sometimes gave me insights about my players that had not occurred to me because he would notice the players in everyday interactions in the hallways, an advantage of teaching in a smaller school. First, however, you have to trust them and they have to trust you. That trust emerges from treating them politely and gratefully. These people are as much a part of the culture as the principal and the students.

An experience at York High School provided insight into the feelings of custodians. One year I had cafeteria supervision for my supervisory assignment. York students had little respect for cleanliness after eating in the cafeteria. I might have well as taken the garbage can and dumped it onto the floor after every period. Come to think of it, there was more litter on the floor than in the garbage cans! Custodians were beyond frustration. What kind of self-respect did students have? Cleaning that cafeteria was a full-time job. Reminders to clean up to students from supervisors like myself or administrators on daily announcements fell on deaf ears. The desperation everyone felt reached the boiling point, so administration and I researched other schools, even visited a few, about some of their methods to activate student awareness about their environment. We began a *First Class* program. Through visits to study halls and support of student leaders, the positive propaganda about school cleanliness and courtesy became a daily reminder to the entire school. Conditions improved and the happiest people were the custodians and maintenance crews who felt some respect and appreciation.

My point defines the importance of great relationships with these saints. They can help with something important or assist in any crisis when you are facilitating an important event for students and parents. Students observe them as keenly as they might their classroom teachers. These unsung heroes are just as valuable as any teacher. Let them know it. Everyone in a school or an organization has a vital role. The stars are only as good as their teammates. The unsung, unnoticed heroes are the oil that makes any machine run well.

VALUE AND ENRICH

Lou Holtz, former head football coach at the University of Notre Dame, said in a speech to a graduating class at Trine University in 2011, "I have been 21; you have never been 74."

Age does possess its value, as does age difference. Perhaps this factor leads to teacher dropout in the first five years of the profession. I witnessed far too many new teachers focus on being "liked." Granted, that feeling is difficult to overcome and to replace with professionalism. The novice teachers who plan and anticipate their lessons every day are just that…young. As teens, like many adults, they will take the easy way out, if shown that door. Many conferences I had as a department chairman with teachers in their first five years resulted in an over abundance of Kleenex: teachers frustrated at student reluctance, disturbed by the all-too-close familiarity, and upset from students' challenges to their authority. Combine that with inexperienced teachers' lack of knowledge of good lesson planning, sound use of verbal inquiry, and the pressure to succeed and we can find teaching on a superficial level. Age difference can also challenge the morale within a department. Combine crusty veterans who believe they know everything with younger teachers who, while talented, do not emit a coachable persona, and you have the basis for some public wars. In this latter situation I found myself very compromising and vulnerable as a department chairman for a few years. The tension that surfaced from the squabbling stifled creativity and productivity for all involved.

Thus, finding answers to the question of how young teachers survive the first few years and develop the comfort zone necessary to be a good teacher is a constant challenge. For that matter, what can be done to value the veterans so that their work becomes *more* effective as time progresses, not less? Here are suggestions:

> **Mentor** programs should cover the first three years for a beginning teacher. Mentor programs can be powerful and their influence permanent.

> **CASE STUDY #1**: The year is 1967. High school Tom awakes at 5:30 feeling ill and complains to his dad who is about ready to leave for work. Dad looks at son and says, "Go to school." Not much to say after that. Funny how those words cured illnesses.

> That mentor program, courtesy of my father, has covered my entire high school life, my college years, and my teaching career. I rarely missed school.

> **CASE STUDY #2**: When I enrolled for classes for the second semester of my senior year at Boston College, the word around campus for a second-semester senior was to take the philosophy course *Slavery and Freedom*, the cake course, taught by a 90-year old Jesuit. I took that advice. On the first day of class, Fr. Jesuit announced that if anyone was not interested in

staying for class, all they had to do was sign in and then could leave. Attendance done! Truth be told, I only missed two of those classes. I guessed I believed in the slavery more than the freedom! Mentor program #1 still reigned.

CASE STUDY #3: After one month as a student-teacher at Newton South High School in Massachusetts in the spring of 1973, I was conferencing with my cooperating teacher. He complimented me about my lesson preparation and about a couple of other things he felt I was doing well. As we continued our discussion, he mentioned that he also noticed the degree with which I seemed to enjoy/love literature. I accepted his compliments silently, thinking, "Boy, am I licking this gig!" His next breath inquired, "Now, do you love kids more than the literature?? If so, you will enjoy a long and fulfilling career." The question brought me back to planet Earth, a question I remembered. We ventured into ways we show we love kids. In the end, that one simple question permeates why one teaches. Good mentors promote the investigation and evaluation of answers to that question.

CASE STUDY #4: Meet Tim and Sandi, Lincoln-Way Central English teachers. Mentors help new teachers or teachers new to a district in two principal ways: learning the curriculum and relaxing enough to enjoy the job. Each district has its respective nuances, its respective culture; Sandi taught me the particular nuances of the L-W English curriculum during my first year at Lincoln-Way in 1999-2000. Her patience and expertise guided me through formal evaluations, always a nerve-jangling experience, no matter the amount of years a teacher possesses, and the long-range goals of the junior and freshmen curricula.

Tim provided the comic relief. Every day that year I had lunch with Tim. That event was a gift and a momentum shift. We laughed and enjoyed those minutes to the point where I sometimes forgot to eat. Tim, an exceptional English teacher still grinding away in the classroom, always insists that his students do more than just the minimum, especially in terms of reading and writing. Thus, I appreciated his continuous example of combining a sense of humor within the serious task of teaching. That year I had to travel to the East campus to complete my day with a section of English 1. The four-mile drive to East often saw other drivers gazing into my car at a stoplight, wondering why the driver was laughing uproariously with no one else present in the vehicle.

Both Sandi and Tim bestowed influence. Later in my time at Lincoln-Way, I worked closely with Sandi as English department chairpersons.

The four case studies are of a personal nature, of course. Yet I hope each provides a glimpse for the ripples of value and enrichment that quality mentors can bestow upon their protégés. That being said, one year of close confidences with a mentor is not sufficient. The first year of teaching is loaded with the powder keg of doubt and self-determined failure. Only one year of poor mentorship can light a fuse toward premature dropouts. Three years of mentoring would save many talented but raw teachers to stay in the profession and thrive. Instead of a Race to the Top, the federal government should throw its funds to that cause, a cause that helps teachers learn how to teach, instead of motivating schools to scrutinize the newspapers once a year for the almighty test score and polling numbers of the best schools.

As already mentioned, there can be such a thing as a poor mentor. Therefore, why not have a simple evaluation of mentors conducted by an administrator, the mentor, and the protégé? This method might consist of a narrative reflection supported by a concise rating and a conference with all three participants. This evaluation would be held one time in the spring in all three years. If mentors are going to be reimbursed, they have to be provided some feedback and provide some feedback themselves. Only fair.

Research abounds for data that determines the teacher fallout rate during their first five years. The expectation does not meet the reality; the workload for a typical teacher cast a far greater shadow and burden than expected; those three months off mean more classes to earn more money. A quality mentor during the first three years can mean survival for new teachers, who are just beginning to find their pulses as instructors in years four and five, and beyond. Who knows how many fine teachers were lost after being cast into the teaching world alone after one year? If our government would show consideration and respect that educators deserve, there would be funding available to all districts for just such a program. Considering some of the outlandish perks many government elected officials have, there is money available. When education becomes a top campaign issue, maybe the tide will turn.

> **Support** from administration for use of teacher time is necessary in two ways: *peer observations* and time for *curriculum discussions.*

Peer observations surfaced through a new evaluation system implemented by Lincoln-Way's district. As the idea of peer observations came about, reluctance was the first reaction. Yet, as a department chairman, I supported the idea based on our department's philosophy of sharing materials; we were always eager to learn and that learning was best exemplified through people's willingness to share materials. If we could share materials, why not share our expertise? The value for the younger staff was a prime consideration, so I took the initiative and paired up our teachers. A more experienced teacher partnered with a less experienced one. This technique was similar to my philosophy of practicing free throws in basketball: a player should never shoot free throws with a poor foul shooter. Peer pressure can instruct and increase concentration. You might think, "What can a newer teacher offer as a tip or as advice to a veteran? Would not a new teacher be intimidated by this experience?" You would be surprised! I received plenty of positive feedback about the observations; the main issue was people finding the time to carry out at least one observation in each semester. Once teachers each observed their partner, they would meet to discuss; I even tried to use some department meeting time for such a conference so I could save the teachers their own valuable time.

I guess a department chair could try to sell this venture to the staff and do it without any blessing from the administration; however, I had to think of gripes from the union who might bark about such an action, saying that this form of observation, *non*-evaluative in nature, constituted a change in working conditions. Many times helpful actions are met with roadblocks.

Regarding curriculum discussions or level meetings, I experienced high degrees of frustration from staff about the lack of time for assessment reform or curriculum changes. When districts hand down mandates that they receive from the state or from their own inspirations, teachers need the time to meet to discuss implementation. I know of many districts that allow meeting time for staff at least twice a month for curriculum matters. Those students will have shorter class periods on those days. Is not the curriculum worth the discussion? With the Common Core push and directives for various types of assessments, districts must provide changes to student schedules that will assist teachers with developing the steps necessary to incorporate mandatory changes. Simply asking teachers to meet on their own time is a sure-fire way for frustration, for half-ass implementation, and for poor morale among staff.

During my time as chairman at Lincoln-Way East, final exams drove me to the point of lunacy. As any good teacher knows, curriculum is always in need of evaluation. Final exams were usually in need of changes and since each level at L-W gave the same exam for evaluation of English skills with reading passages, unity was the bottom line. As any good teacher knows, creating a quality assessment takes time, trial and error, and practice. Teachers need to agree on the product and, more importantly, to provide a similar experience to students. Exams were just one area where time was not provided in the abundance required; nevertheless, we got the job done because my staff knew its importance and sacrificed their own prep time to complete the tasks. Not every district has the same student-first attitude on the part of its teachers. Providing the time within the school calendar is a major responsibility of any district administration. Then, it is up to the department chairs to make sure that that time is fruitful.

Peer evaluations and curriculum discussions are two ways for school faculty to both value and enrich. The real benefactors will be the students,, but teachers won't be far behind.

Laugh

There is little success where there is little laughter.
~Andrew Carnegie

"Apples are fine, but I find today's teacher prefers a nice latte."

I grew up watching cartoons of *Mighty Mouse* at 9:30 every Saturday morning, followed by *Rocky and Bullwinkle*. One of the excerpts on Rocky's show was the cartoon *Fractured Fairy Tales*, satiric spoofs on the beloved stories. I would still watch them today if they were on television. They supplied some community in our home; at times we would all watch them, laughing together. Laughter can supply a sealant for teachers, parents, CEOs. I would propose, rather unoriginally, that the humor ingredient has improved or even saved marriages, organizations, relationships, classrooms, teacher longevity, and a host of other situations. We have all heard, *It takes 17 muscles to smile and 42 muscles to frown.* So as you read this, apply your endorphins, those happy glands, those fire extinguishers for those moments of self-pity, blame, and whining.

In February of 2015, I presented a fifty-minute workshop about the use of humor in the classroom at Wheaton North High School. I outlined some of the ways I try to inject humor into lessons in the most innocuous ways. First though, I asked the participants to make and rank a top-ten list of qualities that make up a good class. Traits such as organization, preparation, engagement, knowledge, personality, and humor were stated, but when we discussed rank, humor was down the list, not in the top five. Then, I asked them to become the students and create the same list. This time sense of humor was in the top three, a very insightful discrepancy. Students need the spice of laughter occasionally to feel a sense of purpose, a sense that school can be enjoyable and that teachers are actual human beings. Faculty, on the other hand, perhaps due to being the more mature ones, felt that while humor is good, their mission of educating kids required a more serious tone. For years, I struggled with humor as a closet form of delivery. I went there if needed, but never stayed in it. If humor happened, great, but then, on with the lesson! It took me many years to see simple ways humor or lighter moments can occur, and can even be planned in a lesson. Here are some ways I suggest, without any ranking. You rank your own.

- Spontaneity
- Personal stories
- Self-deprecation
- Silly answers on tests
- Study of satire: political cartoons, essays, clips
- Students' stories
- Role playing
- Role plays of voices when reading to students
- Dress-ups, props, music
- Love what you do.

Here is a personal story told with sufficient embellishment to certain classes when we were discussing career paths. I realized the value of what I had chosen for a career after I drove a Yellow cab in Chicago in the summer of 1974, thinking it would be an enjoyable job for a few months. Boy, was I wrong. In addition to being robbed of $47, being propositioned twice, fighting all kinds of traffic, feeling occasional wrath from riders, and being the target of various abuse by my boss, I was ignorant about the stress that constant driving can bring. This feeling became more coherent when I did not know where I was going on the vast majority of rides. Having grown up in Chicago, I felt I had a solid knowledge of streets. I considered myself a good driver. I did not need a Bachelor of Arts in English to be hired, just a driver's license, some brains, and a pulse. As I ventured into the streets every day, every day brought a new insight and adventure. Many times I would divert a passenger's doubt about my skills with the question, "What way would you like me to go?" The passenger had one of four distinct reactions: laugh at me and leave the cab; tell me I was an ignorant rookie, then give me directions; curse aloud about the bad day he was having; or sympathize with me, then get out of the cab.

The best trip was an O'Hare airport run since I was responsible for bringing in a minimum of $45 a day in fares. $45 does not sound too challenging, but it was. The O'Hare trip was at least half of that, but that fare did not surface too often. Most of my trips were short ones: bring a Gold Coast shopper to Marshall Field's at State and Washington, bring a shopper from the Loop to her Lake Point Tower apartment. Sometimes, a trip with a total fare of three or four dollars would take thirty minutes due to the traffic. Combine that congestion with the fact that once a driver starts his cab, he turns into a maniac, a skill I still possess today when I drive into Chicago. This skill amazes my wife and sons. Speed limit is 30? To a cabbie, that means there is a 20 mph window. Even drove down a one-way street to save time…you guessed it, the wrong way!

Thus when the shoe fit, I used metaphors from my cab experiences to a lesson in class. No matter whom a teacher might teach, no matter the ages, students enjoy personal stories. They are curious about who the teacher is. The use of personal stories rarely failed as an attention-getter for a lesson or as fillers for a few minutes to reenlist attention within a lesson, an example for an impromptu speech, or a method of introduction in the opening days of school.

Some of my coaching experiences also provided inspirational and uplifting sources of humor. I worked all kinds of basketball camps in the summers between 1976 and 1997. Although they took some years off my life, I will always cherish those experiences. Not only did they teach me so many little things about the game and about meshing personalities within a team framework, but also they supplied the utmost in coaching camaraderie. We worked very hard during the day, and played hard after hours once we thought we had the little campers tuckered out. We were incorrect most of the time about that last assumption. Once we returned to camp in the wee hours of the morning, we might find ten campers in one room fooling around or five toilets gasping for air from a deluge of toilet paper. One particular morning, roughly 5:30 a.m., as I stumbled into the dorm for two hours of sleep before camp resumed at 9:00, I was greeted by a fifth grader who had just showered. He was ready to go, gym shoes tied, hair combed, smiling and eager. "Good morning, coach, what a great day for hoops! You ready??" I just smiled, told him how great he was, and had him help me to my room. "You not feeling good, coach??" the camper inquired. I mumbled as I stumbled.

Keep in mind that these tasks became far more arduous as the week progressed. The coaches were on an endurance test pitting their commitment between work hours and play hours. We passed our own assessments but in wretched physical condition. Saturdays were blessed events.

I found that the basketball camps were just microcosms of the classroom. We asked players to listen to instruction according to the objective we had in mind, complete drill work from precise modeling, apply the instruction to independent practice, assist students individually if they were having trouble doing the task correctly, then watched the assessment unfold in the form of league games in the afternoon. There was always a time later in the day for tutoring sessions for the kids who asked for some individual help. You want engagement?? Plenty of that. Spontaneity? All the time. Student stories, self-deprecation, and coaching tales abounded. Laughter usually surfaced in one way or another, mainly from impromptu, accidental actions by campers.

Humor, present in the right doses and with the right timing, promotes student ownership, togetherness, and engagement. Those pieces don't hurt teacher eagerness either.

Practice

"What you are speaks so loudly, I cannot hear what you say." Ralph Waldo Emerson's eloquent words allow me to offer some details about the essentials for students to see and imitate both during and after their high school years. Offering students practice in the art of good handshakes, the ability to tie a necktie, the courtesy of eye contact, and accurate, polite word choices lend balance and thoroughness to any curriculum, as well as credibility to the teacher. Some might argue that the teachers' role is strictly curriculum and that it is up to the home to instruct their children about social skills and etiquette. However, what if students have no home? Are teachers supposed to accept lack of courtesy and disrespect? How often should teachers ignore students who are ignorant or awkward in social situations? I choose to model or correct issues that I feel I can. In many instances teachers and coaches are new voices; people give chances to new voices. I guess I chose the route of *do it now—get reprimanded later.*

Associating some of those actions to actual events in school allow teachers to offer advice in matters more compelling to students than a recent grade. For example, I showed students methods for tying a necktie during Homecoming week. A few students already knew this skill and they modeled it. The rest of class imitated. Once everyone had the tie in place, I took a class picture, developed it to an 8 x 10, and hanged it in the classroom. Students enjoyed this activity. It offered a break from studies and helped the kids relax. It also encouraged additional rapport and camaraderie.

At York High School I taught my classes the school fight song and on Homecoming Friday we marched down the halls, singing it as loud as we could. Students enjoyed the practice; some teachers were annoyed because they were giving tests. The first time I did this action was particularly upsetting to some staff, but after a couple of years, most teachers looked forward to it. Many even scheduled their tests to Thursdays of that week and got better results since that certain Friday rates high in student distractions.

The handshake. What other form of body language is more telling? Smiles convey warmth and openness; they also relax the teacher. Good posture feels good. A confident walk works. A firm handshake delivers contact and confidence. I practiced handshakes with my students every year: we discussed what those conveyed, then walked around class with handshakes and introduced ourselves to each other. This ritual began on day one as students entered class. I modeled the practice. A variation of handshakes, but less formal, was our "High-Five Fridays." No one entered class without a high five and a verbal, "Happy Friday!!" My being 6'7", the shortest pupils always had fun with that gesture. I even had the assistant principal give me one when he dropped in one Friday for an informal observation. The class rocked with smiles and laughter. And I did have hand sanitizers handy, another item on the teacher supply list that teachers have to buy themselves.

Vocabulary is always a concern with most disciplines. Every subject has its own Tier III words germane to its course and subject matter. Science loves its photosynthesis and amino acids; math enjoys its parabolas and isotopes; history adores its feudalism and Progressive Era; English worships its allusions and anaphora. However, there are three phrases that capture the imagination, which bind us as one, which shatter prejudice and enjoin solid communication. No need for a dictionary. *Please, Thank You,* and *Excuse me* cover all tiers and all subjects, all classes and all cliques. Listen for them; use them frequently;

enjoy the results of courtesy, respect, and equality. Students apply these words but only for select company. I observed with alarming frequency how kids will push past each other in crowded hallways without so much as a word, butt into conversations without invitation in the present Era of Interrupting, walk between two conversants, take items without a thank you, ask for something without the magic word. Teachers have an obligation and a duty to model such positive talk and instruct it when needed. I made it a point to be as courteous as possible in every communication with my colleagues. Self-respect comes from within, but can be taught. Students see much more than we might give them credit for.

We reveal our humanity to our students through our use of words, but we are not their peer. Many an inexperienced teacher falls prey to that trap. The following example offers further evidence that social decorum can be taught to teachers as well as to students. I remember one incident when I was conducting an informal observation on one of my English teachers. A student came in late, the teacher asked for a pass, and the student replied, "I don't have one, (teacher's last name)." The teacher did not correct the student's choice of words or lack of a "Mr." and continued with his class. When that teacher and I discussed the observation, I asked him if all his students address him by last name only, not with a "Mr." He responded, "Well, Tom, no big deal to me. I want them to be comfortable in my class and see me as their friend." We had a pointed discussion and devised ways that the teacher could help students be comfortable without the teacher surrendering his own dignity. I certainly was *un*comfortable with the idea that students saw any of my teachers as their peer, and even addressed this point at the next department meeting. Respect needs to be mutual, but a professional distance must be maintained.

Why is the professional distance a requirement for any teacher? If I gave teachers a choice between being liked or popular and being respected, what would they choose? After forty-two years in the classroom, this choice is a no-brainer for me. However, when first confronted with five classes in a novice's teaching career, the temptation for popularity is overwhelming. All teachers desire to be liked, but if close familiarity is the primary goal, where do the expectations for learning fall? I discovered through plenty of trial and error both the mental battle and the keen preparation needed for accomplishing *learning* for the students as opposed to their *enjoyment* for a lesson. As a matter of fact, as I aged in the profession, I found that planning was one of the hardest parts of good teaching. I also discovered that one can assist the other, but, as mentioned, that partnership is difficult to ascertain and sustain. Once teachers decide that learning is the reason they earn a salary, popularity sinks to a distant second place. Learning motivates clear and rigorous planning, high expectations, and quality assessments. Teachers who focus on the amount of learning for their students demand results from their protégés. Those teachers are relentless in their approach, rarely waste class time, and begin each class with a purpose. Throughout my tenure as an evaluator, I could detect within the first five to ten minutes of a lesson whether that teacher was ready and, more importantly, whether those students knew they were there to learn, not just to spend some time together, have a few laughs, derail the teacher when convenient, or find ways to hinder the learning of others. Students are most adept at figuring out whether a teacher is a true professional or a phony.

The professional distance, once established and sustained, promotes a healthy environment. The professional distance encourages deep learning through inquiry. The professional distance develops sound relationships and trust between teachers and students. Popularity becomes a secondary compliment, rather than a primary label. Once I could verify the damage it could cause, I did not desire popularity; I was too busy worrying and wondering if my students were learning and maturing. Handshakes, neckties, singing, and other props are all setups for learning in the hands of competent teachers.

Prepare

In the summer of 1974 I stood over charred wood in a lot on the west side of Chicago. The house was a victim of an arsonist. My uncle, a precinct captain, helped me get a job as a bulk collector-garbage man for the city. I started at 7:00 and worked until 3:00 under the supervision of my driver named Chuck, a burly, sarcastic chap, and a fellow worker. Chuck doubled as a parking lot manager for Chicago Stadium events. By day he bossed us around; by night, he supervised parking on those days of events. Chuck received a list of jobs in the morning and drove us to the sites on his list. We sat and listened to him, then worked until he said to rest or stop. Most of the time we never worked for more than one hour straight, then it was time for coffee. Those breaks would rival vacations on some days. It all depended on the weather. Hot, humid days meant lots of breaks. More moderate days meant fewer breaks, but let's put it this way: we never felt overworked. Chuck was a stereotypical city employee. If we were able to cover his list of jobs by 2:00, great, if not, those jobs waited until tomorrow.

At that particular charred house, I learned what the unexpected meant. First, I had to wear gloves to do any kind of labor. When we went to that house, I hopped off the truck and started to pick up the debris, mostly charred wood, and toss that detritus into the truck. Chuck took one look and said, "Get a rake, stupid." Chuck was feeling good that day.

"C'mon, Chuck, this is just as easy. Why complicate it?"

"Ok, genius, suit yourself."

I continued to toss wood. I came upon a heap of debris and tried to select the largest piece to level and separate the pile. The piece I selected introduced the unexpected. No sooner had I lifted that wood that a rat the size of a small poodle darted away, uncovering a family of seven or eight babies, about the size of my thumb, pink and thin. I never realized how high I could jump or how high I could scream.

Chuck laughed. "Want that rake now?"

I stared at my foolishness. "I see what you mean." I remained in the truck.

"Next time, listen to me. You suburban white kids don't know shit. Rats love this mess. You're lucky that monster didn't crawl right up your arm or bite you. Always rake that crap out first, so you avoid surprises like that."

A rake became one of my favorite garden tools from that day. About five minutes after that episode, I got the courage to go back into the fracas. I uncovered two more families nestled within the wood with rats that could eat my dog, and with babies, innocent and frail. We worked for an hour and Chuck decided to go for coffee at 10 a.m. We never returned to that site, but I forever wondered about the unexpected.

That wonderment can dovetail into the classroom. I never took a rake into my classroom or for my lectures or activities, but I learned to appreciate the surprises or unanticipated bursts of energy or question from the unlikeliest of sources, the quiet student. One of my most understated habits was my Type-A desire to have everything laid out for the lesson, timed to the minute, then *one* student coming to class having eaten two cold burritos for breakfast, and those burritos deciding to make an unexpected splash onto the floor. How does a teacher recover after that?

Preparing for the unexpected sounds impossible, but this skill is most noticeable in the quickness with which teachers can think on their feet. Many times unprepared occurrences supply teachable moments.

BREATHE AND THINK

"TOMORROW IS ALWAYS FRESH, WITH NO MISTAKES IN IT YET."
~L. M. MONTGOMERY, *ANNE OF GREEN GABLES*

EXHIBIT A:

A proverb states, *God gave us two ears for listening and only one tongue. That should tell us something.* I much prefer to listen rather than speak. When I have something to say of some relevance, I volunteer. I consider myself educated and articulate, but I fail to see the wisdom of talking when I have little original to offer. When I attend or run meetings, I try to offer deliberation and thought as my chief contributions, preferring to shine the spotlight on my teachers or the various participants. Unless I have to announce some decision and its rationale or answer questions, I prefer to listen to what others have to say. I feel that helps people relax, develops more camaraderie, and promotes ownership of issues. Of course if everyone took that route, we would have the fastest meetings in history and achieve very little.

This method of response serves well in classrooms. Nothing is more profound and enlists attention from students better than silence. As a novice teacher, I even faked an answer at times, just so students never drew the conclusion that he didn't know an answer or that he isn't that smart. With more experience and with additional observations from excellent faculty observers, I either announced, "I don't know" to a baffling question, or to stand silent, gazing at the questioner. Amazing what that accomplishes. A teacher might not have a more salient moment in that lesson, a moment where *everyone* is anticipating the next word. Besides, if correct answers are the bottom line for teachers in their classes, I will wager that thinking and inquiry were victims of Houdini.

EXHIBIT B:

Benjamin Franklin once said, *A sound conscience makes for a soft pillow.* Evenings and nights possess many quality options: enjoying a drink, making love, sitting on the patio or deck and surmising about one's situation or plans, working out, dreaming, walking the dog, talking to the neighbor, taking out the garbage, tooling around the house, talking to your spouse, enjoying leisure reading, surveying the stars, catching up on the news, taking a ride for ice cream, letting the big decision cool and simmer, fantasizing about another World Series championship for the Cubs, and/or helping the offspring with an issue or homework. The mind will return to the big issue in the subconscious.

Upon awakening, what does a person feel is the right decision for that big problem? If research has been done and the person is in the contemplation stage, what does one feel immediately in the morning? Whatever that is, is that the same notion a couple of mornings in succession? Then that notion is most likely the thing to do. One has to listen to one's gut and trust it, and I know the gut is clearer in the morning. The night is far too emotional; the day's pressures have been a weight and blurs clear thinking. Let them cool. Enjoy the present. Wake up with new insights. Of course, that wake-up call could come at 2:30 a.m., but settle back and let the sun shine on a new day. Make every attempt to make important decisions in the morning.

EXHIBIT C:

I watched the NFL wild card games with interest over the weekend of January 9-10, 2016. The Cincinnati Bengals threw away their chance at ending a playoff drought by losing their poise when they were winning by a point with less than one minute to play. Two players cost their team a victory by getting one fifteen-yard penalty each for unsportsmanlike conduct, thus giving the Pittsburgh Steelers the field position it needed to kick the game-winning field goal. As I watched this chaos unfold, I reminded myself of my high school basketball coach's definition of poise: Do the job the way you learned the job, no matter the pressure or situation. I sat wondering if the coaching staff of Cincinnati had taught their players anything close to that definition and demanded they follow it. In some ways, I know professional coaches are paid well, but I wonder about their true credibility in the face of their players who make far more money than the coaches do.

Sydney J. Harris was a columnist for *The Sun-Times* and *Chicago Daily News* from the 1940s to his death in 1986. He was considered a master at aphorisms. The author of eleven books, Harris wrote a column titled, *Life's Winners Usually Make the Fewest Mistakes*. The following excerpt is from that column:

> *A great chess master of the past once defined chess as a game in which the player who makes the next to the last mistake is the winner. That description applies to many more pursuits than chess. Every class, every school year, every business, every contest has two basic aims: the positive aim is to have students learn the curriculum or meet or exceed standards, make a good profit, or score the goal (touchdown, putt, etc.). The negative aim is to avoid making as many mistakes as possible.*

> *What many competitors, students, entrepreneurs fail to understand is that the negative aim can be more important than the positive one, or in many cases, more decisive. It is axiomatic that more games, businesses are lost rather than won. Many times uneven temperaments are a root cause of those lost experiences. Human nature dictates that people do not come to work or to class or to a game with the same level of temperament every day. This unevenness is at the heart of this tip.*

> *Gene Littler, a famous golf champion of the past, once remarked, Golf is not a game of great shots. It's a game of the most accurate misses. The people who win make the smallest mistakes. In bridge tournaments, the eventual winners, even if they are world class, rarely average more than a 70% score, which is considered high because there are so many opportunities for errors in the bidding and the play of the band. Perhaps gambling possesses the keenest example of the importance of temperament. The more a player wins, the greater the ego pushes him to keep winning. A façade builds which is tough to diminish. In poker the big winner in the first hour or two is often the biggest loser by the end of the night.*

> *The evolution of consistency is even more evident in a kinetic game like tennis, where all the top players are equally adept at shot-making. The point most often goes not to the one who makes*

a killing return, but to the one who outsteadies and outlasts his opponent. Bjorn Borg was content to stay on the baseline much of the time and allow his opponent to drive the ball into the net or out of bounds.

Thus, those who win, win not because of temporary and isolated brilliancies; they win because they are steady. They play the percentages and are prudent in their decisions. They seek accuracy and control, not a hole in one, and look to make the next to last mistake. A winner knows how much he still has to learn, even when he is considered an expert by others; a loser wants to be considered an expert by others before he has learned enough to know how little he knows (end Harris).

In various fields, Harris's words spell the truth. In the academic world, an A student makes fewer mistakes than a B student; a B student fewer than a C student. Students who earn a C or even a D have made their share of mistakes, but not enough to spell doom in summer school. The student who falls a few points short of passing a course can review the consistency of all the grades and the lack of even completing the assignments. The successful business has fewer returns, fewer complaints, and higher trust. In basketball free throw shooting becomes the litmus test for games decided by eight points or fewer. Missed foul shots are lost opportunities. Turnovers and just about every other area of basketball are examined with numbers: the more mistakes (having over fourteen turnovers in a high school game usually spells defeat), the less chance of victory.

The question remains easy to write, but how does one learn temperament, or teach it? Learning temperament faces challenges, since the patience of many people in today's world is so miniscule; everyone wants instant results. The term *right and privileges* has overcome *obligations and responsibilities*. This mode of thinking transfers to a dislike or diminishing of work ethic and attention to detail. Time itself stands as an enemy to progress: waiting in lines for service, road construction, or a computer fix distract people from patience. These distractions, plus many others, sway society from patient communication and promote the incessant whining or blame we can hear on the news every night. Throw in a sense of entitlement and society squanders opportunities at harmony. If you want to practice patient communication, try writing letters instead of sending emails. Handwritten letters come from the heart and, as with all writing, require some thinking. Emails are all too often misinterpreted or misunderstood.

In school critical thinking steps into the boundaries of temperament. Critical thinking far surpasses objective answers. Critical thinking requires probing, writing, delving beyond the superficial, reaching far into Bloom's taxonomy pocket for new ideas and research. Attaining those skills requires patience and persistence. Many argue that schools should just teach the subjects and leave it at that, ensuring that the kids graduate. That is fine for the average teacher. The superior one always does more than the minimum, and that requires the steely patience and temperament of the teacher who possesses great work capacity, pride, and ego.

Poised and balanced temperament is a requisite for the superior teacher, leader, and coach. Breathe and think.

GROW OR WITHER. YOUR CHOICE.

GROWING "VITAMINS"—TAKE ONE EACH DAY.

- Fake it or make it.
- Smiling decreases pain.
- Love the battle, the competition. The career should follow suit.
- Always do a little more than the minimum.
- Do your best work when you are fatigued.
- Outward resiliency grows from inner toughness.
- How much can you grow sitting in a recliner in front of a television or working a video game for twelve hours every day?
- If you read for fifteen or twenty minutes before you go to bed every night, you can finish three new books every year.
- Find a worthwhile cause and support it.
- Pick up after your pet.
- Spend two minutes each week with the silent student. Two will lead to four.
- Take a class in something you know nothing about.

- Read the same book in the curriculum each year you need to teach it, even though you have read it before. There are ideas you don't understand in those pages.
- Read poetry occasionally; this will slow your life down.
- Write thank you notes promptly.
- Call your mother once a week at the minimum.
- Call fellow faculty or employees by name when you greet them ("Hi, there" is ok, but not as classy.). If you do not know the name, ask the person or find out.
- As you advance in the profession, avoid cynical faculty. Those people kill morale.
- Preparation removes the advance of staleness.
- Exercise for twenty minutes every day or, at the bare minimum, three days in the work week.
- If you are deciding to purchase a dog or a cat, get a dog.
- Take the time to show appreciation, even for the smallest things.
- Every once in a while, go have that drink; the workload can wait.
- Lao-tzu, 6th century B.C. Chinese philosopher, once said, "To love someone deeply gives you strength; being loved deeply by someone gives you courage."
- Do not argue with a spouse who is packing your parachute.
- Focus on your goals, not your problems.
- Take a different route to work or school at least once a week.
- Watch sunsets when possible (I advise Naples, Florida.)
- Rash judgment is fatal to good character.
- Never cheat.
- Smile a lot.
- Avoid negative people.
- Put a marshmallow into your hot chocolate.
- Respect the police, your elders, and teachers.
- Take out the garbage without being told.

- Look people in the eye.
- Be brave. Even if you're not, pretend to be.
- When someone is relating an important personal event, do not interrupt with a story of your own. Let them have the stage.
- Be the first to say, "Hello."
- Sing along with songs you enjoy.
- Stand at attention during the Pledge or the national anthem.
- Be on time.
- Earn trust and learn to trust.
- Make it a habit of doing nice things for people who will never find out.
- Give people a second chance, but not a third.
- The person with big dreams is more powerful than one with all the facts.
- Never take action when you're angry.
- Ask WHY.
- Measure people by the size of their heart.
- Be kinder than necessary.
- Integrity is doing what is right without being told or watched.
- Don't major in minor things.
- Learn to listen; opportunity sometimes knocks very softly.
- Think big thoughts, but relish small pleasures.
- Respect traditions.
- Have periodic conversations with grandparents and parents. Once they are gone, the library closes forever.
- Live your life as an exclamation, not as an explanation.
- Practice empathy.
- Don't litter...and pick up litter that is not yours.
- Never eat the last cookie.
- Pay attention to details.
- Pay your fair share.

- No time to workout? Do pushups, planks, and leg raises.
- When attending meetings or classes, sit in the front.
- Never underestimate the power of forgiveness.
- When someone hugs you, let that person be the first to let go.
- Leave everything a little better than you found it.
- Remember that overnight success usually takes about three years.
- Remain curious about your ability.
- Be modest; a lot was accomplished before you arrived.
- Never waste an opportunity to praise someone or to tell someone you love him or her.
- Wave to children on a school bus.
- Winners do what losers avoid.

YOUR TURN

Identify areas of interest for your own application in your classrooms. Also consider methods you would use to sustain the classroom atmosphere you desire throughout the year.

PERSEVERE

During the Korean War the First Marine Division was fighting forty miles in advance of all other U.S. forces. This type of activity was the norm for marines. Suddenly, the Chinese army crossed the Korean borders with thirty-three divisions comprising 300,000 men. The Americans soon found themselves cut off and heralded by bugles, cymbals, and police whistles announcing the attack of the Chinese. When the commanding general was asked by a war correspondent if the marines were about to make the first retreat in their history, the general snapped, "Retreat, hell, we're only attacking in another direction." But the marine who best expressed the spirit of those Americans was Colonel Lewis B. "Chesty" Puller, who told his regiment, "The enemy is in front of us, behind us, to the left of us and to the right of us. They won't escape this time!" The Marines proceeded to fight their way through 300,000 Chinese and fourteen days of sub-zero cold and blizzards. They had to bury 117 of their fellow Marines in one frozen grave and, lacking a hospital, had to carry each one of their 2,651 casualties to the Port of Hangman and eventual freedom. Why did they last? Why did they win? Dogged determination, the refusal to give up or give in. Standard bearers like those warriors bolstered the culture of the nation at that time in history. Their belief in country and purpose steeled their perseverance.

I wish I could research those Marines' childhoods to see the ways their parents raised them, to witness the ways pride and persistence were ingrained in them. I would wager that no parents put any bumper sticker on their car fenders or windows boasting that their children received multiple trophies or plaques for finishing in seventh place in any sporting competition. More than likely, those Marines were raised on values rather than rights. They took the blame instead of placing it, walked to school instead of being driven, shoveled the snow and cut the grass, put the pressure on themselves rather than on anyone else for bad school performance, and possessed the fear of failure rather than the curse of entitlement. Pragmatism parented those soldiers; self-esteem followed.

Where is my research? My parents. They believed in the words, obligations and responsibilities. I grew up in three different spots in Chicago: a second floor flat on Keating Avenue, a bungalow on west Dickens Street (just south of Shakespeare Avenue-must have been an omen for a future English teacher), and a bungalow on Roscoe St. Each represented an upward rung in the American

Dream, but none of them were mansions. My dad was the only income; Mom took care of the three of us. Self-esteem was a term for the future, a lot of hot air. It is the product of enabling and the window dressing for entitlement. Our term was more like, *Get over here, do this, or else!* We had Sunday dinner in the early afternoon. Mom had a favorite mode of establishing communication with her children, a wooden spoon. It hurt. Sometimes, Mom would take one of Dad's belts and apply to the gluteus maximus. Understand that these were the highest security measures, used only in times of supreme stupidity or subterfuge on the part of her children. Being rude to guests, driving her nuts with brother-sister arguments, or telling her one thing and doing another were also high on her hit list. Today, some parents might be ready to say, *Call DCFS! Parental abuse!* We saw it as normal life and something that was deserved after the punishment was administered, and most of these weapons of mass destruction were verbal threats, not actual consequences. In any event, we did learn courtesy, love, respect for others, and humility. My parents were outstanding people who were generous and loving. First they supplied the discipline, the cause. The love and its effect, followed.

Working with high school students for forty-one years, I came across many teachers and students who felt they had already deserved respect without doing much of anything to merit it or by just doing the minimum. Those people were hard to trust, unlike Marine teammates who charged over any hill to face the enemy or felt the responsibility to watch their partners' backs. Many experts would argue with me, I know, but students who had parents who supplied the discipline and responsible love were easy to spot. They were polite, took criticism well, responded positively to setbacks, and felt that had to earn their status.

One expert who would agree with me is Dr. Leonard Sax whose article excerpt, *The Collapse of Parenting*, appeared in *The Chicago Tribune* on February 1, 2016. In this interview Sax bemoans the transfer of authority from parents to kids. He further states:

> *I wrote about an office visit with a ten-year old boy who is sitting and playing a game on his mobile phone, ignoring me and his mom as I'm talking to his mother about his stomachache. And his mom is describing his stomachache and the boy says, 'Shut up, Mom, you don't know what you're talking about.' And he laughs. That would have been very unusual in 1990 or 2000.*

> *It is now common: children, girls and boys, being disrespectful to their parents, being disrespectful to one another, being disrespectful to themselves, verbally and other wise. The mother did nothing, just looked a little embarrassed. The culture has changed in a profound way in a short period of time in ways that have really harmed kids. (Interview).*

Some might counter with the notion that a pragmatic approach supplies only a means, but not a destination. The skillful parent or leader has a vision of where his child or his organization is headed. Obviously, having both a far-reaching goal along with a method for attainment of that goal creates a potential combination for success. I had a saying in class from the start of many courses: *Pressure makes diamonds.* I dealt in truth to my students. I always felt that soft-soaping what students needed to hear was a form of dishonesty. Want to be fair to your students? Tell them the truth about where they are and supply the evidence, what they need to do to improve, why you are unhappy or dissatisfied. Then, be willing to listen and to supply the support. Those actions exhibit trust. One final note: if teachers want to discover who the Marines are in their classes, observe them in their Physical Education class. Teachers will detect who plays nice with others, who is unselfish, who is competitive, who has no idea about the concept of teamwork, etc. It is amazing what happens to people when they sweat, a substance that never drowned anyone. If you can watch the P.E. classes, take good mental notes. Many times you can observe subtle character traits with which you can empower individual students and increase their sense of responsibility. For example, I had one particularly quiet student in class. As I watched him in P.E. one day in floor hockey, he turned into Mr. Fanatic, competitive and driven, arguing close calls, pushing his team to win. I talked to him the next day and complimented him on his juice during P.E. class. He was at first taken aback that I was even there, but then smiled and thanked me. I asked him to write down two ways he could bring that competitive juice into English class and to describe some positive effects for doing that. He returned with those comments the next day. One of his thoughts was to see how fast he could read a certain book. Considering he had not been reading at all up to that point, I gave it my blessing. He experienced a metamorphosis. When we had a competition in class using *polleverywhere.com*, he became the ringleader for his group. I could detect increasing confidence. Was this student's self-esteem presented to him, wrapped in beautiful paper like a Christmas gift? Hardly. He had to earn that level of confidence. My point here is that confidence came from the work and the relationship. Supply a valid reason for the rigor and a vast majority of students will respond. They will begin to see the value of responsibility and obligations with the effort required for attainment.

Not everyone is a Marine, but everyone can embrace responsibilities and obligations. Part of that equation is for anyone in some type of leadership role to remember to praise people as often as that praise is earned for their work ethic, not just for their intelligence or for the result. Everyone can do his/her part. Relentless persistence sees the job through.

ADAPT

"Congratulations, Tom!" one of my York High School English colleagues offered to me in 1990. "Get ready for twenty years of sleep deprivation." That pronouncement was a few days after my first son, John, was born in 1990. That pronouncement was accurate. John's arrival came in my second year of rebuilding York's basketball program. The truth is, *rebuilding* is never a word a husband would want when it comes to his marriage. When it comes to being a full-time English teacher, having a spouse with a full-time job, and coaching a demanding, time-consuming sport like boys' basketball, children and marriages can be caught in that wringer. I did not want that to happen to me.

Teaching with coaching was my life, my obsession. I poured everything into it. Fortunately for me, I married an understanding wife, Susan, a teacher also. When we met she coached swimming. After I was a head coach for 21 years, and with two boys ages four and seven, the die was cast. That die is called guilt. I was being stretched thin between maintaining and running a quality basketball program at York and finding sufficient time for helping at home. I felt torn during practices when things would surface during or after practice that required me to stay longer, or conversely, when I would receive a call from home where my presence was needed. Saturdays were sometimes eight hour affairs between J-V games in the morning, practice, weight training, etc. Watching film? Another two hours. You get the idea. I wanted to be home and when I felt I was shortchanging the program and my family, I had a choice. I resigned from head coaching in 1997.

In today's world, dual incomes are a reality and families of teacher-coaches, and numerous other occupations of course, have to appraise the type of lifestyle they want to have. With that comes prioritizing the role of the career. After I resigned, many approached me and asked, "How much do you miss it?' and "What do you do with all your free time?" That free time just shifted into the world of fatherhood. People fill their lives with other practicalities after a decision is made to leave something else. I did not miss basketball as much as I thought. The interaction with players—yes; the paperwork and some parents—no. I was too preoccupied with helping at home; children are a full-time love and a precious responsibility.

In 2000, however, I did return to coaching at Lincoln-Way as an assistant for the next thirteen years, and being an assistant absolved me of many of the distractions that a head coach confronts. I was still able to enjoy the game I adored, and the coaching offered my sons an opportunity to be around good athletes and supporting environments. They would accompany me to the gyms, even for some practices when my wife would drop them off and run some errands. When so many parents will worry about where their children might be after hours, we always knew where our kids were. That peace-of-mind is much more vital than any game plan or practice.

Even though there were some tense moments in my marriage, times when Susan just felt alone as a parent, basketball coaching brought some stability to the growth of my boys. They both played high school basketball. I coached them on the Frankfort Warrior travel team I initiated, organized and administered. Susan and I possessed a tool to help steer them toward the values and the dividends competitive sports can bring. When I coached the Warriors, the rides home had a different flavor depending on a win or a loss or in general, the tone of the game. I never started the conversation about my son's level of play; I waited. I waited even more, at times biting my tongue into various sections. I waited until my son started the discussion or asked a question such as, "Dad, what did you think?" or 'Dad, how did I do?" That opening paved the way to a conversation about the game or practice, and I tried to keep as level a tone as possible, yet still supply the necessary honesty. The majority of those times resulted in positive feedback and a continued eagerness from my son for the next time he laced up his sneakers. They are fine adults today. Conversely, a coaching life does not provide the only vehicle for raising good children. There are plenty of terrific kids who never bounced a basketball, swam competitively, or ran track. In the end, though, coaching was worth the time and effort, but coaches need understanding spouses. Adaptability provides a smoother existence between the two.

Couples form a team similar to one in any sports organization. The trials of raising a family while a spouse is coaching, or when both coach, can supply a terrific model for their children to emulate-as long as the spirit of competition is in check and tempered with the instruction of patience and strong values. Watch any Little League game, AAU basketball, or high school competition and you will find parents who belittle officials, blame everyone else for their child's shortcomings, embarrass themselves in front of their kids, or hide the truth from their kids about the child's lack of talent or effort. When I was an assistant at Lincoln-Way, we once cut a boy from the team after tryouts. He played hard, but was not athletic or skillful at 5'5." I received a letter from his sister, castigating me for *my* decision (remember, I was the assistant), criticizing me for curtailing "her brother's NBA dream" and that "her parents felt the same way." He had the ability to play professional basketball, or even college ball, about as much as I do right now. Another prime example is the parent who takes his child's stats during every game. I would have loved to hear those conversations at home after games. Those players were some of the more uncoachable ones, those prima donnas who never met a shot they didn't like. Those examples represent some of the delusion present throughout various levels of athletics. They are also examples to the coaches themselves for how not to raise a student-athlete, so I guess there is some good in them, even though they do make some coaching experiences some degree of miserable.

Raising a family and heading/assisting an athletic program is a tightrope act requiring a steady support system and plenty of adaptability. A safety net fifty feet below the high wire is nice, but excellent communication, time management, and patience supply much better essentials for the teacher-coach family. So does a family vacation every summer, and a dinner just with the spouse on a nonscheduled weekend.

YOUR TURN

Use this space to write some reflections for this section.

SECTION 3-B

COACHES, DO SOMETHING.

(RE)BUILD

Rebuilding and inexperienced equal two potentially lethal descriptions for coaches. I have weathered both a few times. I took over Immaculate Conception in 1976 and the returning players were eager, but green. We averaged only seven wins for the first three years, cracked .500 in my fourth, and won 20 or more in each of my last four seasons to establish one of the best programs in the area. Some of the most dedicated and loyal players and coaches were instrumental in that metamorphosis. That staff contained superb people and coaches. They combined amazing work ethic with the ability to communicate and inspire. They never made excuses. They knew the game, but always put the team first. I owe them a great deal. After I left Immaculate Conception in 1984, I tried the public school scene: Glenbrook North was in worse shape; my first year had no experienced players and little talent. After five wins in the initial year, we finished 14-13 in the second year with five gutsy players, then struggled to be .500 in my remaining three years. Elmhurst-York High School (1989-97) was difficult at first. Only one player had any varsity experience, but he was a solid big man. That team lost its first eight games, but as my post player gained confidence, he blossomed into a constant scoring threat. The Christmas tournament provided the evidence when he earned Most Valuable Player, leading our team to a second place finish out of the sixteen participants. The York program improved each year. I stepped down as a head coach in 1997, but assisted at Lincoln-Way for all but two years for the remainder of my career.

Except for a few highly skilled players and quite a few blessed with an extraordinary work ethic and a will to succeed, my players did not possess tremendous athletic talent. They had to work; I had to supply the direction, the philosophy, and the leadership. What am I driving at here? I enjoyed those challenges because I learned how to coach. I do not buy that coaches who consistently inherit great talent year after year understand all the nuances of coaching. If aspiring coaches really want to learn their trade, they have to go through difficult seasons. Young coaches are too easily spoiled today. If they don't win right away, they become discouraged too easily. If they do win right away for a couple of years, they think they deserve a head coaching position. If they are in a situation where they win a lot right away, they can become egotistical about their own success and might not continue to learn the details in coaching both mediocre players and great ones. Humility can take a back seat instead of staying in the front and driving the improvement.

What details am I talking about? The following lengthy list contains both basic and advanced ingredients; they constitute ways to relish the difficult seasons, to meet lofty expectations, to develop programs, or to sustain success. Many of these concepts revolve around basketball; however, coaches of other sports can find links to their own programs in the majority of these suggestions.

1. For program building, key on your incoming *freshman* class. Depending on the talent level, if a head coach's rebuilding efforts are going to bear fruit, the job will take four years. In the fourth year, the head coach's philosophy and teaching should be part of every player's mantra. For example, the precise execution of the fundamentals has to be consistent for every player. To be more specific with one example, I taught certain technique for the pullback dribble. I expected my coaches to learn this technique and be able to teach it more effortlessly and well each year.

   This is not to say that if the fourth year brings a poor season that that coach's program is a failure. So much depends both upon *each* class bringing something to the table in terms of chemistry and talent and also the continuous improvement of the coaches' ability to teach and to manage both players and situations.

2. Another step equal in importance to the first one is your coaching staff. Not only is it essential to select good people, but also strong teachers who enjoy the game, who will listen to instruction, and

who relish improvement. I would emphasize to avoid yes-men as assistants. Valuable assistant coaches must have the freedom to disagree with the head coach in healthy debates, but also be amenable in supporting the head coach once he or she makes a final decision. For further reading I would recommend Doris Kearns Goodwin, *A Team of Rivals*, an account of Abraham Lincoln's cabinet during one of the most pressure-packed eras in American history, the Civil War. Lincoln purposefully chose men from the opposition party; most of the cabinet did not agree with many of Lincoln's policies and decisions. This kept Lincoln from acting rashly and gave an acute balance to his decisions. This book is a compelling read.

Selection of coaches is only the first step; you must work with them and train them, teaching them the methods you want taught and the detail involved. Attaining and keeping quality assistants is one of the more frustrating responsibilities of a head coach, but it remains a priority. During the pre-season, I invited my coaches over to my house to watch film, discuss players, role-play time-outs or critical game situations, or examine hypothetical scenarios. Each of these evenings built trust among the staff. In addition, encourage attendance at clinics. Better yet, make one clinic a year a staff outing. Here are some examples of more items worth discussion among the staff:

- Your team is struggling. You have just lost a one-point game at home. A father comes into your locker room, visibly upset, and wants to speak with you immediately.

- A player comes to you desiring to discuss lack of playing time.

- It is tryout time and cuts have to be made. How do we handle these?

- The principal calls you into his office and wants an explanation about how you intend to avoid another losing season or how you intend to keep the winning going.

- A transfer athlete appears in your school in the fall. How do you handle transfers?

- You have a very good sophomore or freshman who has the physical ability to play at the varsity level. How do you handle this situation? What are criteria? Explain it to the player in a role-play for either having him on varsity or not.

- You return a team with excellent experience and talent. The group has had winning seasons before this year. Expectations are high. How do you address those expectations on opening day? After a three-game skid? After a six-game winning streak?

3. What is your coaching philosophy? *Why do you coach*? Think long and hard about this. What are you made of as a coach and what will you demand of your athletes? Is your job to win games or to develop players? Or both? How can one support the other?

4. Teach all your perimeter players, most importantly the point guard, a pullback crossover dribble. This dribble has a certain technique and like most fundamentals, can be done incorrectly. Rick Majerus, the late college coach, was a master at this instruction. This dribble is the key to breaking full-court pressure or neutralizing quicker defenders.

   If you do not coach basketball, select three or four fundamentals essential to the effectiveness of the team and program. How will you teach the detail to players for those fundamentals?

5. Fundamentals should be at the core of all your teaching. Players should know them so well they could teach them if necessary. If any basketball aficionados examine games lost by eight points or fewer, they will find a couple of fundamentals missing at key points that cost victory, such as blocking out on freethrows or lack of one defensive rotation.

6. Work a few summer camps. The camps are gold mines for knowledge a coach can acquire by being at colleagues' elbows for a week. Ask

plenty of questions. That last piece is a dimension I found missing from younger coaches when I attended basketball camps. Many novice coaches have a deplorable lack of curiosity or talk far too much rather than listen. In my experience, I found camps more worthwhile than clinics when it came to gaining knowledge about coaching. Clinics are fine, but camps are non-stop exposure to good minds.

7.   Organize and run summer camps for all age groups.

8.   Organize and run clinics at your school in the fall for neighborhood or feeder schools. There is no better practice at teaching fundamentals than practicing those skills in front of a live audience, then fielding questions. Buy pizza for some social time after the clinic.

9.   Attend games at your feeder schools; be very visible. Visibility creates credibility.

10. Study and teach mental training for your athletes. I use basketball as one example:

Matt played point guard for me at York from 1991-93. He was one of those rare creatures who would just try to survive practices, at times play downright poor, but sum up the moxie to be ready at game time, often providing clutch performances. He wasn't much to look at, barely 6' and weighing 140. But did he have the guts and the internal machine. The point most salient about Matt was his mental preparation. A few hours before every game, mainly after school, there he was, in the gym, alone with a ball, dribbling up and down, visualizing every potential move he would have to make against that night's opponent. He epitomized vivid imagination as a powerful tool for success in athletics. I often did mental training, using some valuable practice time to instruct relaxation techniques, visual imagery, and immediate focus. I would leave players alone in the locker room before games to sit quietly and visualize success against that night's opponent.

11. Players weight train all season: heavy in off-season and moderate/light during the season.

12. Learn how to talk to the media. Learn reporters' names; treat them with respect. The media can do a *Marc Antony* on you: praise or bury.

13. Summertime focus for players should be on their *individual* progress, not on the amount of wins their AAU team or their school summer team accumulates.

14. Learn how to attack any defense. Then, teach those defenses' weaknesses to the players.

15. Never underestimate last-second plays. A coach should have plays from full-court, half-court, under out-of-bounds against any defense and each dependent on being up or down. Coaches can have a very sick feeling in the gut when they discover through a last-second situation in an actual game that they have not prepared their team to execute a play when it is needed to have a chance to win. As a matter of fact, they don't even have a play!

16. Practice *diagraming* end-of-game situations on your own and with a timer. You do not have time to plan the family vacation in a one-minute timeout.

17. Measure your team's success, strengths and limitations, and toughness against the eight best teams on the schedule. Forget the cupcakes when measuring the level of toughness and skills your team possesses.

18. Love your non-starters (your bench). Never ignore them; you need them. Find every opportunity to praise their effort and their contributions.

19. Practice organization compares to the relevance of sun to life. Do all your drills seamlessly flow into the big picture of your overall offensive and defensive strategy? If a drill does not correlate to a game situation, why are you using it? [Sounds like a part of the classroom, does it not? Do your classroom activities support the lesson's target and correlate to relevant assessments?]

20. Dedicate some time in almost every practice to end-of-game situations. I used to practice diagramming plays at home under time pressure and tutored my assistant coaches to do the same at meetings. I discovered that no matter the level of interest from the players up to that point, practice of last-second situations increased energy and attention from the players. By the way, when your team has the ball for a last second shot attempt, at what time do you want the shot? I say 5-6 seconds, so there is time for an offensive rebound. I see plenty of college teams, coached by millionaire head coaches, who do not drill these time sequences into their players. In today's game the most observers might see is a screen and roll. I appreciate the simplicity of this basic set; however, the lack of creativity on offenses is astounding. The lack of execution for screening a spot and not a body is awful.

21. Be versatile enough to adapt your offenses to your talent. Never get too complicated. If players know and can apply the fundamentals under game speed, any offense becomes easier to digest and execute.

22. Reliable seniors make for good teams. Oh, by the way, they should also be good players. Oh, and the most unselfish. When I would speak with freshmen and sophomores about their futures in basketball, I would direct their attention to excellent seniors. That example is the model the underclassmen's attitude and work habits should emulate. If seniors do not practice the example you as their coach desire, you might have an uneven, inconsistent season.

23. When your best player is your hardest worker, get ready to enjoy a good, maybe a great season.

24. Who is the *glue guy* on your team? This player might lack many of the skills of the better players, might not be a great shooter, and might not be the most athletic. He is, however, the leader in the details that make any team a winner: hustle, teamwork, and unselfishness. A coach can detect his glue guy as he watches his team unravel or lack execution when this player has to take a breather.

25. How players treat and speak to their parents speaks volumes about the player's character.

26. Both coaches and players should read about the game they coach/ play. Every summer assign one basketball-related book or a book related to the sport you coach to your players for summer reading. Here are some possibilities for basketball teams. Other suggestions appear in Appendix C.

- *My Losing Season*, Pat Conroy
- *Jordan Rules*, Sam Smith
- *Sacred Hoops*, Phil Jackson
- *Pistol (The Life of Pete Maravich)*, Mark Kriegel
- *The Miracle of St. Anthony*, Adrian Wojnarowski
- *A Season on the Brink*, John Feinstein
- *The Fab Five*, Mitch Albom
- *Heaven is a Playground*, Rick Telander
- *The Breaks of the Game*, David Halberstam
- *Larry Bird/Magic Johnson – When the Game Was Ours*, Jackie McMullen
- *Drive—The Story of My Life*, Larry Bird
- *Life on the Run*, Bill Bradley

Why is book reading a good idea? A short list of reasons begins with the simple belief that athletes do not read as nearly as much as they should; consequently, they know a mere paucity of the history of the game they profess to love so much. Second, a coach can catch a glimpse of their players' intellectual talents: their ability to discuss and/or interpret what they read. Third, reading a basketball or respective sport-related book just might inspire the team to play the game at a higher level.

If a coach's budget allows for the purchase of the same book for every player in the program, this activity can solidify team unity and provide the coach with practical applications during the actual season. When I was at York High School, I once had the players read *The Old Man and the Sea* by Ernest Hemingway. We were facing Oak Park-River Forest, a conference rival and a team hard for us to beat. I devised a game plan based on the struggles of Santiago as he tried to land his big fish, his dream fish. The players bought both the book and the plan. We nearly upset Oak Park at their place, losing by 3. I believed that the game plan and the reading inspired the players to play at a level they had not yet achieved. We used the loss as a springboard of new confidence and won 5 of the next 6. Moreover, this unique approach instilled freshness and curiosity into the middle of the long basketball season.

Why not give this approach a try? Coaches are teachers. Applying this technique would further support reading across the curriculum and enhance the coach's credibility in the eyes of the faculty.

27. "Play hard; play smart; play together." Need I say more? That mantra came from the late Coach Rick Majerus.

28. Can your team adjust on the spot on offense when a defense switches from a zone to a man-to-man?

29. Ever have a *program practice* for a portion of time after school? All the kids in the program work together on skills. This practice could combine station work, position breakdown, etc. The lower levels really enjoy working with varsity players, plus the head coach gets to see how hard they work.

30. As a follow-up to the previous suggestion, assigning a varsity player as a Big Brother to one or two sophomores or freshmen is another method for program unity. Those pairs would work together during a program practice. When the schedules permit, the varsity players watched their little brothers in games. In essence, the big brothers took on a coaching persona. These moments supplied opportunities for leadership development.

31. There are exceptions to every rule, but I believe if your point guard is your leading scorer, you might lack the balance in scoring necessary to win big games. Point guards should be facilitators first, be in the best shape on the team, be one of the best foul shooters, and know what the head coach wants in situations, especially end-of-game. Communication between head coach and point guard has to be steady, clear, and daily.

32. Part of our daily warmup was having players go to baskets and practice offensive moves *without* a ball. Having the basketball in hand can be a distraction for players; they think too much about the end result and not the process. A good example is footwork faking, a skill lost in today's players. Without a ball, players will see the details in execution of correct fundamentals more clearly, pushing the growth of muscle memory. For your sport, what skills could your players do *without a ball* that would enhance their technique and muscle-memory?

33. Are the three best scorers shooting the ball the majority of the time? That aspect is worth charting by a manager and worth studying by the coach. I am sure that there are relative statistics for every other sport.

34. Do your players know their roles? Each player needs a role for a sense of ownership and belonging. Roles become more challenging as players mature and improve their skills. Specific roles also constitute a baseline for building confidence in players. For example, nowadays I do some individual tutoring of high school players. One young man, a 6'6" junior in 2016-17, has some solid athleticism, listens well, and can play both inside and outside from about 17'. I tried to simplify his vision for improvement when we discussed the question, "What one part of the game would determine your best value to the team and to your own ability? What will you contribute the most to a winning season?" After some thought, he replied, "Rebounding" which was just the answer I desired. If this player focuses on that one aspect as his primary contribution, his play will blossom and his team will be in position to win many

games. Rebounding takes work and passion, and it is a skill that ensures a team can control its own destiny in games. So, consider definition of roles as a useful factor in determining both a team's success and each individual player's level of confidence. Roles also assist a coach's discussions with each of his/her players when questions about playing time or lack of improvement surface, as they inevitably will.

35. Make practices more challenging than games for your players.

36. Do not let up toward the end of seasons. You might shorten the practice time, but do not let up on the rigor or the expectations, whether having a winning or a losing season. You are teaching persistence every day.

37. Pass out one article every two weeks for players to read. Keep a brain food binder as a collection of articles for players' metal, physical, and emotional development. If possible, take the team to a college practice, so they can see high levels of work and talent.

38. The *coach* determines the quality of effort by every player, *not* the player. If the coach explains and justifies a lack of effort by a player, the player needs to adjust. This factor creates more misunderstanding between parent and coaches than any other one (see #47).

39. Can your team run a delay and smoothly transition to an effective closing set or play?

40. Try to have individual conferences with each player at least twice a month. Put the tape over your mouth and let them talk, vent, etc.

41. A team gathering (dinner, bowling, movie) once a month or more is a good idea.

42. Is your team still winning after losses? The answer to this question should lie in your philosophy for coaching. John Wooden's books are a great starting point for young coaches, no matter what sport.

43. Always be on time. Tolerate no tardiness.

44. Be tougher, yet positive on your best players; go easier and be more supportive on the less skilled. Yet another form of differentiated instruction in the athletic arena.

45. Avoid at all costs the *IWCS* illness. *If* we only- *would* that have not happened-*could* have done it-*should* have done it. The *If em-Would've-Could a-Should a* disease shortens life spans, raises blood pressure to heights unknown to physicians, promotes all kinds of excuses, and leads to more *IWCS*. As Yoda states in *Star Wars*, "Luke, *do*. There is no try." Jedi knights should know, would you not agree?

46. Shot selection is an individual discussion to have with every player. Enforce the results of this discussion. This aspect is a necessary part of defining roles for players (see #34).

47. The three most important statistics: rebound differential (Can your team average a minimum of eight offensive rebounds a game and double that for defensive), free throw differential (Does your team make more free throws than your opponent attempts?), and turnover differential (Can your team average fewer than 12 turnovers per game?). What are the three key statistics in your sport?

48. The skill of screening has become as neglected as sound passing. Teach the ball handler to wait until the screener has set his feet. Teach the screener to aim the middle of his body toward the near shoulder of the man he is screening. For execution of this fundamental, the screener has to welcome body contact and roll to the basket upon impact. Teach the roller to slide his feet, avoiding running. The sliding of feet on the roll helps the roller to catch any pass with better balance. Teach players how to accept screens as well as to set them.

49. A hard cut is as good as an effective pick.

50. When running sprints, do the players touch every necessary line? Line awareness is important in the game. Furthermore, stopwatches do not lie. Maintain and enforce a baseline time for completing sprints, one for guards and one for forwards.

51. Yes, coaches, you can evaluate *heart*.

    H=hustle for loose balls

    E=enthusiasm for positive verbal and nonverbal communication on the floor, especially on defense

    A=attitude toward everyone in the program

    R=relentlessness of effort and attendance during season *and* off-season

    T=toughness: drawing charges, rebounding in a crowd on offense, finding and blocking a body out on defense, being able to lock down the dribble-drive. Jay Bilas, the college basketball analyst on ESPN, wrote a thorough article defining toughness in basketball. (See Appendix C.)

52. Use a majority of bounce passes against zones to inside players. These passes are rarely deflected. Instead of teaching only plays or sets vs. zones, begin instruction of zone offense by teaching the key *concepts*: inside-out passing, dribbling into gaps, crashing offensive boards, moving the ball from side to side, establishing sufficient patience. Any zone offense worth its salt will rely on those principles.

53. Good coaches learn as much as the players. I once heard the following statement from one of the guest speakers at a summer basketball camp I worked, "Campers, you will leave camp a worse player from when you started on Sunday." At first this did not make sense. Then the speaker clarified, "You will be trying to apply all the tips these coaches give you and you will make more mistakes. After you go home and steadily work on those tips, your game will improve." I believe the same mantra can be applied to teaching and coaching. Students apply the lessons and at times, that can be a struggle. Months later, they acknowledge what they learned in a particular class. What they learned came from who the teacher was, not necessarily the curriculum. Moral of this tip…working camps beats sitting at clinics.

54. GREAT PLAYERS...

- have the ability to focus, no matter what the conditions.

- ask questions and are always willing to learn–nothing from the coach is beneath him or her.

- want to do the work everyday.

- make the work the star.

- go every bit as hard in practices as they do in games.

- know the little things separate them from the rest of the players; thus, they pay great attention to details.

- mistrust players who do not work hard.

- want to hear the truth.

- are committed to all aspects of the game: skills, body, training, conditioning, *everything*.

- hold themselves personally responsible and avoid blaming others for shortcomings.

- despise losing.

- understand that they need great teammates. They appreciate team basketball and are the first to acknowledge everyone on the team.

55. The first two or three weeks of a season are similar to the first few minutes of classes. Students and players will test teachers and coaches to detect their instructors' mettle, resolve, and enforcement of the particular culture. Conveying credibility during these days qualifies the teacher-coach and promotes a better morale that will sustain throughout the year.

56. A word about officials...the less you talk to them, the more they will listen to you. I wish I had realized that notion 40 years ago.

57. Lectures dull the brain; interactive lectures engage. Speak not for more than ten minutes to your players; then interact, drill, discuss, allow students the control. Control extends to the boundary of effort. I have always maintained that I, as head coach, determined effort on the part of each player. Human nature being what it is, people will slack off when they have the opportunity. If I told a player he was not providing enough effort, he simply wasn't. I provided the reasons for my judgment; then it was up to the player to provide the cure. Rarely did I compromise this judgment.

58. Whatever you do, do not listen to faculty who downplay your program, but do not ignore them. There will be a few. Invite them to a game or two; stay positive about your players and about yourself, especially in a losing streak. It is amazing how quick word-of-mouth can spread. During rough years, I said as little as possible. During winning seasons, I said even less, except to the media. I let the players and the teamwork do the talking.

59. Some statements to discuss with staff and players at meetings:

   • "Players don't care how much you know until they know how much you care."

   • "Remember you are coaching someone else's son/daughter."

   • "Are you coaching to make a living or coaching to make a difference?"

   • "An army of deer led by a lion will defeat an army of lions led by a deer."

   • "Never complain about something you allow."

   • "Two are better than one when two act as one."

   • "Are you afraid to look bad?"

   • "Listening is never casual" (Russell 55).

   • "If you cannot listen, you cannot win."

60. The GRAND SLAM for big men:

    - score inside,

    - score off offensive rebounds,

    - run the floor to score (second shots, early post, cuts to hole in fastbreak situations for early inside position, etc.),

    - score off effective and tough screens.

    There is always a way for the big man to be involved. Bottom line: for a post player, no rebounding is a *bad* night. Rebounding is passion and a constant way for any player, much less the postmen, to contribute. Rebounding determines a team's control of a game. *Note*: if you have a good big man, get him the ball one out of every three times down the floor. If the big loses touch with the ball, he will stop playing. They are spoiled that way; I should know.

    In addition, post players should have one solid move to the baseline and one counter to the middle. A basic dictum of good post players is to realize that the closer they are to the basket, the slower they should play.

61. One commandment: Judge not by a player's physical size, especially during freshman tryouts. Check players' shoe sizes and, if possible, the heights of the parents. Bonus commandment: Underestimate not the freshman B players, especially the uncoordinated big kids. A couple will come back to school in the fall for their sophomore year having grown 3 or 4 inches!

62. Shooting form must be taught, no matter what the skill set of the player. At Lincoln-Way East, the acronym was B.E.E.F.: balance, eyes, elbow, follow-through. I wonder how thoroughly shooting form is taught and emphasized by coaches at all levels today?

63. When guarding the ball, players must be taught correct defense sliding; the outside foot lifts and slides before the inside foot. So many players have no understanding of this essential fundamental. When players do this slide incorrectly, fouls result.

64. Fouls are committed three to five seconds before the actual whistle sounds.

65. Teach and talk more after winning; talk less after losing.

66. The use of video. Instrumental for team improvement, but watching an entire game has its weakness: players' attention span. Prepare certain segments for key moments for winning or losing the game. If filming a nonconference game, try this idea: spend a certain amount of minutes following one player at a time. This tactic can be a very good learning tool for the respective player. Seeing what players do when off the ball or when on defense can illustrate the type of habits that player possesses.

67. Just an idea...each week or month players vote for best hustler, most inspirational player, best rebounder, etc. Those players are awarded a t-shirt with that title; they wear that t-short for the duration you determine before you vote again (every two weeks?). Occasionally, ask players to vote for the *hardest worker* and the *best player*. Usually, those two results are not identical. Great discussions can result.

68. There is a major difference between being a coach and being a spectator on the bench. Always try to have a *feel* for the game. With that feel, a coach understands what is happening in the game and what needs to be done to improve the play at the right time. Being a cheerleader for the players removes the coach from a clear perspective of what is needed at the time to change momentum in one's favor.

I recommend that any young, aspiring basketball coach not begin his/her career in a public high school. Begin at the earliest level possible, grade school. If unmarried, do both. This start will push you to develop your ability to teach the game to players who have few fundamentals or little discipline. This start will push you to determine how badly you want to coach and that nothing will be easy in this career. In a way, coach and player both start at ground zero.

69. What better way to decrease players' sense of entitlement than involving them in a couple of community projects. Groups such as needy families at Christmas time, soup kitchens, clothing drives, litter pickups on weekends are all worthy ventures for coaches to enlist their players' help and spirit of volunteerism. These activities are incredible ways to foster more team unity and unselfishness.

70. Do you know the five principles of balance? These concepts were one of the first things I learned as a coach in the 70s. I taught them religiously to players in every attempt to avoid turnovers, the Public Enemy #1 of victory. Here they are:

    • middle stance of legs and trunk (not too high, not too low)

    • legs are just outside of the shoulders with a wide base instead of a narrow one

    • head splits the distance between the legs

    • weight is put on the inside of the thighs and the balls of the feet

    • chin is parallel to the floor-one of the most essential concepts of the five

71. Discuss your school's summer camps with the other sports' coaches for times and days together. Keep off each other's toes so that you do not force students to have to decide which camp to attend. If a student does have to make that decision, let him or her make it without any repercussions in terms of making the team in the fall. Those students will either make it or not depending on their skills and attitude.

72. Basketball coaches, play much more 3 on 3 than 5 on 5 during summer camps. 3 on 3, shooting, offensive fundamentals, and 1 on 1 should be the staples of all camps and each of those methods should be preceded by instruction and/or a certain focus. Teaching the game through breakdowns such as 3 on 3 reinforce coaches' credibility that they are teachers first. 3 on 3 isolates players more clearly. Coaches can evaluate players far more easily when they touch the

ball more often and reveal players' instincts for passing correctly and their ability to move without the ball. If you coach a different sport, what essential concepts would you isolate for drill work?

73. Other than a t-shirt, no trophies should be distributed; haven't we heard enough about the disease of trophy saturation? Plaques and trophies collect dust and are quite meaningless in the big picture. They supply some short-term motivation, but become as significant as last month's news over the long haul. The award is making the team in the fall. How about awarding a new basketball or a t-shirt for program promotion to a contest winner or to the camper with the best attitude?

74. Players should be required to keep personal notebooks on a daily basis that record goals and reflection, along with shot charts. Summer is about individual progress, not team finishes. No one remembers what a team did in the summer; it's the winter that counts. If individuals improve and the talent is there, the team will flourish.

75. Keep track of players' academic progress. Discuss grades with each player once a month at the very least. When I was a head coach, at the start of the basketball season, I would put a list of every player's name on one sheet (listed by year) into every faculty member's mailbox. I wanted the faculty to know who played on their school's team, and yes, wanted to know if there were any issues in the classroom with either the players' work ethic or behavior. I would communicate this action to the program the day after I put the list into teachers' mailboxes. Overall, I was pleased I did this action. Most teachers appreciated knowing those athletes and would come to me if the need arose. I would then have some feedback for the player when we discussed grades. If the issue was disrespect or a failing grade, I tried to drop what I was doing to find the player at an appropriate time. I had every player's class schedule with me at all times. I took the teacher's side in 99% of the cases. My players knew they had to toe the line in school. After all, I was the one who determined playing time and I was most careful to treat each player equally, whether a starter or the twelfth man.

76. Name the team sport: volleyball, baseball, basketball, football, etc. I maintain if any team cannot defend well, there is no real team, and I care little for how many points per game a team might score. I realize teams have to be able to put points on the board, but the esprit de corps of any winning team, and certainly a championship team, is team defense. Offense will have nights both good and mediocre; team defense cannot have off nights. Off nights on defense is non-negotiable. In basketball team defense begins with guarding the basketball and ends with the defensive rebound. I expressed a core belief to my teams: *No shot, Bad shot, One shot* for emphasis on every defensive possession. Team defense is not hard to teach, but it is challenging to sell and challenging to sustain. Once any team believes in its defense, enjoyment and winning follow.

77. Whatever peaks and valleys a particular season might hold for you and your team(s), try to keep in mind you are never as good as on your best days and never as bad as on your worst ones. You are somewhere in the middle. Find that middle and improve from there.

If you follow all these steps within your own creativity, things still might not work out. As Don McGee, the great high school coach at Wheaton Central High School in Wheaton, Illinois in the 1980s, said, "The degree of players' mental toughness is in direct correlation to the quickness of their discouragement."

So, coaches, take some time to evaluate the following questions:

A. What is your degree of mental toughness? Give some examples where you exhibited mental toughness or the lack of it?

B. From the aforementioned list, select the ones you want to improve the most in any leadership capacity you have at the moment.

C. Note a few reflections in the space below. What are <u>three</u> big ideas from the list you will apply?

The BBC-Bonuses for Basketball Coaches

Want a more fundamentally sound team? Here are ten situations/skills for players to avoid and for coaches to emphasize during practices. These ten items constitute my ten pet peeves (in no particular order) as a basketball coach.

1. giving up the baseline on defense

2. no blocking out on opponent's missed free throws or not blocking out at all

3. driving baseline and picking up the dribble, instead of pulling it back out

4. fouling a jump shooter

5. players who have all kinds of energy on offense, but can't sprint back on defense

6. immediate dribbling upon the catch (there are some exceptions to this one)

7. shooting too early (with more than five or six seconds left) at end of quarters, halves, or games

8. lack of body contact on screens

9. leaving the feet to pass, especially not knowing to whom to pass

10. for point guards: not knowing the score, the situation, and/or the time

FOSTER AND NURTURE

Coaches constantly foster habits. I preached to my teams that one time is a mistake, and two times a habit. Players who repeat the same mistakes signals both a lack of commitment from the player and a lack of sound teaching by the coach. Applying this tenet accelerates the growth in a team. To some, this concept may seem harsh and impatient. I came to discover that "impatient patience" should belong in every coach's philosophy. Impatient patience delivers constant communication between players and coach that improvement is required every day. Improvement stems from sound practice habits. Players and teams blossom from those habits through the *correct* repetition of fundamentals. Please notice the descriptor *correct*. If coaches allow players to perform modes of practice incorrectly, coaches only have themselves to blame for poor game performances. A coach must explain this form of coaching to the players and go one step ahead, a step any good teacher would provide: show each player what he needs to improve, the steps necessary to gain confidence, and the accountability if the player does not respond. Accountability might be all forms of interaction and relationship: conferences, video, extra practice, recognition when a player fixes the problem, extra running. Coaches have to know what buttons to push for each player. Fostering good habits requires the three steps for mental toughness:

1. Know the problem.

2. Know the way(s) to fix the problem.

3. *Fix it.*

The third step provides the difference between the winners in a program and the whiners. Welcoming, but not accepting, errors and providing the insights and the knowledge to correct those errors define good programs, ever-improving players, and quality coaches. The best teams find the ways to fix their own shortcomings and don't waste much time in doing so.

Point players in the right directions for models of positive habits. Manage and control the models to watch for aspiring basketball players. Here are my top suggestions from professional players, both current and retired:

- For shooting and off the ball screening: Stephen Curry or Klay Thompson (Golden State Warriors)

- For rebounding: Dennis Rodman (Detroit Pistons, Chicago Bulls)

- For post moves: Kevin McHale (Boston Celtics)

- For defense and toughness: Jerry Sloan (Chicago Bulls)

- For an all-round game: Michael Jordan (Chicago Bulls)

- For emotional temperament: Kawhi Leonard (San Antonio Spurs)

- For poise, belief in a system: Tim Duncan (San Antonio Spurs)

- For point guard play: Magic Johnson (Los Angeles Lakers), Tony Parker (San Antonio Spurs), or John Stockton (Utah Jazz)

- For basketball IQ and court presence: Larry Bird (Boston Celtics)

- For best, young fundamental specialist: Gordon Hayward (Utah Jazz)

YOUR TURN

If you coach a different sport, make your own list here.

POSITION	SKILL TO EMULATE

VARY

Variety of methodology trickles down to coaching, for there is nothing worse at practices than boredom. When I was devising practices each night for the next day and/or week, I was mindful to employ a variety of competition and drills, so that players would never be bored. I rarely wrote the same practice plan two days in a row or the same plan for the same day week after week. Boys need variety. My goals for practices remained quite similar, but my methods for attaining those goals had plenty of variance. Some of that variance depended upon the upcoming opponent. For example, if we were practicing half-court defense and the opponent had a very good post player, we might work on a swarming, double-team defense once that player caught the ball. The next opponent might need a different form of defense. All practices had one thing which the classroom does not contain-kinetic energy. For boys that energy commands their attention. Here are some other examples of the variety I tried to employ:

- 3 on 3—one day the emphasis might be on offense where the scoring team keeps the ball. The next day or situation would be defensive play where the scoring team became the defense and win that game according to the amount of stops. I limited the amount of dribbles each offensive player would have (three at most).

- Bring the team together before each 5 on 5 scrimmage to emphasize what is to be accomplished. These talks never totaled more than three minutes. Ask the team to reflect after each one about the level of performance or achievement of the emphasis. This assessment is relative to the classroom where students might use a learning log at the end of activities to evaluate their understanding of the lesson's goal. For the coach these talks targeted the strategies we would employ against the next opponent.

- 1 on 1—off a pass one time where the offensive player has to free himself. The next would be from half court with the offensive player having only four dribbles to get a shot. Another form might be rapid-fire cutthroat with three players. In most games the offensive player cannot start his play from the same spot on the court on each possession.

- Shooting drills were rarely the same two days in a row, but I relied on the same shooting drills in order to capture player efficiency running those drills. Almost all shooting drills are charted so field goal percentage is known. If a player does not know his shooting percentage, how would he know if he was improving form week to week?

- At times during January and February weekends, we played volleyball or swam together for short durations, just to break up the routine a bit and supply some creativity and fun.

- Players kept a season-long notebook, preferably a three-ring spiral for handouts, containing reflections, weekly goals, game goals, and self-evaluations. I also provided players with one basketball article per week for more knowledge or information about the game, its history, etc. Sometimes I asked each player to bring in an article of interest.

PERSEVERE (MEMOIR)

82-22...the score of the first conference basketball game I coached for my sophomore squad at Quigley-North in 1973. My team owned the 22. The game was at St. Benedict High School on Chicago's northwest side, a mismatch from the start. St. Benedict's sophomores, the Bengals, overpowered us inside, ran the ball whenever they desired, and laughed at us once they were up by 40.

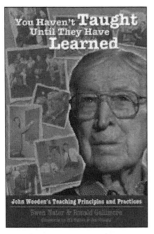

There were few moments in my coaching career where I needed the concept to *teach more on the court; coach more in the classroom*, and I was still thirty-five years away from hearing it. As a rookie coach, I perceived my team was fired up and ready to play. They were yelling to each other before the game, so the emotion and enthusiasm were present for a good effort. So I thought; educated guessing has to belong in any coach's job description. We had practiced well, and is not practice a good indicator of game readiness? That game proved the efficacy of the following statement, the cover of the book written by Swen Nater, who played for Coach John Wooden at UCLA, *You Haven't Taught Until They Have Learned.*

After the humiliation, I stood staring at a wall outside the stone-silent locker room. Bill Schaefer, my varsity coach, just looked at me as I stood outside the locker room and said, "Welcome to coaching." Painfully obvious to me were the facts: we were not physical enough, we did not apply the fundamentals enough; we were not tough enough to stand up to an opponent's arrogance and bravado. Once I stopped moping and gathered sufficient composure, I walked into the locker room, and told the players, "You might think I am nuts, but I believe we can beat that team." Nuts being a given, something inside told me that I had gutsy kids who would not give up. I told the players to shower and dress. That was all I said, remembering the words of Al McGuire: "You can teach better after wins; keep the talk brief after losses because you teach through winning. The players don't listen after losses." There was no one to blame except myself; it was up to me to improve my teaching methods on the court. We had another crack against St. Benedict's in a February home game, a date my mind ingrained. I would use that future game to gauge the effectiveness of my coaching; I had two months to prepare them, day by day, week by week, game by game.

As the season wore on, we were a .500 team but the scales were tipping in our favor. I scrutinized my practice plans and devised more competitive drills and scrimmages. Accountability was a premium. The players enjoyed practices and were extremely competitive in games, many of which were against teams with greater talent, a challenge I confronted through the majority of my career. We were improving our instincts, our team play, and our ability to compete in certain games devoid of any semblance of offensive execution and scoring. February loomed. I had not spoken one word about the St. Benedict game. We focused on the moment, even though I was not acutely realizing exactly what I was doing. As a coach you constantly gauge the collective temperature of your team, and I felt the collective confidence rising.

At the beginning of February, two weeks before we played St. Benedict, on the advice of Schaefer, I started to build in the plan for that game. We had one game to play the Friday before. It was then that I started to discuss St. Benedict and what I had in mind. At that point I was looking at a team with renewed confidence. Our guards were handling pressure well, a key focus for beating Goliath. We were shooting free throws well, a huge asset for the plan I wanted to install. The idea was to run some delay game on most half-court possessions, make the Bengals impatient, hoping they gamble and foul. With good shot selection off the delays, we hoped to take them by surprise. Only four players had the collective green light to take the majority of shots. Those shots had to go in. I was also hoping they would be taking us lightly. Who could blame them?

The locker room before warmup resembled the scene before the state final in Hoosiers, the delicious basketball film starring Gene Hackman. Tense, yet focused. Anxious, but alert. I talked about our improvement since that first conference game and gave reasons why we would be in a position to win. I mentioned it did not matter what they did; we had to run our plan and stay together. Then, we would let the chips fall where they might. I also recalled what I said to them after the first crushing loss, "You might think I am nuts, but I believe we can beat that team." That seemed to relax the players. Michael, our quiet leader who rarely spoke, smiled. I asked them, "Do you believe?" We huddled, said our prayer like good Catholic school seminarians, and sprinted onto the court. As I looked in the mirror before taking the court, I thought of Coach Schaefer's famous words, "It's in the hands of the basketball gods now."

The gods were smiling that day. We beat St. Benedict 40-31, making 80% of our foul shots, making twice as many free throws as St. Benedict attempted. Our delays caught them off guard, forcing them out of fastbreaks and into stagnant half-court basketball. We forced them into anxious decisions and ball handling miscues, and took them out of their arrogance with tough rebounding. We played stifling, half-court defense without needless fouls. Two different St. Ben's players got one technical foul each for arguing with the officials. With a minute left and Quigley up by ten, I was still nervous, still sweating. My captain came over during a freethrow and stared at me as I was barking out all kinds of nonsense. He interrupted with five more words than he had spoken the entire season, "Coach, relax, we got them!" I did not say another word, just enjoyed the realization that they had learned because I had finally taught. It was one of the most joyous coaching experiences I had in 42 years on the sidelines.

Through moments like this, the coaching and the teaching worlds were melding into one entity. They partner in forming the identity and the resilience of a teacher-coach. Those teachers who have never coached will find it difficult to understand that special relationship. Where classroom teachers can close the door and conduct their lessons, coaches have no door; their works of art are observed by plenty of bleacher assistants who are all too ready to offer suggestions for improvement. Where classroom teachers are observed once or twice a year, coaches have as many final exams as games on their schedules. On the other hand, both the compassion and the intensity of coaching filter into classroom instruction. Teachers want their students to learn the material; they can take a student aside and attempt to find the right button to push; they can become the master motivators many coaches believe they might be. All in all, the two ingredients both teachers and coaches must collect and use on a daily basis are *relentlessness* and *perseverance*. You think I needed both those qualities after losing 82-22 in the days and weeks ahead leading to the rematch? In time I realized I was learning these traits due to my quick temper and my youthful desire to improve everything and everyone by the next day, that *impatient-patience*. Relentlessness and perseverance are what teachers and coaches need for any arena of student engagement. Temper each with the right dose of patience and there lies a winning formula. The rest will come in its own time, as long as the owner remains curious about knowledge.

EXPLORE

I would be remiss if I did not acknowledge one of the more insightful and gifted teachers in Illinois. In his book *Teaching From the Deep End*, Golden Apple President Dominic Belmonte, my English chairman at York High School from 1989-1996, explains an essential activity for discovering self-exploration. In Chapter 6 in that book, Dom describes the importance for teachers to ponder and explain their educational philosophy. He states:

> *This is truly the key to everything—why are you up there? What is your reason for teaching? This challenge faces new teachers soon after September hellos fade into October obstacles, November nuisances, or December dilemmas. Your reliance on work sheets and your struggles with uncomfortable silences and hesitations and ebbing confidence are all the result of too little reflection on the essential question: Why are you up there?" (35)*

Dom continues to detail some of the steps for personal identification of a philosophy. Teaching tenets, affirmations of one's belief system, *give your teaching purpose and meaning. Without purpose and meaning, you are marking time and time will become your enemy* (36). He recommends that every teacher sit down and write personal tenets on one sheet of paper. I maintain that there are few better techniques for classroom management than teachers knowing why they are teaching. When teachers value their own importance and meaning, they model reliable practices. They then empower students to follow their leads.

This principle holds true in any organization. What do the CEOs or presidents of companies stand for and how do they communicate that message to employees? Where would good coaches be without a belief in their understanding of what they hold dear and what they want to accomplish with a certain team? On a personal level, I can say that I had a scattered idea of my beliefs when I first took over a varsity program in 1976. Of course, I knew certain things: we will play man-to-man defense; we will be unselfish; we will work hard, etc. However, I did not yet know myself or the standards I desired to instill in each player. How might I react to the selfish player, to the limited player, to the benchwarmers? How should I develop each player? How would my coaching influence players beyond the court? I never really thought about the values that are most necessary in coaching or teaching, patience being a prime example. Many questions, with few answers. Experience becomes the watery benchmark and into that pool every coach and teacher must dive. Belmonte's words were highly accurate when he comments, *you are marking time and time will become your enemy* (37). This feeling was exactly mine in that disastrous basketball year of 1977 when I nearly had a nervous breakdown coaching the varsity. There is no worse feeling as a coach or a teacher when you are looking at the clock more than at your students or players.

One of my best personal experiences for this tip is my seven-year journey as the cross country coach at Immaculate Conception. My athletic director called me into his office in early August of 1977. He mentioned that he needed a cross country coach and he wanted me to assume that duty. I sat stunned. I had never run cross country, except for the ten-mile march of death via Coach Schaefer, nor did I have any inkling about coaching it. He wouldn't hear it. "Tom, you can teach, so you can do this. Read up on it and do it." As if coaching was that easy. Talk about feeling unprepared and untried, reminiscent of soldiers confronted with a field of land mines. Tryouts were in one week. I had no idea who the runners were or who would try out. I sped to Elmhurst Public Library and found York High School's Joe Newton's famous book, *The Long Green Line*. Newton was the long-time successful distance coach at the neighborhood public school. I read the book in one night, consumed by the detail and the dedication, by his love for his runners, and by his practice regime.

Seven runners, five boys and two girls, came out for the squad. Each one survived a coach who learned along the way. We had one runner who made it downstate. He set a prime example for the younger runners. We grew into a powerhouse, capturing third place in the state in 1979. Another young winner developed, one of the most mentally tough athletes I have ever had the pleasure to coach in any sport, who won the state title in 1980 and finished second as a senior in 1981. In 1982 we finished in fifth place in state. Coaching cross country helped me to define why I taught. Plus, coaching enabled me to take methods from that particular arena into the classroom.

With their work capacity and capacity for generosity, cross country runners floored me. I marveled at kids who ran all those miles just to throw up at the finish. Runners have such a unique mentality. They loved running in the rain and through mud puddles; they would dogpile each other after a team victory or an advancement to state, their minds and hearts were always with their teammates; they did not care about popularity and were the athletes with the highest degrees of self-respect. I wished at times for heart transplants from those athletes to a few of the basketball players. Moreover, their willingness to sacrifice themselves for a greater good was astonishing. The aforementioned state champion was one such example. He came out for the team after school in his freshman year. He showed up to East End Park wearing baseball spikes. When I questioned that, he responded, "I thought spikes were needed when you run." He ran the entire workout, but during the last part, he left the group, went off to the side, and proceeded to expel the Caesar salad he had consumed right before practice. After that episode, he promptly rejoined the group and finished the run, no questions asked. That moment was when I knew he had that special something that separates some athletes from the thoroughbreds. He thrived on hard practices. Never possessing great speed for finishing kicks, he would run a steady first mile, demolish the opposition in the second, and just drive himself throughout the third. With 100 yards remaining, he typically had built up an insurmountable lead on his pursuers and would just be able to hold off any last-second challengers. That was his exact formula when he beat his rival from Cornell High School in the Class A state final in Peoria in 1980.

Plenty of hardy souls helped me discover why I taught and why I coached. All the runners I coached during those seven years were the core of one of my tenets when I decided to write them down: *Relentlessness is the heart of a superior teacher; I never give up on anyone.* When I saw and nurtured what everyday, skinny, unnoticeable teenagers could accomplish when they delivered heart and desire, how could I do any different?

The cross country experience prompted many a personal tenet I practice to this day, even in retirement. Here are a few more examples of my own:

- Start the car, don't over pump the accelerator; press the gas, apply the brakes when necessary, then carefully steer. Observe the scenery astutely.

- Strive for excellence, not perfection.

- The most essential vocabulary assignment: use please, thank you, and excuse me whenever appropriate.

- Look at both kids and colleagues with your eyes, your brain, and your heart. One of those assets will deliver what you need.

We sleep in the bed we make, so now it is your turn. Research to discover the compelling reasons you teach and coach with a sheet of paper and pen in front of you. *Why do you what you do?* Make that list. Check it twice. Then sleep in your tenet bed. Don't forget to change the sheets with annual reflection. Early August might prove to be a good time for evaluating those tenets.

I included teaching tenets in this section for coaches to reinforce a central theme in this book: *teaching is coaching and coaching is teaching.* Consider a list for both classroom teaching and for coaching, or make the list and see the ones that crossover. However you make your list, write down what you truly are and what you stand for day in and day out as a teacher and/or coach.

YOUR TURN

My Teaching Tenets:

INSPIRE

Effective language arts curriculum will include readings from the ancient Greeks, whether it is mythology, philosophy, the *Odyssey*, or the *Iliad*. In my experience I related to students the concept of hubris, false pride, within the theme of reasons for a man's downfall from a pinnacle of success. One concept that escaped my clutches was that of thumos, the desire for recognition or for eternal fame. In his book *The Social Animal: the Hidden Sources of Love, Character, and Achievement*, David Brooks explains this concept relative to a fictional teenager named Harold as he attempts to find a place in the world. In his attempt to write a research paper for his course, Harold discovers:

> *...he had been surrounded by people with a set of socially approved motivations: to make money, to get good grades, to get into a good college. But none of those really explained why Harold did what he did, or why the Greeks heroes did what they did...Harold's culture didn't really have a word for that desire, but this Greek word (thumos) helped explain Harold to himself. (96)*

Brooks continues to explain that Harold's penchant for imagining himself in winning, glorifying situations was the result of thumos which underscores the other drives for success and money (97). My own instruction of the Transcendentalism era in American literature was part of trying to help students understand that they were not the centers of the universe as many young people so think. A core tenet of this philosophy maintains that God, man, and nature are all a part of a higher union, a goal, perhaps, for people to strive to find a place where significance, not material success, would equal what the Greeks desired and what the excellent basketball coach John Wooden described through his life and in his books.

Ever read the books by Coach John Wooden, the significant basketball coach at UCLA from 1948-1975 or listen to his talks? Wooden started as a high school English teacher and basketball coach in Indiana. He is recognized today as one of the finest teachers who ever lived. For fourteen years he worked on his own definition of success, a definition inspiring people today. Wooden defined success as *the peace of mind attained only through self-satisfaction in knowing you made the effort to do the best of what you're capable of doing.* Wooden's definition surfaces through his dissatisfaction with the pursuit of materialism as the measure of a person's success. It stands to reason that few people at death's door wonder why their golf handicap was not lower or why their annual salary was not higher.

Success is finding the *significance* in one's life, the result of which is the peace of mind Wooden believes or the thumos the Greeks admired. That level of self-achievement continues to be one of the toughest things for anyone to find. On a personal level, my significance began with a life of service in teaching; that life of service was born in my early desire to become a priest. While in college, I determined that if I was not going to offer my life to the priesthood, teaching was the next best form of service. Teachers are some of the most selfless, humble people, a premise reinforced by the humble, selfless faculty I worked with throughout 42 years. My world of significance enlarged when I met and married my wife Susan, a teacher herself. She taught me, and daily teaches me, the continuation of service, especially when we became parents. Until that time, I did not really understand what sacrifice meant on a more global scale. Now, I believe that any form of significance comes with legacy and influence. Our legacy exists in our two sons, John and Tim. They will carry our spirit and our character after Susan and I are gone. In any case, my wife and I imparted some degree of legacy to the students we have instructed. We will never know the true impact on our protégés, but we know we have had some effect. Significance, then, embodies the *ripple effect*.

Drop a Pebble in the Water

Drop a pebble in the water:
just a splash, and it is gone;
But there's half-a-hundred ripples
Circling on and on and on,
Spreading, spreading from the center,
flowing on out to the sea.
And there is no way of telling
where the end is going to be.

Drop a pebble in the water:
in a minute you forget,
But there's little waves a-flowing,
and there's ripples circling yet,
And those little waves a-flowing

to a great big wave have grown;
You've disturbed a mighty river
just by dropping in a stone.

Drop an unkind word, or careless:
in a minute it is gone;
But there's half-a-hundred ripples
circling on and on and on.
They keep spreading, spreading, spreading
from the center as they go,
And there is no way to stop them,
once you've started them to flow.

Drop an unkind word, or careless:
in a minute you forget;
But there's little waves a-flowing,
and there's ripples circling yet,
And perhaps in some sad heart
a mighty wave of tears you've stirred,
And disturbed a life was happy
ere you dropped that unkind word.

Drop a word of cheer and kindness:
just a flash and it is gone;
But there's half-a-hundred ripples
circling on and on and on,
Bearing hope and joy and comfort
on each splashing, dashing wave
Till you wouldn't believe the volume
of the one kind word you gave.

Drop a word of cheer and kindness:
in a minute you forget;
But there's gladness still a-swelling,
and there's joy circling yet,
And you've rolled a wave of comfort
whose sweet music can be heard
Over miles and miles of water
just by dropping one kind word.

~By James W. Foley~

YOUR TURN

Robert Fulgham, in his best-selling book *Everything I Need to Know I Learned in Kindergarten,* writes, "Leave everything in better shape than you found it." I suggest we use this as a starting point for what significance implies as I turn the spotlight on people from various occupations who answered my request to respond to the question, What or how do you make your life significant? Before you read a sampling of the responses, please take the time to write down your response to that question in the space below:

SECTION 4

THE END RESULT

IN THE BOOK *BUSH AT WAR*, author Bob Woodward recounts a war meeting President George W. Bush held about one month after 9/11. Bush was preparing a speech to the nation that would alert the country that the United States had begun attacking al Qaeda and Taliban sites in Afghanistan. He stated,

> *I know many Americans feel fear today,' as he outlined the preparations the government had taken. He addressed the military, 'Your mission is defined; your objectives are clear; your goal is just; you have my full confidence; and you will have every tool you need to carry out your duty.' He then read a letter he had received from a fourth grade girl whose father was in the military. She had written, "As much as I don't want my dad to fight, I'm willing to give him to you.' (209)*

Sometimes the voices with the most clarity come from our children. Talk about significance! Her nineteen words empower the self-sacrifice, the generosity, the courage, the commitment, and the simplicity that true significance contains.

What is the *end result* of stopping the whining and starting the winning? We are all interested in results and we want those results yesterday, desiring immediate satisfaction. Fortunately, we can't detect the desired gains overnight. I say *fortunately* because those gains are too precious, too arduous, too satisfying to be discovered in the blink of an eye. They take time and effort; they take less blaming, less expecting, and more doing. They take selflessness. Thus, I asked a collection of people from a variety of professions and age groups to describe the significance in their lives. As you ponder their responses, please notice the paucity of blame or whining and the plethora of self-actualization and individual responsibility.

Elizabeth Hauck
HR Professional

As both mother, friend, HR Professional, I measure quality of my life by having a positive impact on other's lives. To be a resource, a mentor, an example, to hear things like "thank you for all your help" and have the person actually mean it. That brings me feelings of worth, success, etc.

Carl Dumele
Owner of the Aeromotive Company in Elgin, Illinois

For me, it's self awareness. I cherish everyday I have among most of my fellow man. Recognizing a given situation and placing it into perspective or priority has always been good to me. In turn, I'm happy. I enjoy sharing that feeling with others. When I search even deeper, I realize it is my faith that opens my heart and mind, making me aware of our limited time here on earth. In turn, making my life more significant.

Linda Miserendino
Housewife and Mother of Two Boys

My life is significant because I brought into the world two beautiful sons who will continue to grow and teach (they are teachers) our youth of America the importance of life. I hope with our teachings of love and family, they will have children and teach them the importance of a good and loving life.

Pat Sullivan (retired)
Providence High School Basketball Coach, Assistant to the President and Head Men's Basketball Coach at the University of St. Francis in Joliet, Illinois:

I think that helping one student through a difficult time in his/

her life makes an educator's life significant. Albert Einstein's statement says it all for teachers and coaches, 'I know no reason why we are here except to help others.'

Matt Gross
English Teacher at Ottawa High School (Ottawa, IL)

At school, I am significant because I do my best to model good behavior every day for my students. My behavior hopefully helps establish a pattern of how to live a productive, positive life. Another area is by giving. Whether I was donating my blood or donating food and/or clothing to Goodwill or the needy, I felt like I was playing a significant role in someone else's life. In providing my kids with the tools necessary to be successful, I am significant also. I think that later in life, when my kids are grown, I will feel like I lived a significant life that was very meaningful to them.

Dan Galligan
English Teacher and Baseball Coach
(Lincoln-Way East High School in Frankfort, IL)

To me being significant is about influence. The people and events that have shaped my life and influenced me are significant. As a teacher, coach, and parent, my goal is to be influential in the right way. If kids I've taught or coached or eventually my own children can say I was the right type of influence on them, then I believe my life will have been truly significant. That is as important or more so than more traditional definitions of success.

Brianna Korczak
English Teacher at Lincoln-Way Central High School
(Frankfort, IL)

In my life, the people I share my life with make my life significant. In my profession as a teacher, learning about the students and showing the students that their interests and lives are important to someone (me) is significant because it shows that even for one hour a day, the students know they are important to someone and that someone expects them to work and grow. An example: a challenging senior last year asked me, in front of the class, what can I do after I graduate? In response, I knew he liked sports, he liked to talk (in my class especially), he loved music, and his writing was not bad. He didn't expect me to respond, but I mentioned he could be a sports reporter, a sports broadcaster, or a deejay for a radio station. I told him communications might be a route he would want to explore. As I brought these professions up and showed him that I took an interest in him and knew what he was interested in, he had an epiphany. The significance is that I was able to provide some direction for him. That moment of respect, understanding, and hope is what makes my job significant. The students I am allowed to help grow and learn are what make my profession significant. The relationships are what makes my career significant, which is why I am in the greatest profession there is.

Karen McConnell
English Teacher at Lincoln-Way East High School (Frankfort, IL)

I look at significance as something small, something that has simple meaning, yet in the most personal and intimate way. People talk about success all the time, but real significance is something a person doesn't always talk about, doesn't always share, and doesn't ever need to define verbally.

Steve Tomczak
Owner of BodyTech Total Fitness (Mokena, IL)

I am drawn away from material things and centered more on my importance as a person. Whether or not I am living a significant life is determined, most importantly, by how I have raised my kids. Am I teaching my kids to live a life of high integrity and character and with a strong work ethic? Have I taught them to strive to live a productive life in whatever they choose to do? These factors, to me, are the biggest indicators of whether or not I had a significant life.

As a side note, being in the health club industry for the majority of my life, it has always been important to me to provide a platform for people to live healthier, happier, more productive lives. To see this happen to many people has also given a strong sense of significance in my life.

JAMES PHELAN
DISTINGUISHED PROFESSOR OF ENGLISH AT THE OHIO STATE UNIVERSITY (COLUMBUS, OH)

What makes my life significant is the effect it has on other people. First in importance are my wife, children, and grandchild. If I can be a loving, supportive, helpful husband, father, and grandfather, someone whom the others can both enjoy time with and count on in times of need, then I'm doing something significant. Second in importance are my colleagues and students. If I can connect with colleague in ways that enable us to work better and make good decisions about our teaching and research, then I'm doing something significant. If I can be an effective teacher and open students up to the riches of literature and to the rewards of thinking seriously and well about it, then I'm doing something significant. Third are the readers of my scholarship. If I can give them food for thought and help them advance their own work, I am doing something significant. In a way, scholarship is an extension of teaching. Fourth are the many authors I work with as an editor. If I can connect with them and their work and help them make it better so that other readers can connect with it, then I am doing something significant.

ROBERT J. KOWALSKI
LAW ENFORCEMENT FOR 35 YEARS, CURRENTLY CHIEF OF POLICE IN SAUK VILLAGE, IL

I attribute all my success in law enforcement to the education I received. Throughout my education I had individuals who had a significant impact on leading me in the right direction and showing me what moral character and integrity mean.

(THE LATE) BILL SCHAEFER, SR.
PHYSICAL EDUCATION, HEALTH, AND ENGLISH TEACHER AND HEAD
BASKETBALL COACH AT QUIGLEY SEMINARY NORTH, FENTON HIGH SCHOOL,
ROSARY COLLEGE, AND BAKER COLLEGE IN MICHIGAN

I think my life has been significant in the many ways that I influenced people in a positive way... everything from showing folks how to live to how to handle the dying processes and death... deaths of loved ones and of myself. I think I have made a significant difference in showing people how to handle tough times, period. I have taught my 4 kids and 11 grandkids how to lead significant, good lives, always putting others before ourselves, even if it means going to extremes.

GARY DEITELHOFF
SALES FOR THE HEALTH CARE INDUSTRY (ARLINGTON HEIGHTS, IL)

How significant is it to volunteer your time to help underprivileged children, or help pour soup for the homeless in a soup line?

How significant is it for a person to help someone who is disabled to simply get through a heavy door?

How significant is it for someone to give up much of the life they love so s/he can care for a sick loved one who may never get better?

How significant is it for someone to donate a kidney to a complete stranger, who happens to be a perfect match?

These are pretty dramatic examples of things that are very significant. The impacts of these things on the recipients/the beneficiaries are beyond measure. However, they are not quantifiable....not measureable by the numbers, and most of these significant things go completely unrecognized. No awards, no World Records, no mention in the Guinness Book of Records.

In addition, significance usually involves at least two people, one to give and the other to receive. Also, significance is rarely quantifiable, not measureable by numbers and not weighed by even the most highly accurate digital scale. The undefined level of appreciation of the person who receives it can only measure it.

There have always been awards presented by companies to celebrate the successes of their employees. The awards that come to these recipients are all well-deserved and should be recognized. I work in a sales capacity within the healthcare industry, but I did not begin my business career in sales. Initially I was in human resources. When I first entered sales as a career, I was very fortunate to work for Jim Herrmann in a small distributorship in Chicago From the very beginning, Jim advised me to treat every client in every transaction with the highest level of dignity, respect and fairness. He also trained me not to focus only on company profits, but to focus instead on whom our products would impact the most....the patients. He said that if I continued to keep the patient as the primary focus of my business dealings, not only would I be "successful" (compensation, awards, etc.) but also every patient would receive the significant benefits from state-of-the-art products. Even though we all understood the importance of turning a profit in order to keep the company in the black, Jim trained us to keep the patient as our focal point and let the profits take care of themselves....and they did! With our distributorship, I was successful, and grateful to receive the "Top Gun" award as the #1 rep in the company. I received similar awards from other companies I've worked with. Even after our distributorship was sold, and we all went in different directions with our careers, I kept Jim's advice as the cornerstone on which I would build my career, and have passed that same advice on to many other fine people I have trained over the years.

Jim Herrmann is a very smart man, but even more importantly he is one of the great human beings and leaders I have been blessed to know. He taught me that when I focus on "significance," the "successes" are not far behind.

Jerry Pius (retired)
Former Teacher and High School Principal
at Lincoln-Way High School

My goal each day when teaching and coaching was to significantly make a difference in students' lives by giving them new information, as well as leaving them with a smile via a compliment or pat on the back. As an administrator I tried to make sure those many staff members regardless of job description were appreciated. I also assigned the most troublesome and misbehaving students as my office aides during their free times or study halls, two or three a period. Besides shocking them as well as staff members, this effort was successful. The students saw me as someone who cared because I gave them responsible assignments and gained their trust and mine in theirs. This cooperation made them feel a part of the school and to this day, I still hear from some of them. They are doing well.

Jeff Keller
Math Department Chairman and Teacher,
Lincoln-Way East High School (Frankfort, IL)

I live a significant life by living God's will: thinking of others first and living by the motto JOY—Jesus, Others, You—in that order. That concept brings significance to my life. I fill the photocopier with paper until it is full even when I only use thirty sheets. I pay the bill of the person behind me in the drive-up. I volunteer at homeless shelters, etc. Significance is not in my eyes, but in the eyes of God.

John Janulis
Assistant Director of Housing and Residence Life
at St. Louis University

How do I lead a significant life? I lead by believing that people live their lives with unyielding fidelity to compassion, and are guided by an unwavering faith in the overall goodness in humanity. They trust that they are not spiritually alone, and believe in a power greater than themselves. They can dare to be vulnerable knowing that somebody will walk alongside them to pick up the pieces to make them whole. I believe that it's our collective responsibility to help make each other whole.

John Anstett
Sales Team Leader, Schneider National (Green Bay, WI)
I feel that my life is significant mostly because I live beyond the importance of just my life. In a way I am always prepared to give up everything and expect nothing in return for my family. I've always wanted to have a family of my own, so, my life is significant because I live for the people I care about most in this world-Kelly and Noah. I am able to do that because of all the great people that enabled me to do so throughout my life. Those people can be talked about in an entire book by itself but it would start and end with my incredible parents.

Barbara Kuhn
Mother of Three (Scottsdale, AZ)
Significant—Large enough to be noticed or have an effect (Merriam Webster)

In my view success is measured in various ways; significance, however, stands on its own understanding. Leading a significant life for me involves a continuum of inquiry; am I making a difference, am I doing enough? These are constant cues to attain an existent and meaningful life.

My legacy may not be large enough to be noticed but hopefully significant enough to have had an effect.

Tom McCormack
Physical Education Teacher and Head Boys' Basketball Coach, Conant High School (Hoffman Estates, IL)
As teachers and coaches, we'll never know about some our most significant influences on the people we have taught and/or coached, and that's OK.

I like to think that if they "get it" while they're actually with us, or later on in life, really doesn't matter as long as they get it at some point.

I have a former player that I actually had to let go before his senior season (who ended being a scholarship Division-1 player) that calls or comes to see me about once a month to ask for advice or just talk. I probably have more kids thank me for making the tough calls during their young lives than anything else.

To that point, the feedback that I get the most from former players 5, 10, 15, 20, and 25 years later, is how practicing on a regular basis at 5:30 in the morning affected their lives.

Even though they got used to it, it was a tough adjustment. However, many of them tell me that it had a very positive influence on many of the things in their lives, from family to work to coaching their kids, etc. I know I've told you this before, but the idea for morning practice came to me when you and I attended a Medalist clinic with John Chaney as the speaker over 30 years ago. So in a way, your taking me to that clinic is responsible for all this!

Rich Weigel (retired)
Assistant Vice President Sales & Marketing in the Logistics Industry (Lisle, IL)

"One man can make a difference in the world." It wasn't until I was much older that I learned that this phrase is very true. For example, my dad (who is 96) has 7 kids, 23 grandchildren and 15 (so far) great grandchildren. In this group, there are doctors, lawyers, accountants, engineers, teachers, social workers, etc. Imagine how many lives they have touched for the better. Imagine what a void they would have left if Dad had been killed in WW II.

On a smaller scale, I have a wonderful wife, 4 great daughters and 6 grandchildren. Before retirement, I traveled across the US, Mexico and Canada for work. I met a lot of people, made many friends and treated people as I would like to be treated. It's amazing what you can accomplish with a warm smile, firm handshake and strong ethics. In my spare time, I coached both boys' and girls' basketball, served on the local school board and volunteered for many parish activities, and taught my daughters the important things in life with the help of our Catholic schools. My wife and I have also been involved with Encounter (retreats for engaged couples) for over 35 years and touched the lives of over 700 couples.

When I retired, I wanted to do all the things I couldn't do while working. Now my daughter calls me a "wannabe social worker." So I volunteer at a few different agencies helping people with their finances, taxes, rent, utilities, transportation, etc. My wife and I also mentor families (usually single moms) that were formerly homeless. All this and our grandkids keep us really busy! But life is good! And God has blessed us in many ways including family and many friends! My motto is based on an old biblical saying: To whom much is given, much is expected. Winners don't whine; they're too busy living up to God's expectations!

John Barrett
Teacher in his 21st Year at Pleasant Plains Middle School (IL)

It is important to keep oneself humble to be significant. After winning the IESA championship in 2008, I swept the floor before each practice, not a manager, ME, the HEAD COACH. Also, recently, I was awarded a trophy in recognition for 25 years of service as a catechist, AT MASS, by the BISHOP of our diocese. At the reception following mass, I took out all the garbage to the dumpster. That action wasn›t for show. Because when I accomplish something remarkable, I attempt to remind myself ANYBODY COULD have done it, but I DID.

Bill Russell
(qtd. in Russell Rules 31):

As I have come to understand curiosity as an active, working part of my life, it has led me to some important conclusions about commitment I might not have reached otherwise. What must be done to achieve success (significance) is often something where the doer is not the direct beneficiary. This is especially true for any type of team player. Trying to figure out how something is done automatically pushes one toward commitment.

Steve Little (retired)
Physical Education Teacher and Head Boys' Basketball Coach, Lincoln-Way Central High School (New Lenox, IL):
After getting over the shock that someone you love has a life threatening illness, you pull things together. Faith, always first, family, friends and lastly, forgetting you are not the only thing that matters in our universe! As the caretaker, forget yourself. The patient and medical staff are all that matter. You cannot go overboard enough! Be a great listener and cherish the moments together. Some of the worse days are better than the best days because you are building this great bond between your loved one and the Lord. Stay in the moment: I cannot emphasize that enough. Your love for your special person will grow 100 times over, and you will always be happy and content knowing you did your best.

Matt Blackall (retired)
English Teacher and Wrestling Coach at Glenbrook North High School (Northbrook, IL):
Sometime during the first week of school every year, I would walk over to the pencil sharpener in the room and just start turning the handle. At first, the kids paid no attention. I'd say nothing and continue cranking the sharpener. Slowly, the kids quieted down as they began to wonder if they needed to go and see their counselors about getting a new teacher. Once I had everyone's attention (and concern), I'd ask him or her what I was doing. The literal minded and practical students would always answer first. They'd usually roll their eyes and say with that tone that only an adolescent can manage, "You're turning the pencil sharpener." I'd say, " No, that's not it." Or if the kid was particularly sarcastic, just "Wrong answer." The planning to

visit the counselors would ratchet up at this point. Then I would tell them that what I was doing was winding the world. That if I didn't do that every day, the world would stop turning. So my task was particularly important. Then the planning for trips to guidance became audible. Finally, I would explain to them that in reading Carl Jung, I came on a narrative of a trip he took to the American Southwest. He visited an Indian tribe there and noticed that every morning a group of elders would leave the village before dawn and go to the top of a mountain. He inquired about what they were doing, but couldn't get answers. Finally, one of the elders told him that they went to the mountaintop every morning to greet the sun. They believed that failure to carry out that task would lead to the sun not appearing. Jung reflected on the importance and significance this gave to their lives and their task. I would tell students that finding a meaning and purpose like that for your life's work and activity was invaluable. It's also a notion that I would recall throughout the school year.

Fast forward to a couple of years ago. In the mail one day I received a package from California. Inside was an old, beat up pencil sharpener with a note that said it was a flea market find. The student, Carolyn, said that she thought I might be able to use an auxiliary world winder. Moments like those make me realize that my work went way beyond curriculum and grades and GPAs. I was a participant in something much bigger and more important. I can certainly live with that.

ADAM GETTIS
OFFENSIVE LINEMAN FOR THE NEW YORK GIANTS IN THE NATIONAL FOOTBALL LEAGUE:
In order to live a significant life, I have to find something or someone that motivates me to want more. With my career as a professional football player, every time I walk on and off the field, I play and act according to give all glory to God my lord and savior. Next thing I work for is my family. Knowing that I want to give them the world, I do everything in my power to excel in everything I do, which also makes me better.

Kristin Schaefer Mazanowski
Teacher at Maine West High School
(Des Plaines, IL):

I lead a life of significance by making sure there is always someone for me to care about before myself. Depending on the stage of my life, it may be my friends, spouse, children, students, players, parents, siblings or community, but I try to focus on others before myself. When I go to bed having fed my kids healthy meals, texted college friends to plan an upcoming outing, visited a bed ridden uncle, volunteered for my parish, and made my sister laugh (all of which I did today), I know I am leading a significant life.

Patrick Shehane
A Senior at Illinois State University
(Bloomington-Normal, IL):

In my time here I have come know many different role models. These role models include professors, fellow students, and upper classmen on the rugby team. All have taught me, took me under their wing, and showed me how rewarding helping others on the journey through life can be. Now that I am in my senior year, I try to fill a similar role for others. Leading a significant life to me means showing others kindness and compassion. As a board member of my major's club, I try to include new members in all social events and teach them the different career paths that are possible with our degree. I try to give back to those who are in need with St. Jude Children's Hospital fundraising events. I attempt to show new players on the rugby team how to act on and off the field. I also show compassion in educating patients about healthy lifestyles and body maintenance at an outpatient physical therapy clinic. After ISU I hope to lead a significant life by continuing to help others in need. I will be applying to medical school and hope to specialize in emergency medicine. Being able to help others for a living, to me, is the definition of a significant life.

All the above excerpts are written first-hand by those specific people. Now, I take the liberty to add two examples, one from personal experience, and the other from a recent National Book Award winner.

One of my many Boston College benefits gave me Dr. David Freitag. The son of Dr. Irwin and Bernadine Freitag, and sibling to six others, David was my roommate at Boston College during freshman year. We became instant friends, and his enthusiasm soon dissolved any dire homesickness I experienced. "Frog," as he is known world-wide, personifies the ultimate people collector. He is the tremendous model I described to many of my students in high school classes when they were on the ledge, obsessed with college acceptance. I mentioned to them that David took the circuitous path to his present occupation, MOHS surgeon for skin cancers. Dave began in the School of Arts and Sciences, switched in sophomore year to the School of Business, graduating with a degree in finance. He played basketball in Belgium for a year, then joined the Navy. He decided to go to medical school at Georgetown where he earned his license to practice dermatology. He first established a practice in Washington D.C., his hometown, then moved to Naples, Florida, where he currently lives and works. Currently, David has been rated one of the top 20% of all doctors in the nation. So what was my point to students? *Listen carefully; opportunity sometimes knocks very softly.* The changes people undergo in their 20s can be sudden and dramatic. Look at David. College had little to do with his ultimate career, but it had its role. College is not about competitions won, but about connections made (Atchley speech), and David is a prime example of this last statement.

David has been a gift to me and to my entire family. He instructed me early about the difference between vodka and water, a lesson not learned without some pain. He helped hone my competitiveness in basketball, but when things deteriorated for him in hoops due to injuries, he always supported and encouraged me. He has been ever so kind to my wife and to my sons; whenever we are in Naples, Florida, he makes his home ours. His generosity is famous: he once donated his outdated x-ray machine to a doctor friend in Russia without charge. Moreover, he flew to Russia with that machine and spent the time showing his friend how to use it. His penchant for playing pranks, dropping in on his friends for sudden visits, and reaching out to satisfy his delightful curiosity are all his personal trademarks. Perhaps his most salient trait is his empathy. When my mother died in 1994, I received a tap on my shoulder at her wake. David stood behind me. He flew in just for a couple of hours that night to be with my dad, me, Susan, and my siblings. When my father was declining in health years later, he dropped in at his condo to see him.

Those are just a few reasons why he would have been an excellent teacher, a *significant* teacher: humor, empathy, time, and care-those necessary traits for the teacher in all of us. David has never stopped improving his curiosity or his love of life. Those reasons are why I love him. Those traits embellish every other positive about him, and those traits define good teachers. As mentioned, we are all teachers in the ways we live our lives. David would have been a successful ditch digger; he possesses all the intangibles that life can offer, and he continues to help me improve my own life and the lives of my family. Due to my athletic career, I was able to meet David-a friendship forged that has endured. Through the trials of heated competition, some of those friendships become unbreakable, a link of steel trust. Dr. David Freitag is a prime example of a person leading a life of significance.

The New York Times rated *Redeployment* as one of the ten best books of the year. The author, Phil Klay, served in Iraq as a Marine during the surge and provides a memorable first-hand account of the dire results of this war on soldiers' minds, bodies, and souls. To me, the book also provides an honest glimpse into what significance truly means. In one of the late chapters titled *War Stories*, a vet named Jenks recalls the IED ambush he survived, although he was burned to the brink of death and lives today earless and hairless, with a face full of scar tissue, nerve damage, and skin grafts:

> *I am alive because of so many people. More people than I will ever know saved my life not once, but repeatedly. They tell me I fought, kicking and screaming, before they drugged me. And some techniques that saved my life didn't even exist until Iraq, like giving patients fresh plasma along with packed red blood cells to help clotting. I needed clot, and I couldn't do it just with my blood. I needed the blood that the soldiers and airmen whom I will never know lined up to give me, and I needed the docs to have the knowledge to give it to me. So I owe my life to the doc who figured out the best way to push trauma victims' blood, and I owe it to all the Marines that doc watched die before he figured it out.*

Whether I am a poor disfigured vet who got exactly what he volunteered for, or the luckiest man on earth, surrounded by love and care at what is unquestionably the worst period of my life, is really a matter of perspective. There's no upside to bitterness, so why be bitter? Perhaps I've sacrificed more for my country than most, but I've sacrificed far, far less than some. I have good friends. I have all my limbs. I have my brain and my soul and hope for the future. What sort of fool would I have to be, to not accept these gifts with the joy they deserve? (228-9)

I don't see much whining, blaming, or expecting handouts within Jenks's perspective, do you? Of course, the context is far different from what teachers and coaches experience, but the essence of Jenks's significance is, at heart, identical.

To conclude, why is significance so vital for consistent reflection? One answer to this question is with a question. *If you could start your life or career over, would you choose to lead the same life or career?* I suggest that if the answer is yes, you feel you have made a positive and uplifting impact on people. You feel you have made sacrifices when you have lost a part of yourself so that others can benefit. Legacy is not a concept most people think about on a day-to-day basis, but legacy remains a poignant and credible outcome for any life. Lou Holtz described this concept well in his speech to the graduates at Trine University in Indiana in 2012, when he stated, "If you didn't show up to work, would anyone miss you?" George Bailey in the Frank Capra film, *It's a Wonderful Life,* echoes this question when he eventually understands what the awful effects would have been on his family and friends if he had never been born. We can experience this impact by imagining a similar concept to motivate ourselves to live a more significant and meaningful life by giving all we have. Chicago Bears' Super Bowl champion football coach, Mike Ditka, stated, "Strong people motivate themselves." Strong people expect no handouts, blame less often, and take the proactive steps to find meaning for others.

To put the end result another way, hunger develops: hunger for learning more than ever since we expect no handouts; hunger for more responsibility since we refrain from the dead end of blaming others for hassles and problems everyone faces; hunger for self-action since we do more than the minimum.

Significance can be summed with the words of the late Al McGuire, who won a national championship in 1977 as head coach at Marquette University, "Don't buy me flowers after I die; buy me a drink while I am alive."

SECTION 5

CONCLUSION:
EVERY STUDENT WAS SOMEONE'S NEWBORN

A TIMELINE

1918:   Carl Anstett born of Joseph and Barbara Anstett in Clausen, Germany, July 21.

1922:   Christine Anstett, born of Frank and Mary Kornfeind in Austria, May 15.

1944-45: Carl maneuvers from duck boat to Omaha Beach on D-Day. He survives, marches into Germany, kills Nazis, borrows a tank to visit his family in Clausen, returns the tank, returns to U.S. after war ends.

1946:   Carl Anstett marries Christine Kornfeind, January 19.

1947:   Diane Anstett, born of Carl and Christine, April 2.

1951:   Thomas Anstett, born of Carl and Christine, April 15.

1962:   Mark Anstett, born of Carl and Christine, December 24.

1968:   Michael Barta, born of Louie and Diane Barta, October 30.

1976:   Diane Anstett marries Richard Breman, June 12.

1988:   Tom Anstett marries Susan Prachar, April 9.

1989:   Mark Anstett marries Carol Chaplin, April 22.

1990:   John Anstett, born of Tom & Susan, May 30.

1992:   Michael Anstett, born of Mark and Carol, January 20.

1993:   Timothy Anstett, born of Tom & Susan, September 24.

1994:   Christine Anstett, R.I.P., after a nine-month bout with pancreatic cancer, November 24.

2008:   Carl Anstett, R.I.P., after two battles with bladder cancer, October 30.

2014:   John Anstett marries Kelly Dunaway, November 27.

2015:   Noah John Anstett, born of John and Kelly, August 27.

Dr. Garlovsky had delivered the ignoble news. "The tumor is far too aggressive, nothing we can do. It should only be a few days, if that. I'm sorry...of all people for this to happen to. He is such a nice man, a true warrior."

"Are you going to tell him or should I?" My sister Diane waited for me to respond.

"I'll tell him." I thought a son should show some courage and tell his father his end was immediate. I was unsteady. I looked at my crestfallen sister. How many times do we tell people they will die, much less one of our parents? To me befell that obligation.

We walked into the hospital room. Dad lay in bed. He hadn't spoken much at all the last few days. His gaunt face told the truth: the stark moments of pain, a sliver of the manliness. His eyes contained their glimmer and optimism, however, fresh and alive.

"Dad?" No response. "Dad, I got something to tell you. You hear me?" His eyes glinted after a slight turn of the head. "Dr. Garlovsky said that your tumor cannot be controlled, too aggressive. He said you might have a few days left, maybe not. I'm sorry, Dad."

Dad looked at me and sighed, "What a deal." He turned and stared at the ceiling. Never said another word. I kissed him on the forehead, a kiss sealed with an *I love you* and a *thank you*.

Dad received a military tribute at his funeral, complete with Taps, a 21-gun salute, and a folded American flag presented to my sister.

The late Francis Cardinal George stated, "The only thing we take away in death is what we have given away in life." Among many his many assets, my dad gave part of his life for America and its posterity, his seed, his unearthly patience with his children, his devotion to his wife, his universal generosity, his impeccable talent for solving mechanical problems, and his love for his grandchildren. I believe his last thoughts lay somewhere in that list.

As teacher and coaches, we know not where the lives of our understudies will take them. All we try to do is to influence our charges to take the right bus. We can influence, not control. Influence has the lasting power, but the rest is up to them and to the uncertain wand life will wave. We strive to do right for them; we treat them as our own, knowing they are someone's newborn. We *hesitate to blame* in order to understand better. We *expect nothing* handed to us in order to own and to model true responsibility. We *do more* than the minimum.

Epilogue

IN AN INTERVIEW WITH JEAN STEIN in 1956, the American novelist William Faulkner responded to Stein's question, "Is there any possible formula to follow in order to be a good novelist or writer?"

Faulkner answered, "99% talent...99% discipline...99% work. He must never be satisfied with what he does. It never is as good as it can be done. Always dream and shoot higher than you know you can do. Don't bother just to be better than your contemporaries or predecessors. Try to be better than yourself."

I guess that the final sentence of Faulkner's has been my main purpose in writing this book. I found myself dreaming of my friends, family members, past colleagues, or unknown people reading this book and being inspired in small ways to be better than they are. When I was teaching, I challenged students to discover a true work ethic through consistent effort. When I was coaching, I pounded into players' heads that they had to win the battle over themselves in order to win any battle against any team or competitor. Those battles are hard to first accept, then to win, but they must be waged. Only then can life open our eyes to what can be accomplished. I don't know if I accomplished much for you, dear reader, with this effort. I do know that I feel a better person for it. Writing is such a difficult task, much more arduous than I envisioned. That this book took over three years to complete is just one example of the challenge, but I feel both relieved and satisfied with what I have penned. Through it all I accomplished one dream of mine, and as Coach Krzyzewski from Duke University has said, "In your dreams you always win." I hope and expect you to win in yours.

ACKNOWLEDGEMENTS

To my parents, Carl and Christine,
who made sure I was traveling on the right bus.

To my wife, Susan, who provides constant love, wisdom, and support.

To my sister Diane and brother Mark, always part of my life.

To my sons, John and T.J., for teaching me fatherhood.

To my extended family: Michael and Tina, Mary and Jerry, Jane and Doug,
aunts and uncles, nephews and nieces, cousins galore, thanks for all the love.

To all the dedicated teachers, in English and all other subjects,
I have had the honor to know and to work with at five schools:
Quigley Seminary North in Chicago (1973-76), Immaculate Conception
High School in Elmhurst (1976-84), Glenbrook North High School in
Northbrook (1884-89), York Community High School in Elmhurst (1989-99),
Lincoln-Way District 210 at the East and Central campuses in Frankfort &
New Lenox (1999-2014): you have epitomized what Alfred Lord Tennyson
writes in *Ulysses*, "I am part of all I have met."

To the many committed coaches (in all sports) I have known, heard,
witnessed, befriended, and emulated, outstanding examples of tenacity,
knowledge, competition, and good sportsmanship.

To my many teammates throughout my high school, college,
and amateur playing days, friends and worthy examples of what a good
person and a real basketball player mean.

To the late Mr. William Schaefer, my high school basketball coach,
personal savior and hero.

To Mr. Jim Bloch, athletic director at Glenbrook North High School during my tenure there, confidant and booster.

To Mr. Dominic Belmonte, CEO at the Golden Apple Foundation in Chicago, role model.

To Mr. Tim Reilly, assistant superintendent for curriculum, Lincoln-Way District 210, a model for any teacher and a expert in differentiation.

To Coach Pat Sullivan, (retired) head basketball coach, University of St. Francis, one of the most knowledgeable and generous people I know.

To Coach Hubie Brown, NBA commentator at ESPN, previous professional basketball head coach & secret mentor.

To the late coach Rick Majerus, men's college basketball coach supreme and friend, who forgot more basketball than I know.

To (the late) Mr. Frank McCourt, renowned author (*Angela's Ashes*, *'Tis*, and *Teacher Man*) and my hidden motivator. He wrote his first book at age 66.

To Mr. Tom McCormack, head boys' basketball coach, Conant High School in Hoffman Estates (IL), friend/colleague/supporter/hoops expert.

To Mr. Gary Deitelhoff, a better friend never existed.

To all the thousands of English students and basketball players over 42 years in my teaching career, teachers themselves.

To those I might have neglected, but will never forget…

THANK YOU

Appendix A

Bonus Points...A Letter to English Teachers

Dear English guru,

Congratulations on your choice of career. Wherever you fall on the salary scale, you deserve a special pat on the back and well-earned praise. This letter is my way of looking back, so that you can look ahead. I hope one or two of these ideas catch fire in your belly. So, if I had a second chance and if I had my way...

1. **All literature in English courses should be taught *thematically*.**

Rationale: Chronological literature instruction has its place, but not in English curricula. I often tried to astound my students with dramatic readings of Anne Bradstreet's poem *Upon the Burning of Our House*, then correlate the subject matter to Puritan concepts and ideology. I did most of the work. The assessment was multiple choice questions and short answer responses that did little to enlarge the thinking of the students. The end result was a lot of yawns with the majority of students thinking, "What for?"

Now, imagine using Bradstreet's poem within the theme of *Materialism in American Society* instead of it being just a forgettable example of 17th century literature. Quite a contrast. Imagine further, if you will, contrasting Bradstreet's poem with *Shine, Perishing Republic* by Robinson Jeffers, with students writing a comparison-contrast essay after Socratic Seminar discussions. Which one puts more onus on the students? Which one has more potential for student engagement? Which one incorporates some contemporary literature; you know, that literature that sits in comfort and anonymity at the end of the Table of Contents within that massive literature anthology that English teachers never instruct by the end of the chronological year?

Just think. Students might actually find some relevance about the world they share within thematic-driven study. I was bothered by the fact that today's students know so little about today's world. Thematic study links current events to the lives of the characters in the literature. A second thematic example might study *Personal Dignity within a Society*. Imagine blending the following pieces into one unit: fiction such as *White Tiger* by Aravind Adiga and/or *The Scarlet Letter* by Nathaniel Hawthorne, nonfiction such as *Black Men in Public Spaces* by Brent Staples and/or *Shooting an Elephant* by George Orwell, poetry such as *Thought* by Walt Whitman and *Still I Rise* by Maya Angelou. Students get a taste of various genres, eras, and authors while discussing and writing about a topic in the news on a daily basis. What could be better? Might you couple those pieces with short clips from the film *Hotel Rwanda*?

Finally, one of the themes must contain lessons on achieving a level of personal grit. Far too many students sell themselves short. This notion is a codicil of adolescence, to be sure, yet why not bring that challenge in the open and read about people who have grit, that ability to persevere no matter the odds or brick walls? Many times a student's and/or an adult's ability to succeed is not a matter of intelligence; it is a matter of sustaining effort over a long period of time and conquering those moments of whining and blaming. Worth the effort.

2.   **Start each English course with instruction on research methods, plagiarism, citation creation, etc. because the entire school's mode of writing is based upon the art of *rhetoric*.**

Rationale: After you and your students take a couple of days to set the tone for learning in the class, begin the curriculum with research. Thus, an academic tone is set. Since your entire school believes in rhetoric as the basis for writing instruction (hint, hint…), students begin to develop their synthesis skills in the area of research. Teachers blend various genres for both reading and writing. Voice, tone, and audience are the bedrocks for instruction and student application. Begin with small doses, dependent on the students' year in school, and as the year progresses, move to more complex ones. In the instruction, combine the sufficient amount of work with the complexity of inquiry, so that the appropriate level of rigor is established and sustained.

3. **Provide sound instruction to all staff on methodology and strategies for close reading skills.**

Rationale: Assume your students do not read, moreover, cannot read well for comprehension. You are assuming correctly. Research on close reading skills has taken on light-year speed and improvement; I wish I had known some of the current strategies when I was teaching. These skills can raise the confidence level of all students in all subjects. Lincoln-Way District 210 was a pioneer in secondary schools in the area of reading when the district decided to have all freshmen take a reading course. I suggest that even those teachers of that course will benefit from learning more about close reading skills. I do mention quite a few earlier in this book, but here is one to whet your appetite. When you present a new article, or even a novel, to your students, ask them to look at the title and make a question for that title. Students have an immediate focus for reading, searching for the answer to that question they devised. Dr. Douglas Fisher and Carol Jago, among others, have written a surplus of excellent material and strategies for this focus of instruction. You can also find them online through *YouTube* videos.

All staff needs more professional development in this area. If students cannot read with some level of accuracy and comprehension, what type of confidence will they have as thinkers and writers?

4. **Sentence combining must be a *priority* for instruction and practice in English classes.**

Rationale: There has always been so much debate and angst over methodology for the instruction of grammar and usage. High school English teachers are held in relative bondage over the level of readiness of junior high students regarding grammar. For the most part over the past thirty years, grammar has been mistaught, ignored, and/or irrelevant within the English curricula of elementary and junior highs. If I could do it over, I would integrate the instruction of grammar within sentence combining skills and target certain emphases for student revisions of writing for the areas of pronoun and subject-verb agreement, punctuation, and spelling. Worksheets might be decent as an introduction, but supply little concrete or practical application when it comes to students' putting a pen to paper. For the most part, worksheets are a waste of teaching and learning time and give the term homework a bad reputation, "busy work" I believe is the term.

What can sentence combining accomplish? Try these for starters:

- Promote thorough understanding of clauses (necessary ACT and SAT preparation, by the way),
- Clarify types and usefulness of various phrases
- Help students understand useless redundancies in writing,
- Assist students to realize the rhythm and purpose(s) that both long and short(er) sentences can communicate,
- Integrate the instruction of parts of speech,
- Avoid unnecessary sentence style repetition,
- Clarify the best choice and purpose for conjunctions.
- Provide avenues for helping students to understand why revisions and redrafts are two primary components to their improvement as writers.

For more information about this topic, I suggest reading the document *Writing Next* (Carnegie Corporation of New York, 2007), a comprehensive study by Steve Graham and Dolores Perin about effective strategies to improve adolescent and middle school writing. In addition, ask your districts to require the **Writing to Read** program for a presentation as part of an all-school Institute.

5.   **To quote a past President:** *Ask not what your school can do for you; ask what you can do for your school.* (John F. Kennedy)

Rationale: Throughout my career I witnessed too many teachers too anxious to escape school. They reminded me of the escape scene in *Shawshank Redemption* when Andy Dufrain had to engineer the most arduous plan for fleeing the prison. All staff must coach or sponsor at least one team or organization for a minimum of five years. Discover the other side of school, the school's personality, and students' personal interests. Discover methods that coaching can enhance your own teaching methods in the classroom. Discover more time management. Discover more patience. Discover what you can and cannot do. Discover the positive without the whine. *Do something* for your school besides the classroom duties.

6. *Words, words, words. (Hamlet, II.2.)*

Rationale: One of my previous English colleagues used a small white board every day to post a favorite quotation or original saying for students to read. There he stood every day outside his classroom door at the start of each period. Students, whether his or not, would flock like curious sheep to that shepherd's room to read the quotation. This ritual became a favorite for faculty as well; this habit earned a spot in one of the Yearbooks. These small ways prove significant in the long run; they gave us some small, at times humorous, encouragement to hang onto throughout the day.

Here's another example: In the movie *Mr. Holland's Opus*, Holland's first principal, Mrs. Jacobs, says to him at one point, "A teacher has two jobs: fill their minds with knowledge, yes, but more important, give those minds a compass so that the knowledge doesn't go to waste." Teachers point students in a variety of directions. Talk to them as people from time to time, not just as students. Give students something tangible to ponder or to respond to in writing. More importantly, you must strive to support each other's efforts with verbal encouragement. An adage states, *It's nice to be great, but it's greater to be nice.*

7. Want to be the coolest person in your department? Join the I.A.T.E.

Rationale: That's the Illinois Association of Teachers of English, English colleagues. If you are a first-year teacher, you can join for free. Even if you are not, dues are only $25 per year. Moreover, the IATE has a three-day conference every year, complete with fifty to ninety minute workshops that you can choose to attend. English teachers from all over the state present these workshops. I have presented six of these workshops, my topics ranging from close reading skills to Socratic Seminar methods. What a terrific way to increase your professional development, in addition to missing a day of school when your students can torture a sub, so you can pick up the shreds of evidence on the following Monday. Don't let that piece of information discourage you, however. Joining the association gives you four quarterly booklets with timely articles about English pedagogical methods and creative approaches. Furthermore after you return, your department chairman might ask you to present information you heard at the conference to the entire department. What great presenting experience awaits you! In addition, the conference is typically held at a nice hotel where there are at least two bars in the lobby area. There you can find some downtime to join other colleagues to trade war stories to complain about your administrators or blame parents for your students' failures. Plenty of advantages. Hope I have convinced you to join; far too many teachers find all kinds of reasons not to become members. They lose. Start winning.

Avoid counting the days; make the days count. I wish you all the best that an English teaching career offers.

~Tom

"COWARDLY THOUGHTS, ANXIOUS HESITATION
WOMANISH TIMIDITY, TIMOROUS COMPLAINTS
WON'T KEEP MISERY AWAY FROM YOU
AND WILL NOT SET YOU FREE.
TO PRESERVE ALL YOUR POWER DESPITE EVERYTHING,
TO NEVER BEND AND SHOW YOURSELF TO BE STRONG,
BRING THE MIGHT OF THE GODS TO YOUR AID."
(QTD. IN BEER 88)

Appendix B

A Model for Prompt Differentiation

Little did I realize back in 1985 when I created the following prompts for student assessment for *The Great Gatsby* that I was opening a door to differentiated instruction. I called it *Tom's ever-present boredom for reading similar essays about one prompt* syndrome. I looked at Bloom's taxonomy and decided to ask students to contract for a grade on the essay of their choice. I refused to write a prompt for the bottom tier of remembering. All of our class work tried to move the students a little to a lot above minimal critical thinking. Students contracted for a certain grade (Ds were not allowed). If they did not meet the grade on the first attempt, a rewrite after a conference was in order. They were allowed two rewrites; after that last one, the last grade stood firm. Perhaps this model can inspire you to do a similar task for your students, no matter the discipline.

CREATE

Develop and write a possible Chapter 10 for this novel. Continue using the point-of-view of Nick Carraway to write this narrative. Consider what Nick does in the aftermath of Chapter 9, but refer to Gatsby or other appropriate characters within the chapter.

EVALUATE

Argue for the validity for the title of the novel. Support, reject, or qualify the notion of *great* for Gatsby. Consider text evidence, personal observation, or historical examples for support.

(or)

Argue for or against the continuation of *The Great Gatsby* as a required reading for English 3 curriculum.

ANALYZE

Examine Fitzgerald's use of imagery and formulate an argument for that imagery's support or criticism of the American Dream.

APPLY

Apply the meaning of the American Dream as Fitzgerald sees it to the meaning of that dream today in 1985 (2017).

UNDERSTAND

Discuss the importance of Tom Buchanan (or another character other than Nick, Gatsby, or Daisy) in the novel.

A LIST OF BRAIN FOOD

CLASSROOM/ENGLISH INSTRUCTION

I Read It, but I Don't Get It (and) Do I Really Have To Teach Reading? by Cris Tovani

Teaching From the Deep End & Teaching on Solid Ground by Dominic Belmonte

Classics in the Classroom & With Rigor For All by Carol Jago

Teaching With Your Mouth Shut by Donald L. Finkel

Opening Dialogue by Martin Nystrand

On Writing by Steven King

You Haven't Taught Until They Have Learned by Swen Nater

LENCIONI LIBRARY

The Five Temptations of a CEO

The Five Dysfunctions of a Team

The Four Obsessions of an Extraordinary Administrator

The Three Signs of a Miserable Job

WOODEN LIBRARY

Wooden, A Lifetime of Observations and Reflections On and Off the Court

Coach Wooden, One on One

Wooden on Leadership

The Essential Wooden

Inch and Miles (for young children)

HOLTZ LIBRARY

Winning Every Day: The Game Plan for Success

Wins, Losses, and Lessons

OTHER QUALITY READS

Quiet Strength by Tony Dungy

On Becoming a Leader by Warren Bennis

The Art of War by Sun Tzu

The Last Lecture by Randy Pausch

My Losing Season by Pat Conroy

Leading with the Heart by Mike Krzyzewski

First Things First by Stephen Covey

Good to Great by Jim Collins

Teacher Man by Frank McCourt

The Winner Within by Pat Riley

Coaches of Chicago by Dr. Paul Pryma

Attitude by Pat Sullivan

The Smart Take from the Strong by Pete Carril

Russell Rules by Bill Russell

Toughness by Jay Bilas

The Purpose Driven Life by Rick Warren

Values of the Game by Bill Bradley

Team of Rivals by Doris Kearns Goodwin

Thank You Power by Deborah Norville

The Boys in the Boat: Nine Americans and Their Epic Quest for Gold at the 1936 Berlin Olympics by Daniel James Brown

Masters of the Games: Essays and Stories on Sport by Joseph Epstein

The Match: The Day the Game of Golf Changed Forever by Mark Frost

The Road to Character and *The Social Animal: The Hidden Sources of Love, Character, and Achievement* by David Brooks

Managing Anger by Terry London

The Last Lecture by Randy Pausch

SPEECHES

Rick Atchley: to Abilene Christian University, 2013.

Lou Holtz: to Trine University, 2014 and to Franciscan University/Steubenville, 2015.

Steve Jobs: to Stanford University Commencement, 2005

APPENDIX D

WHAT'S THE DIFF?

You might be in a state of flux as to the differences between "teaching" and "coaching." Try the activity below. You will see a list of –ing participles. Determine where each belongs and write it in the spaces. Use each descriptor only once.

CHOICES:

empowering	supporting	educating	improving	facilitating	criticizing
advising	imploring	tutoring	encouraging	enhancing	training
developing	learning	inspiring	partnering	motivating	helping
targeting	yelling	humoring	challenging	promoting	harping

TEACHING	COACHING

If your process of choice was similar to mine, I felt utter confusion by the end of my attempt. "Inspiring" can be placed in both, right? Wait…teachers *and* coaches both motivate. I can put "inspiring" in one column and even out the other with "motivating." "Empowering"?? Your guess is as good as mine.

My point? Wherever you put each term, do you not see that there is a parallelism, karma, between both? The denotations for teaching are quite simplistic and direct: "educating, tutoring, training, and helping (people to learn)." Coaching covers a plethora of actions. Whatever you decided, is there little doubt that both actions are a part of the education of students, whether in the classroom or in the athletic arena? Teachers need coaching methods to excite their protégés; coaches need to become the better teachers in the school. There is plenty to learn from both personae. Perhaps administrators who might be reading this book can stimulate their staffs by providing the time to the faculty where coaches can lend their expertise to the pedagogical side, and teachers can provide coaches with insights about their methods and the athletes. Sharing what you know is a concept I explore in this book.

BLAME OR BUILD?

I watched them tearing a building down,
A gang of men in a busy town.
With a ho-heave-ho and a lusty yell,
They swung a beam, and the side wall fell.

I asked the foreman: "Are these skilled—
And the men you'd hire if you had to build?"
He gave me a laugh and said: "No, indeed!
Just common labor is all I need.
I can wreck in a day or two
What builders have taken a year to do."

And I thought to myself as I went my way,
Which of these roles have I tried to play?
Am I a builder who works with care
Measuring life by a rule and square?
Am I shaping my deeds to a well made Plan,
Patiently doing the best I can?
Or am I a wrecker, who walks the town
Content with the labor of tearing down?

~Edgar A. Guest

BIBLIOGRAPHY

Anderson, Mark. *Andertoons*. n.d. n.p. n.d. Web. 8 August 2015.

Assessment and Accountability. Guiding Principles for Classroom Assessment. Illinois State Board of Education. 2015.

Belmonte, Dominic. *Teaching From the Deep End*. Thousand Oaks: Corwin Press, 2003.

Beer, Edith Hahn. *The Nazi Officer's Wife – How One Jewish Woman Survived the Holocaust*. New York: Harper, 2000. Print.

Berkas, Nancy & Pattison, Cynthia. *Critical Issue: Integrating Standards into the Curriculum. 2000*. www.ncrel.orr. 1 June 2015. Internet.

Brooks, David. *The Social Animal: the Hidden Sources of Love, Character, and Achievement*. New York: Random House, 2011.

Buehl, Doug. *Developing Readers in Academic Disciplines* (2011). Newark: The International Reading Association, 2011.

Di Carlo, Matthew. Update on Teacher Turnover in the U. S. 22 January 2015. Internet. 7 June 2015.

Dickey, Jack. *Who Killed Summer Vacation? Time*. 2015.

D'Souza, Dinesh. *Ronald Reagan*. New York: The Free Press (Simon and Schuster), 1997. Print.

Dykstra, Lenny. House of Nails. New York: Harper Collins, 2016. Print.

Fine, Sarah. *Education Week*. 2010.

French, Ron. *Building a better teacher: Michigan classrooms loaded with rookie teachers who soon wash out*. 14 October 2013. Internet. 7 June 2015.

Frost, Mark. *The Grand Slam: Bobby Jones, America, and the Story of Golf*. New York: Hyperion Books, 2004. Print.

Glasbergen, Randy. *Glasbergen Cartoon Service*. n.d. Web. 20 December 2015.

Hackney, Sean and Newman, Brian. *Using the Rhetorical Situation to Inform Literacy Instruction and Assessment Across the Discipline. English Journal*: 103-1. 2013. 60-65.

Klay, Phil. *Redeployment*. New York: Penguin Books, 2014. Print.

Jago, Carol. *Classics in the Classroom*. New York: Heinemann, 2004.

---. *With Rigor for All*. 2000.

Markazi, Arash. *Kobe: Europe's Players More Skillful*. ESPN.com. 3 January 2015. Retrieved 7 February 2016. Web.

A Modern Southern Reader. Eds. Ben Forkner, Patrick Samaway, S.J. Atlanta: Peachtree Publishers, 1986.

---. Faulkner, William. *Interview with Jean Stein*. 1956. 661-663. Print.

---. Warren, Robert Penn. *Old Photographs of the Future*. 333. Print.

Nystrand, Martin. *Opening Dialogue: Understanding the Dynamics of Language and Learning in the English Classroom*. New York: Teachers College Press, 1997. Print.

O'Sullivan, John. *Is it Wise to Specialize?* Problems in Youth Sports Specialization, Sports Parenting. 13 January 2014. Web.

Richardson, Will. "Change Agent." *Teacher PD Sourcebook. Education Week*, 2010. Online. 15 June 2015.

Russell, Bill. *Russell Rules*. New York: Penguin Group, 2001. Print.

Sax, Leonard, Dr. "The Collapse of Parenting: Parents need to take charge or kids will suffer." *Chicago Tribune*. 1 February 2016. Interview.

Sperry, Chris. *Baseball Life*. Retrieved 12 August 2016. http://www.sperrybaseballlife.com/stay-at-17-inches

Stories for Preaching. Story of Rome's fall found in T. Cahill, *How the Irish Saved Civilisation*. (Hodder, 1995). 23 January 2016. Web.

Woodward, Bob. *Bush at War*. New York: Simon and Schuster, 2002. Print.

ABOUT THE AUTHOR

TOM ANSTETT has four decades of teaching and coaching under his belt. A Golden Apple nominee and two-time inductee into the Illinois Basketball Coaches Hall of Fame is a clear reflection of the passion and mastery of his craft. Before retiring, Anstett poured his vast experience and wisdom into his students and athletes, and is doing the same for educators and mentors today. *Stop Whining; Start Winning* provides teachers and coaches with a wide-ranging perspective on how to captivate, motivate, and develop students and athletes.

Anstett played basketball at Boston College and then immediately began teaching in the Chicago area. He earned his Master's in Literature in 1989 and his Type-75 Administration Certification in 1997, both at Northeastern Illinois University. While teaching English and Spanish, Anstett published multiple poetry and English-related articles, and has presented at several Illinois Association of Teachers of English conferences. He was awarded District Coach of the Year on two occasions, and was also inducted into the Illinois Basketball Coaches Hall of Fame as both a player and as a coach.

Currently in retirement, Anstett is still tutoring high school students and frequently presenting at teacher workshops through the Joliet Professional Development Alliance.

Made in the USA
Lexington, KY
22 July 2019